# Challenges and Innovation in Education

# Challenges and Innovation in Education

**Dr. G. VISVANATHAN**
Professor, Department of Education,
Annamalai University, T.N
and
**Dr.S.K.PANNEER SELVAM**
Assistant Professor, Department of Education,
Bharathidasan University, T.N

RANDOM

**RANDOM PUBLICATIONS**
**NEW DELHI (INDIA)**

**Challenges and Innovation in Education**

---

ISBN 978-93-5111-537-3


Published in 2015 in India by

**RANDOM PUBLICATIONS**

4376-A/4B, Gali Murari Lal, Ansari Road
New Delhi-110 002
Phone : +9111-43580356, 011-43142548, 011-23289044
e-mail : sales@randompublications.com
info@randompublications.com
randomexports@gmail.com

Reprint 2021

*Type Setting by :* Shah Computer Graphics, Delhi-110094
*Digitally Printed at* : Replika Press Pvt. Ltd.

# Contents

## 14

## Similar Systems on Cloud Computing in Education 87



## 15

## System Approach in Higher Education 96

## 18



## 19



## 20

## 21



## 22



## 23

47



48



49

# 1

# Developing Learning Environments of Tomorrow

## Introduction

The role of education in the knowledge society is to provide innovative learning environments for tomorrow's knowledge workers and wider community. Our learning systems, our curriculum and assessment models, our teaching methods, and the whole culture of education and learning demand radical change to be adequately equipped for the emerging knowledge-based economy. School buildings and their surroundings are a useful resource for teaching and for fostering independent, enquiry-based learning. The traditional design of a school is beginning to transform, as specialized teaching spaces and classrooms, with a set school day and curriculum, accommodated at a school site shift towards multi-purpose spaces, with flexible timetables and individual learning plans accommodated at multiple locations across the neighborhood. The way that teachers are developed professionally, the school curriculum, management, assessment and testing systems, parental engagement, expectations and entitlements all intermesh with the design of schools to create the learning environment.

The learning environments of the future should be:

1. Flexible at different scales and timescales, allowing for variation in use, occupancy and layout
2. Inspiring to those working, learning and visiting, and embodying organizational aims
3. Supportive of effective teaching and learning, accommodating a wide range of experiences and activities
4. Involving of the users and the wider community, and linking with other learning places

The role of education in the knowledge society is to provide innova-tive learning environments for tomorrow's knowledge workers and wider community. Our learning systems, our curriculum and assessment models, our teaching methods, and the whole culture of education and learning demand radical change to be adequately equipped for the emerging knowledge-based economy. School buildings and their surroundings are a useful resource for teaching and for fostering independent, enquiry-based learning.

They aspire to shape minds, both inside and beyond the classroom. In schools of the future, students, teachers and designers will be turning to concepts of sustainable design to address comfort-related issues such as hygiene, safety, security, acoustics and availability of space, natural daylight and natural ventilation.

## Role of Students, Teachers And Designers

Involving students in the design phase will result in facilities that reflect their needs, desires and creative ideas. If the project is completed quickly or in short phases, students can also see their ideas come to fruition, resulting in a greater feeling of ownership. As the educational process becomes more learner-centered and technology- driven, teachers must learn to use new and more flexible learning environments to the best effect.

School buildings and their surroundings are a useful resource for teaching and for fostering independent, enquiry-based learning. Building designers can use the architectural elements, the building systems and the external spaces to provide many different learning opportunities for students in new and existing schools.

## Architectural Elements as A Learning Tool

For many students "learning by doing" is more effective and motivating than other methods of learning. Designers can incorporate learning features from core subjects and concepts such as environmental sustainability in both new and existing schools to foster more experiential forms of learning. Teachers can use these elements from the internal and external environment to enhance and complement the curriculum.

## Creating Flexible Spaces For Flexible Learning

More interactive models replace the traditional teacher- centered model of learning to place students and teachers at the centre of educational process. Educational spaces must be sufficiently flexible to accommodate an ever- increasing range of teaching and learning scenarios and technologies. To best facilitate flexible learning environments, new and existing facilities must consider.

### Space For Group Learning

Large spaces need to be broken into smaller units to facilitate group work and cross- curricular learning and to cater to students with different learning styles.

### Space For Individual Learning

Schools can allocate areas for personal study with individual desks.

### Open, Multi-purpose Spaces

Open areas can serve as social spaces, open access learning areas, quiet study areas or central briefing areas. Multipurpose classrooms facilitate flexible teaching by creating an open multipurpose space at the front of the classroom separated by a glass partition.

### Specialised Spaces

Design provision must be made for specialized activities such as vocational training, sport and the performing arts.

### New Learning Environment

The traditional design of a school is beginning to transform, as specialized teaching spaces and classrooms, with a set school day and curriculum, accommodated at a school site shift towards multi-purpose spaces, with flexible timetables and individual learning plans accommodated at multiple locations across the neighborhood. The way that teachers are developed professionally, the school curriculum, management, assessment and testing systems, parental engagement, expectations and entitlements all intermesh with the design of schools to create the learning environment.

"A learning environment is a place or community where people can draw upon resources to make sense out of things and construct meaningful solutions to problems"-(Manninen, J.)

## Embrace Innovation And Challenge Assumptions In Design

Creating opportunities for innovation and experiment, and sharing good practice are required, alongside removing the barriers to innovation. Integrate management, pedagogy and technology with design: Design of the learning environment should be considered in tandem with the management framework, pedagogy and technology. Achieve flexible and agile design solutions: The design solution should integrate the underlying elements of infrastructure (management, pedagogy and technology), whilst allowing for flexibility, both in the short-term and the long-term.

## Inspirational Spaces

Learning spaces should be inspirational. They will never compete with the other engaging spaces in which young people spend their time – retail, leisure and other public environments – if they continue to look, feel and smell like institutions. We need therefore to rethink not just the buildings in which learning is housed but every element that makes up the learning environment – internal spaces, furniture, technology, school dinners, lighting, storage systems, communication and ensure that we continue to provide innovative solutions designed to improve the experience of learning. The future of learning environments demands that architects, designers and manufacturers work together with students, teaching staff and educationalists to translate both emerging educational trends and day to day interactions into spaces, products and systems that truly support learning.

The way we live, work and the skills and knowledge that business and society demand stand in contrast to the priorities on which the education system was originally designed. Our learning systems, our curriculum and assessment models, our teaching methods, and the whole culture of education and learning demand radical change to be adequately equipped for the emerging knowledge-based economy.

## Using Ict

ICT is a central element in education and also in learners' life; ubiquitous and immersive technology.ICT offers unlimited scope for improving access to education both within and between schools. Tools such as wireless connections and interacting multimedia can connect schools in remote areas to schools anywhere in the world. ICT classroom features high speed broadband connection to the internet; interactive whiteboards linked to the internet; virtual reality tools and image projection; high quality video conferencing equipment.

## Scaffolding Learning

The ideal role of the teacher is that of providing scaffolding (collaborative dialogue) to assist students on tasks within their zones of proximal development"(Hamilton and Ghatala, 1994). "During scaffolding the first step is to build interest and engage the learner. Once the learner is actively participating, the given task should be simplified by breaking it into smaller sub-tasks. During this task, the teacher needs to keep the learner focused, while concentrating on the most important ideas of the assignment. One of the most integral steps in scaffolding consists of keeping the learner from becoming frustrated. The final task associated with scaffolding involves the teacher modelling possible ways of completing tasks, which the learner can then imitate and eventually internalise" (Dahms et al., 2007).

Social media and particularly video present rich opportunities for the modelling of ways of completing a task, especially given the ability of using social networking software to support communities of practice. However, imitation alone may not be sufficient in the context of advanced knowledge work. Rather, refection is required both to understand more abstract models and at the same time to reapply models to particular contexts and instances of application in practice.

## The Future of Learning Environments

The development and use of Personal Learning Networks and Personal Learning Environments can support and mediate individual and group based learning in multiple contexts and promote learner autonomy and control. The role of teachers in such an environment would be to support, model and scaffold learning. Such an approach will allow the development and exploration of Personal Learning Pathways, based on the interests and needs of the learners and participation in culturally rich collaborative forms of knowledge construction. Such approaches to learning recognise the role of informal learning and the role of context.

Schools can only form one part of such collaborative and networked knowledge constellation. Indeed the focus moves from schools as institutional embodiments of learning to focus on the process and forms of learning. Hence institutions must rethink and recast their role as part of community and distributed networks supporting learning and collaborative knowledge development. Indeed, the major impact of the uses of new technologies and social networking for learning is to move learning out of the institutions and into wider society. For schools to continue to play a role in that learning, they too have to reposition themselves within wider social networks and communities. This is a two way process, not only schools reaching outwards, but also opening up to the community, distributed or otherwise, to join in collaborative learning processes. The future development of technology looks likely to increase pressures for such change.

Social networks and social networking practicc is continuing to grow and is increasingly integrated in different areas of society and economy. At the same time new interfaces to computers and networks are likely to render the keyboard obsolescent, allowing the integration of computers and learning in everyday life and activity. Personal Learning Pathways will guide and mediate progression through this expanded learning environment.

## Conclusion

In the future, the boundaries between formal and informal learning will blur and the school as an institution will dematerialize. The focus will shift from creating the right buildings to creating the right environments, interactions and conditions for learning, and these may appear in a variety of physical and non-physical spaces. The quality of learning environments will appear on educational league tables and assessment structures will have been redesigned to encourage collaborative and creative work.
The learning environments of the future should be:

- Flexible at different scales and timescales, allowing for variation in use, occupancy and layout
- Inspiring to those working, learning and visiting, and embodying organisational aims
- Supportive of effective teaching and learning, accommodating a wide range of experiences and activities
- Involving of the users and the wider community, and linking with other learning places

## References

1. Maturing Learning: Mashup Personal Learning Environments, CEUR Workshops proceedings

2. Rachel Jupp, 'Creating a learning society', Education Review vol 15 no 2,200 Manninen, J. 2011. Re-thinking education: from teaching practicesto Learning Environments.

# 2

# Intra, Inter and Emotional Intelligences

## Introduction

Digital age is the age of globalization and information. The learners in this age can acquire information about any concept of science, technology, culture, religion, and values from any part of the globe from where ever they are. The transfer of information into knowledge, competency and capability requires cognitive and non cognitive skills and intelligence. Employability requires higher knowledge, competencies and capabilities. In this article an attempt is made to find out the influence of non cognitive skills and intelligence such as intra personal intelligence, inter personal intelligence and emotional intelligence on promoting capabilities and competencies of the learners for employability. By descriptive research methodology, first employability is analysed in different dimensions and the needed skills and competencies for the same is derived. Second the intra, inter and emotional intelligences are discussed and derived to what extent the said intelligences, promotes the learners capabilities for employability. Third the strategies and techniques to inculcate these intelligences to learners through the educational process are interpreted. The article is concluded with the finding that the above said intelligences play dominant role i.e. Ten competencies are determined by them in making the learners/ individual's employability. If the Educational process inculcates proper knowledge and application strategies of the intra, inter and emotional intelligences then the individuals become highly employable and they satisfy themselves and do better service to the society.

Digital age refers to the present time use of machines and computers to present information in digital format. Some of the commonly used digital form is the use of information technology and the Internet. Digital age is the age of globalization and information. The learners in this age can acquire information about any concept of science, technology, culture, religion, and values from any part of the globe from where they are. The transfer of information into knowledge, competencies and capabilities requires cognitive and non cognitive skills and intelligences

## Employability

Employability is a set of skills, understandings and personal attributes that make graduates more likely to gain employment and be successful in their chosen occupations which benefits themselves, the work force, the community and the economy.

Employability skills are classified into two categories as General skills and Specific skills. General skill are needed to get most jobs, they also help the graduate to stay in a job and work to get progress in the job. Specific skills are job-specific skills

The three intelligences described and interpreted with employability skills are briefly described below.

## Multiple Intelligences

The idea of multiple intelligences was introduced by Howard Gardner in 1983. Gardner proposed that instead of there being one general intelligence, there are different kinds of intelligence. Two among them are intrapersonal intelligence and interpersonal intelligence and these intelligences are discussed and analysed and interpreted with employability.

## Intrapersonal intelligence

Intrapersonal Intelligence is explained as having the following criteria. Highly developed self-knowledge, defined as having accurate knowledge of one's dreams, goals strengths, limitations, moods, anxieties, desires and motivations. The ability to act on the basis of self-knowledge, creating environments, guiding behavior, and making decisions based on an accurate picture of oneself. People that have intrapersonal intelligence know themselves well. They aren't forced into molds and they make decisions base on what is right for themselves. They possess a strong sense of identity and purpose.

### Interpersonal intelligence

Interpersonal intelligence is the ability to recognize distinctions between other people to know their faces and voices, to react appropriately to their needs, to understand their motives, feelings and moods and to appreciate such perspectives with sensitivity and empathy., the social skills like Social sensitivity, Socially influential and Interpersonal work towards people are those typically characteristic of individuals with interpersonal intelligence.

### Emotional Intelligence

The third intelligence discussed and interpreted with employability is emotional intelligence Daniel Goleman (1995, 1998) terms other kind of intelligence quite distinct from that measured by IQ tests, is more important for a happy, productive life than IQ is Emotional Intelligence. Goleman (1995) defines it as Emotional intelligence is cluster of traits or abilities relating to the emotional side of life- abilities such as recognizing and managing one's own emotions, being able to motivate oneself and restrain one's impulses, recognizing and managing others' emotions, and handling interpersonal relationships in an effective manner.

### Objectives

1. To find out the needed skills and competencies for the employability by analyzing / reviewing the literature in different dimensions.
2. To understand the extent to which the intra, inter and emotional intelligences promotes the learners capabilities for employability.
3. Strategies and techniques to inculcate these intelligences to learners through the educational process.

### Objective 1

From the review of literature the following ten skills are derived to be more important for employability

1. Communication: Graduates have to be confident about speaking to people fact-to-face or over the phone, and write well enough to be understood.
2. Team Work: Graduates have to be good at working with people.

This means both workmates and other people that come into contact with the organization

3. Problem Solving: Graduates have to able to find solutions when faced with difficulties or set-backs. Even if they can't think of a solution straight away, they need to have a logical process for figuring things out.
4. Drive: Determination to get things done. Make things happen & constantly looking for better ways of doing things.
5. Initiative and Enterprise: Graduates need to be able to think about the bigger picture and the future of the organization they are working for. Employers will value Graduates ability to think creatively and to make improvements to the way things are.
6. Planning and Organising: Graduates need to be able to organize them, plan project timelines and meet deadlines.
7. Independence: Accepts responsibility for views and actions and able to work under their own direction & initiative.
8. Self-Management: Graduates need to be able to get on with their work without someone having to check up on them every five minutes. Graduates should also be able to delegate tasks to make sure things get done on time.
9. Learning: Learn new things and be able to pick them up quickly. There are likely to be some changes to the job and to the structure of the work place while they are in work.
10. Information Management: Locate, select, organize, and document information using appropriate technology and information systems.

## Objective 2

To understand the extent to which the intra, inter and emotional intelligences promotes the learners capabilities for employability.

By descriptive analysis of the existing literature on intra, inter and emotional intelligences, the characters and skills of people with the said intelligences are derived and presented in the following paragraphs.

## Intra personal Intelligence

People with intrapersonal intelligence know themselves well. They aren't forced into molds, and they make decisions based on what is right for themselves. People with intrapersonal intelligence often:

1. Accurate knowledge of one's strengths and goals
2. Accurate knowledge of their limitations

3. Accurate understandings of their motivations.
4. Understanding of their anxieties and desires
5. Ability to act on the basis of self-knowledge.
6. Ability for creating environment
7. Guiding behavior
8. Making decisions based on accurate picture of oneself.
9. Possess a strong sense of identity and purpose
10. Possess a high level of organizing abilities

**Interpersonal Intelligence**

People with interpersonal intelligence are able to pick up on the mood, characteristics, emotions, and intentions of those around them. They are also able to use this information to tailor their approach of interacting with each individual. People with interpersonal intelligence often:

1. Work well with others
2. Are skilled verbal and nonverbal communicators
3. Enjoy being around others
4. Are natural leaders among peers and groups
5. Have good problem solving skills
6. Are empathetic
7. Are good at socializing with others and enjoy discussion
8. Can examine a situation from multiple point of views
9. Easily form strong, positive relationships with others
10. Are able to influence the opinions and actions of others.

**Emotional Intelligence**

People with high emotional intelligence are usually successful in most things they do. People with high EI make others feel good, they go through life much more easily than people who are easily angered or upset.

People with emotional intelligence are

1. They understand their emotions
2. They are confident
3. Ability to control emotions
4. Know their strengths and weaknesses
5. Highly motivated
6. High productive love a challenge
7. Understands wants needs and viewpoints of others
8. Good in listening, lives in a very open and honest way

9. Help others to develop and shine
10. Manage disputes, excellent communicators and are building relationships.

**Table showing employability skills and corresponding abilities and competencies derived from intra, inter and emotional intelligences**

| Sl.No | Employability Skills | People with Intra personal intelligence | People with inter personal intelligence | People with Emotional intelligence |
|---|---|---|---|---|
| 1 | Communication | Knowledge of one's strengths and goals | Skilled verbal and nonverbal communications | Understand their emotions Control emotions |
| 2 | Team Work | Knowledge of their limitations | Work well with others | |
| 3 | Problem Solving | Understanding of their motivation. | Good problem solving skills | Confident |
| 4 | Drive | Understanding of their desires and anxieties | Empathetic | Know Strength and weakness |
| 5 | Initiative and Enterprise | Ability to act on the basis of self knowledge | Examine a situation from multiple point of views | Highly Motivated |
| 6 | Planning and Organising | Ability for creating environment | Enjoy being around others | High productive and love a challenge |
| 7 | Independence | Guiding behavior | Good at socializing and enjoy discussion | Understands wants needs and viewpoints of others |
| 8 | Self-Management | Making decisions based on accurate picture oneself | Easily form strong, positive relationships with others | Good in listening, lives in a very open and honest way |
| 9 | Learning | Possess a strong sense of identity and purpose | Able to influence the opinions and actions of others | Help others to develop and shine |
| 10 | Information Management | Possess a high level of organizing abilities | Natural leaders among peers and groups | Manage disputes excellent communicators |

From the above table of skills and competencies we infer the extent to which the intra, inter and emotional intelligence promotes the learners capabilities and employability. In educational process the three intelligences are properly inculcated learners acquire capabilities and competencies for employability.

## Objective 3

Strategies and techniques to inculcate these intelligences to learners through the educational process. For the above said objective strategies and techniques are developed and practiced in different workshops and also implemented in the pre service professional courses including teacher preparation programmes. Highly reliable, valid, practicable techniques for promoting intra, inter and emotional intelligence are listed below.

## Strategies to promote emotional intelligence

All information to the brain come through our senses, and when this information is overwhelmingly stressful or emotional, instinct will take over and our ability to act will be limited to the flight, fight or freeze response. Therefore, to have access to the wide range of choices and the ability to make good decisions, we need to be able to bring our emotions into balance at will. Emotional intelligence is built by reducing stress, remaining focused, and staying connected to yourself and others. Key skills are

1. The ability to quickly reduce stress in the moment in a variety of settings
2. The ability to recognized your emotions and keep them from overwhelming you
3. The ability to connect emotionally with others by using nonverbal communication.
4. The ability to use humor and play to stay connected in challenging situations
5. The ability to resolve conflicts positively and with confidence.

## Conclusions

In Digital age transfer of information into knowledge, competency and capability requires cognitive and non cognitive skills and intelligence. Employability requires higher knowledge, competencies and capabilities. The skills needed to get job, stay in job and progress in job are achieved by acquiring proper Intra personal intelligence, Interpersonal intelligence and Emotional intelligence.

## References

1. Bigge. M.L and Shermis. S.S (2003) Learning theories for Teachers. 6th Edn. Newyork: Harper Colins.
2. Calvin. W.H (1966). How brains think. Newyork: Basic Books
3. Engelbrecht.P. & Green. L (2001) Promoting learner development: Preventing and working with barriers to learning. Pretoria: Van Schaik

4. Mayer.J.D Caruso. D. & Salovey. P (1999). Emotional intelligence meets traditional standards for intelligence. Intelligence. Cambridge: Cambridge University Press.
5. Mayer.J.D. Caruso, D.R. (2000) Models of emotional intelligence. In R.J Sternberg (Ed). Handbook of Intelligence. Cambridge, England: Cambridge University Press.

# 3

# Blended Learning of Educational Prosses

"To combine any form of instructional technology (e.g., videotape, CD-ROM, Web-based training, film) with face-to-face instructor-led training." names of blended learning."You may hear blended learning described as"integrated learning, "hybrid learning", "multi-method learning". "The term "blended learning" is being used with increasing frequency in both academic and corporate circles. Blended learning can be delivered in a variety of ways. A common model is delivery of "theory" content by e-learning prior to actual attendance at a training course or program to put the "theory" into practice. Integrated learning is also seen as a stepping stone to blended learning. This term shows a need for more methods of teaching than the traditional classroom can offer. The point of creating blended learning was to allow flexible learning for the students. This term then is also a major aspect of blended learning. It needs to be recognized and understood by users in order to better create and deliver a blended learning unit to students. " In differentiated instruction, educators look at students' learning styles, interests, and abilities. "Virtual fieldtrips benefit students, families, schools, teachers, and communities" . Virtual fieldtrips can take students to places they have personally visited, will be personally visiting. In most blended learning classrooms, there is the ability to study whenever the student chooses to do so. If a student is absent, she/he may view some of the missed materials at the same time that the rest of the class does, even though the student cannot be physically in the classroom.

## Meaning

While teachers have always used a variety of teaching methods and media, it includes the recent availability of digital learning technologies and Internet-based tools that facilitate communication, interaction, and collaborative learning. Neither e-learning nor the traditional classrooms are ideal for all types of learning. Blended learning offers the opportunity to incorporate the 'best of both worlds' to improve teaching and learning, to take "advantage of the strengths of both learning environments and be more successful in avoiding their weaknesses." Evidence from a study conducted by Alfred P. Rovai and Hope M. Jordan "suggest that blended courses produce a stronger sense of community among students than either traditional or fully online courses"

## Dr. Margaret Driscoll identifies four different concepts in defining

The first defines blended learning as meaning "to combine or mix modes of Web-based technology (e.g., live virtual classroom, self-paced instruction, collaborative learning, streaming video, audio, and text) to accomplish an educational goal. "Second definition describes blended learning as meaning "to combine various pedagogical approaches (e.g., constructivism, behaviorism, cognitive) to produce an optimal learning outcome with or without instructional technology." (Driscoll, 2002)

The third definition from Dr. Driscoll (2002) defines blended learning as meaning "to combine any form of instructional technology (e.g., videotape, CD-ROM, Web-based training, film) with face-to-face instructor-led training." The fourth concept from Dr. Driscoll defines blended learning as meaning "to mix or combine instructional technology with actual job tasks in order to create a harmonious effect of learning and working."

## The Many Names of Blended Learning

Blended learning is something that is used in the world of education as well as the world of business. Blended learning is not a new concept, but may be a new term to many users. Below is a list and explanation of just a few of the more common, but older, names of blended learning.

"You may hear blended learning described as"integrated learning, "hybrid learning", "multi-method learning". "The term "blended learning" is being used with increasing frequency in both academic and corporate circles. In 2003, blended learning as one of the top ten trends to emerge in the knowledge delivery industry".

## Descriptions

Blended Learning: Learning methods that combine e-learning with other forms of flexible learning and more traditional forms of learning.

Blended learning (also called hybrid learning) is the term used to describe learning or training events or activities where e-learning, in its various forms, is combined with more traditional forms of training such as "class room" training blended learning is usually defined as the combination of multiple approaches to teaching. It can also be defined as educational processes, which involves the use of diversity of methods and resources or to learning experiences, which are derived from more than one kind of information source.

Examples include combining technology-based materials and traditional print materials, group and individual study, structured pace study and self-paced study, or tutorial and coaching.

Blended learning can be delivered in a variety of ways. A common model is delivery of "theory" content by e-learning prior to actual attendance at a training course or program to put the "theory" into practice. This can be a very efficient and effective method of delivery, particularly if travel and accommodation costs are involved. This mixture of methods reflects the hybrid nature of the training.

These show how blended learning is viewed in different situations, different environments, and by different people. Blended learning involves the use of some technology as well as the use of more traditional methods to allow the student to work and learn at his/her own pace. Blended learning is a relatively new term. However, the ideas of this style of teaching and learning behind it are more common. The following is a list of synonyms or previous terms that are linked to blended learning.

## Hybrid Learning

The goal of hybrid courses is to pair the best features of face-to-face teaching with the best options of online learning to promote active and independent learning and reduce class seat time. Using instructional technologies, the hybrid model forces the redesign of some lecture or lab content into new online learning activities, such as case studies, tutorials, self-testing exercises, simulations, and online group collaborations (NJIT, 2005).

Using computer-based technologies, instructors use the hybrid model to redesign some lecture or lab content into new activities, such as case studies, tutorials, self-testing exercises, simulations, and online group collaborations.

Hybrid courses seem to be the pre-step to blended learning. Hybrid courses involve a great amount of technology. They also greatly increase the independence of the student by allowing him/her to work at his/her own pace outside of the typical classroom.

## Integrated Learning

Teaching strategies that enhance brain-based learning include controlling, active learning, field trips, guest speakers, and real-life projects that allow students to use many learning styles and multiple intelligences. An interdisciplinary curriculum or integrated learning also reinforces brain-based learning, because the brain can better make connections when material is presented in an integrated way, rather than as isolated bits of information.

## Integrated Learning System

A complete software, hardware, and network system used for instruction. In addition to providing curriculum and lessons organized by level, an ILS usually includes a number of tools such as assessments, record keeping, report writing, and user information files that help to identify learning needs, monitor progress, and maintain student records

Integrated learning is also seen as a stepping stone to blended learning. This term shows a need for more methods of teaching than the traditional classroom can offer. This is of course the basis for blended learning. Integrated learning allows a teacher to provided instruction to students in a way that will be meaningful and interesting to each learner. This again is the main concept behind blended learning.

## Mixed Mode Learning

As a capability, learning is often thought of as one of the necessary conditions for intelligence in an agent. Some systems extend this requirement by including a plethora of mechanisms for learning in order to obtain as much as possible from the system, or to allow various components of their system to learn in their own ways On the other hand, multiple methods are included in a system in order to measure the performance of one method .

## E-learning

E-learning is not a synonym of blended learning, but is a major component of a successful blended learning unit. Without e-learning, there would be no real technology. Without technology, there would be little hope of blended learning. Therefore the concept of e-learning is a major aspect of blended learning and one that needs to be recognized and understood by those interested in blended learning.

## Flexible Learning

"The term flexible learning is referred broadly to mean increased learner choice in content, sequence, method, time, and place of learning. In addition it is also associated with increased flexibility in administrative and course management processes. However it is interesting to note that most literature refers to online learning as only a form of flexible learning, but there is a clear emphasis on the use of online technologies to achieve flexible learning goals" learning styles and preferences - the availability of a range of learning resources and tasks to suit individual needs; Flexible learning is the main concept and reasoning behind blended learning. The point of creating blended learning was to allow flexible learning for the students. This term then is also a major aspect of blended learning. It needs to be recognized and understood by users in order to better create and deliver a blended learning unit to students.

As can be seen from the above examples and explanations, technology may not be a given to blended learning, but an addition. Instead we need to look at blended learning as using methods outside the traditional classroom and teaching to help interest and reach all learners. These methods could be using technology, or just some other form of teaching, like speakers or manipulative, to help all student learning, to reach all the students in the class.

## In Education

Educators seem to have the most interest in blended learning, for obvious reasons. Because of this, much of the research on blended learning has been based around classroom situations. All level of education has been researched with blended learning, from the elementary school grades up to graduate school.

Good classroom teachers have always blended their methods—reading, writing, lecture, discussion, practice and projects, to name just a few, are all part of an effective blend. Blending is only a revelation for those who have been trying to do everything with just one tool—usually the computer—and ending up with less than ideal results. Understanding that using the right tool, in the right situation, for the right purpose should be a guiding design principle.

One clear advantage of blended learning in education is its connection with differentiated instruction. Differentiated instruction involves "custom-designing instruction based on student needs." In differentiated instruction, educators look at students' learning styles, interests, and abilities. Once these factors have been determined, educators decide which curriculum content, learning activities, products, and learning environment will best serve those individual students' needs. Blended learning can fit into a number of these areas. By using blended learning, educators are definitely altering the learning environment when students work collaboratively in learning communities online. For example, Teachers could also add relevant curriculum content that would be unavailable or difficult to comprehend outside of the internet. Learning activities and products can also be changed to use technologies in a classroom that uses blended learning.

So what does the research say? In a study by Dean and associates, research showed that providing several online option in addition to traditional classroom training actually increased what students learned. Another study showed that student interaction and satisfaction improved, along with students learning more, in courses that incorporated blended learning.

Another advantage of blended learning is pacing and attendance. In most blended learning classrooms, there is the ability to study whenever the student chooses to do so. If a student is absent, she/he may view some of the missed materials at the same time that the rest of the class does, even though the student cannot be physically in the classroom. This helps students stay on track and not fall behind, which is especially helpful for students with prolonged sicknesses or injuries that prevent them from attending school. These "self-study modules" also allow learners to review certain content at any time for help in understanding a concept or to work ahead for those students who learn at a faster pace.

Because of the ability of students to self-pace, there is a higher completion rate for students in blended learning classrooms than to those in strictly e-learning situations. This self-pacing allows for the engagement of every learner in the classroom at any given time. Students also see that the learning involved becomes a process, not individual learning events. This revelation allows for an increased application of the learning done in the classroom.

With the given research, it is clear that using blended learning in education improves the teaching and learning done in a given course. Educators want to teach in a way that best reaches all of their students. If blended learning accomplishes this, then more teachers will begin to use these methods. When teachers begin to explore blended learning and the resources that can be found through the internet and other technologies, they can structure their classroom in a way that best suits their teaching style and their students' learning styles. Blended learning allows "teachers and their students to have the best of both worlds." The traditional classroom and e-learning both have advantages and disadvantages. As Alvarez states, "the online environment is not the ideal setting for all types of learning. Classrooms are not perfect either.... That's why so many teachers and corporate trainers are concentrating their efforts on integrating internet-based technologies and classrooms to create blended learning environments. It just makes good sense."

As stated above blended learning should provide students and teachers with the best of both worlds. Teachers that have been teaching for numerous years may be stuck in their traditional teaching methods. These same teachers may not be technology literate which in turn limits what they can do with technology. Teachers must be trained and required to use some type of technology in the classroom if blended learning is going to successfully take place. The teachers may use a variety of teaching styles, but without technology the students are being cheated out of what they need to be successful in today's world.

## Multimedia Virtual Internet

1. This section focuses on blended learning in the classroom with the use of multimedia and internet resources. This includes the use of videos, virtual field trips, interactive websites, software packages, and broadcasting.
2. Blended learning often requires a reliance on technology use in the classroom. Because there is often a lack of access to technology outside of school, blending learning for many students, must occur in the classroom. The use of the internet for blending learning is wonderful. However, if students do not have access outside of the school day, the blended learning must occur in the classroom.

## Video/Dvd

Blended learning can include technology as common place today as using a video/DVD clip, segment, or movie. What is a video? According to the Corporation for Public Broadcasting (2002) the characteristics of video media are as follows

1. Video is the medium that you...are most familiar with.
2. Video can be distributed as "hard copy" on videocassette or DVD, digitized and delivered on the Web or CD, or distributed through specialized educational channels.
3. Video is especially good at telling a story or showing things that require narrative structure or moving images.
4. Video often has an emotional impact. It's great at "taking you there and making you care." Today, VCRs (or DVD players) are widely accessible in classrooms and informal educational settings.
5. Provide a common experience for all students.
6. Generate Interest and stimulate imagination.
7. Offer a different perspective on or another approach to a topic.
8. Connect students with faraway places.
9. Demonstrate abstract ideas.
10. Stimulate the development of critical thinking skills.
11. Equalize educational opportunities.
12. Enhance self-respect and break down social stereotypes.
13. Promote critical viewing skills and media awareness.

There are many processes that are taught and interest could be gained with a training video. The process of check writing is complicated for some, see the process unfold in a video could increase the knowledge and interest of the process. This would save instructional time and provide more time for the teacher to work one-on-one with students needing further instruction.

## Virtual Field Trips

Blended learning "Virtual Field Trips can be used in any number of ways to serve a variety of educational goals". Fieldtrips have been a method of blending the learning and teaching methods of a class for a many years. The reality of funding shortages force schools to remain on campus. Using blended learning through the virtual fieldtrip is a wonderful opportunity. The virtual fieldtrip experience is an excellent model of a teaching strategy that was not possible before the advent of computers in the (school) classroom (Beal & Mason 1999). Going on a field trip has usually meant taking students out of the school building for some purpose. Today, due to budget restraints and other issues, it is becoming more and more difficult to take students out of the classroom to see things first hand. Schools with computer and internet access have the opportunity to go on fieldtrips without spending any additional money or ever leaving the school building. "Virtual fieldtrips benefit students, families, schools, teachers, and communities". Virtual fieldtrips can take students to places they have personally visited, will be personally visiting.

### Interactive Websites

Blended learning oftentimes includes the use of interactive websites. The use of interactive web sites requires computer and internet access in the school. These sites provide another opportunity for teachers to use technology in their classroom, thus promoting blended learning. Interactive websites can be utilized within the class for those students who do not have internet access and can give other students the opportunity to expand knowledge if access is available privately. For these purposes, when we use the web, we are referring to the Internet.

### Conclusion

The use of information and communication technologies has been found to improve access to as well as student attitudes towards learning. By incorporating information technology into class projects, communication between lecturers and part-time students was improved, and students were able to better evaluate their understanding of course material via the use of "computer-based study.

Blended learning has a strong dependence on the technical resources with which the blended learning experience is delivered these tools need to be reliable, easy to use, and up to date in order for the use of the Internet to have a meaningful impact on the learning experience.

### Reference

1. Http://en.wikibooks.org/wiki/Blended Learning in K-12/Blended Learning in Grades 9-12
2. Http://www.edutopia.org/blog/blended-online-learning-heather-wolpert-gawron
3. Http://www.blendedlearningnow.com/

# 4

# Blended Learning: Mixture of F 2f Learning and U-learning

Blended is a name commonly used to describe a class that combines fact-to-face classroom instruction with online learning? A major part of the activities take place online, while traditional classroom time is reduced but not eliminated. This type of class allows you, the student, to have a more flexible schedule. It still allows for face-to-face contact with your instructor and other classmates just like in a traditional class. Blended learning, sometimes called "Blended learning," provides the best opportunities for learning transition from classroom to e-learning. It provides students with an option of taking some learning materials fully online and some in class, or blended. This article explores the importance of blended learning.

## Blended Learning (H-learning)

The most common reason that an instructor, a learner, or a trainer might pick Blended learning over other learning options is that Blended learning combines the best of both worlds. Based on this, Blended learning provides various benefits over using any single learning delivery type alone, such as pedagogical richness, learning effectiveness, access to knowledge, cost-effectiveness, ease of revision, etc. In fact, Blended learning brings a more natural way to learn and work. A blend is an integrated strategy that involves a planned combination of approaches, such as coaching by a supervisor; participation in an online class; reference to a manual and participation in seminars,

## Characteristics of Blended learning

H-learning means that learning requires students to meet for face to face classes while providing much of the learning content and interaction online via delivery software and instructional tools. The main characteristics of H-learning can be concluded as:

1. Mixed Mode: H-learning combines the socialization, group learning and hands-on opportunities of the classroom (face to face) with the learning possibilities of the online environment (U-learning).
2. Student Centered: Learning shifts from lecture to student-centered instruction.
3. Communications Important: The key element behind a Blended learning environment is the scope and nature of the communication channels provided to support learners.
4. Access flexibility: Blending is used to provide a balance between flexible learning options and knowledge access.
5. Cost-effectiveness: Blended learning provides an opportunity for reaching a large, globally dispersed audience in a short period of time with consistent, semi-personal content delivery.

## Purpose of Blended Learning

A critical element to the blended learning concept is reduced seat time. Reduction of time that students spend in a face-to-face, traditional classroom format serves several purposes that offer several benefits including:

1. Institutions have the potential to manage instructional and facility resources more efficiently, teaching more students within a semester. This approach is beneficial for students, providing the convenience and flexibility associated with online learning, freeing up time for work, family obligations or extra-curricular activities.
2. Blended learning develops a skill set for students that otherwise would not be possible in exclusive face-to-face instruction. Skills include digital citizenship, information management skills, self-directed learning, and web research and collaboration skills.

## Principles of Blended Learning

The following seven pedagogical goals for constructivist Blended learning environments

1. *Provide experience with the knowledge construction process:* Students created rather than used a multimedia learning environment. They were supposed to collect information from a variety of sources. Relevant information had to be selected, analysed and related to their individual prior knowledge. This had then to be structured and edited in accordance with the demands of a web-based learning environment.
2. *Provide experience in appreciation for multiple perspectives:* As students had to acquire declarative knowledge and prepare and edit learning material, they experienced being both in the roles of learners and instructional designers. Furthermore, the media created had to be presented and evaluated in class.
3. *Embed learning in realistic and relevant contexts:* The course dealt with realistic and authentic situations for psychology and education students. Not only did they write a theoretical learning text for the web based learning environment, they also had to come forward with practical examples and exercises for their particular topic. The applied principles of instructional design were especially relevant for their future work in schools and other educational institutions.
4. *Encourage ownership and voice in the learning process:* All participants of the course took responsibility for the project. Personal contributions had to be presented and defended in class. Thus, the degree of individual achievement was made apparent in the course of production and at the end, when the learning environment was put online.
5. *Embed learning in social experience:* The project was planned, run, evaluated and modified within an active dialogue in class as well as in small working groups. Aspects concerning the entity of the web-based learning environment (e.g., the structure and layout of the learning environment) were negotiated in class.
6. *Encourage the use of multiple modes of representation:* Students had to design various learning media: learning texts, different modes of exercises including informative feedback, practical examples, slides, as well as commented links to Internet resources. The specific demands that arise from the particular character of a certain medium had to be recognised.
7. *Encourage self-awareness in the knowledge construction process:* The process of creating a web-based learning environment was

articulated and reflected during the complete period of course. This included continuously working on the personal contributions in small working groups and continuously evaluating the contributions already presented in class. Results of the class' evaluations were used to revise the presented contributions.

We expected that pursuing these goals in a Blended learning course would enable students to engage in active, mindful and purposeful knowledge acquisition and reflection as well as in the development of critical thinking skills.

## Benefits of Blended Learning

1. Enhanced learning: Students usually receive more feedback, and more frequent feedback, from their instructors. Students can acquire useful skills from using the Internet and computer technology. (Live instructor presence, technological enhancements) Students have more time to reflect and refer to relevant course and other research materials when working and writing online than when responding in class.
2. Support for student collaboration: Real-time real-space interactivity and asynchronous online interactions, synchronous online interactions
3. Course accessibility: Students have access to unlimited up-to-date resources available via the Web. Live signing in live courses, transcription of audio and video, labeling of images with alt text online.
4. Rich learner assessment: Automated assessments, live instructor-led assessments, peer assessments live or via the online classroom.
5. 24/7 Accesses: Students often develop or enhance skills in time management, critical thinking, and problem solving. Students typically have 24/7 access to online course materials.
6. Multi-use / Dual use resources: Course contents may often be used in both contexts (F2F and online)

Many students say that they learn more in a Blended course, because they can use outside resources more easily than in a traditional course, but they still have face-to-face access to the instructor and the other students in the course. Almost all students who take Blended courses appreciate the convenience and flexibility to adapt to individual work and family schedules.

## Conclusion

When developing a Blended learning experience we need to contemplate the whole spectrum with learning opportunities that are appropriate to the learner and the situation. It does involve very careful planning and preparation for it to be successful. It is necessary for us to look beyond the traditional boundaries of classroom instruction by augmenting their current best practices with new advances in learning and collaboration technologies to maximize results. More importantly, we should seek to empower every learner to become an active participant in the learning and collaboration process. Anyway, not today also tomorrow, Blended learning will be the best solution for learning.

## References

1. Bersin & Associates. (2003). *Blended learning: What works?: An industry study of the strategy, implementation, and impact of blended learning*: Bersin & Associates.
2. Cottrell, D., & Robison, R. (2003). Blended learning in an accounting course. *Quarterly Review of Distance Education, 4*(3), 261-269.
3. Graham, C. R., Allen, S., & Ure, D. (2003). *Blended learning environments: A review of the research literature.* Unpublished manuscript, Provo, UT.
4. Hadidi, R., & Sung, C. (2000). *Pedagogy of online instruction - Can it be as good as face-to-face?* Proceedings of the Americas Conference of Information Systems, Long Beach, CA.
5. Hara, N., & Kling, R (2000). Students' Distress with a Web-Based Distance Education Course: An Ethnographic Study of Participants' Experiences. *Information, Communication and Society, 3*(4), 557-579.
6. Martyn, M. (2003). The Blended online model: Good practice. Educause Quarterly, 26(1), 18-23.
7. Thiyagu, K., & Amirthagowri.K. (2009, Feb). Mobile learning is future learning, Edutrack, vol.8. No.6. PP.5 to 8.
8. Young, J. R. (2002, March 22). 'Blended' teaching seeks to end the divide between traditional and online instruction. *Chronicle of Higher Education,* pp. A33.

# 5

# Blended Learning in Teacher Education

## Introduction

Blended learning is a term increasingly used to describe the way e-learning is being combined with traditional classroom methods and independent study to create a new, hybrid teaching methodology. It represents a much greater change in basic technique than simply adding computers to classrooms; it represents, in many cases, a fundamental change in the way teachers and students approach the learning experience. It has already produced an offshoot–the flipped classroom – that has quickly become a distinct approach of its own.

## Definition Of Blended Learning

1. "The thoughtful integration of classroom face-to- face learning experiences with online learning experiences"
2. "Blended learning combines online with face-to-face learning. The goal of blended learning is to provide the most efficient and effective instruction experience by combining delivery modalities".
3. "Blended learning - mixed mode or hybrid - learning is the integration of face-to-face (F2F) learning with online learning activities"
4. A solution that combines several different delivery methods, such as collaboration software, Web-based courses, EPSS, and knowledge management practices"

5. "Learning that mixes various event-based activities, including face-to-face classrooms, live e-learning, and self-paced instruction. "
6. "Blended learning is the effective combination of different modes of delivery, models of teaching and styles of learning"
7. Blended learning is the combination of multiple approaches to pedagogy or teaching. For example:- self-paced, collaborative or inquiry-based study.

## Objectives of Blended Learning

1. Increase the amount and quality of faculty-to-student and student-to-student interaction;
2. Increase opportunities for active and collaborative learning and assessment before, during and after lectures;
3. Help students prepare for class discussions or lab work;
4. Facilitate more varied and engaging media for presenting course content;
5. Address learning bottlenecks via new types of interactive and independent learning activities;
6. Allow class time to be spent on active learning activities by shifting background or foundational content to the online environment;
7. Help to create a sense of community in large classes;
8. Allow students to access course materials when and where they want, at their own pace.
9. Build a community of teachers driven by learning from one another
10. Empower teachers
11. Structure learning around the needs of teachers and their classroom practices
12. Drive collaborative teacher problem-solving

## History of Blended Learning

The concept of blended learning, in which multiple learning environments and activities are combined, has existed for quite some time. Long before the advent of computers and social networks, teachers created blended learning experiences using simple technologies like paper and pencil. Educators have always crafted learning experiences that incorporate a variety of activities in different environments for the purpose of reinforcing learning material. For example, consider the concept of the apprenticeship. Prior to the hands-on experience, the apprentice studied the work of the master through observation, conversation, and possibly through reading.

Contemporary definitions of blended learning take into account the role that technology can play. Technologies like CD-ROM and later the internet made it possible to create new environments for learning, new opportunities for synchronous and asynchronous collaboration, and new modes of delivery for learning materials, self-directed guides, and tutorials. More recently, blended learning figures prominently in conversations about online learning. In this context, blended learning represents a convergence of online and face-to-face experiences. Interactions across both environments are mitigated by space, time, fidelity, and personal interaction. While some research indicates that blended learning solutions have a positive impact on student learning, most research has taken place in higher education and adult learning, so care should be taken when extending this research to the K-12 arena.

### Components of Blended Learning

1. Synchronous Physical/Face-to-Face Components
2. Synchronous Electronic Components
3. Asynchronous Components

### Synchronous Physical/Face-to-to-Face Components

1. Face-to-face Tutoring
2. Coaching or Mentoring Sessions
3. Classroom
4. Workshops
5. Conferences
6. Meetings
7. Labs

### Synchronous Electronic components

1. Internet conferencing
2. Audio Conferencing (i.e., phone conferencing)
3. Live Video via satellite or Videoconferencing
4. Virtual Online Classroom

### Asynchronous Components

1. On-line self-paced Learning Content (Web pages)
2. E-mail, Discussion Forums
3. EPSS (Electronic Support Systems) & Job Aids
4. Web/Computer-Based instruction

5. Books
6. Articles
7. CD-ROM
8. Audio (disc/tape)
9. Video (disc/tape)
10. White papers
11. Archived Live Events

There is a general consensus among education innovators that blended learning has three primary components:

1. In-person classroom activities facilitated by a trained educator.
2. Online learning materials, often including pre-recorded lectures given by that same instructor.
3. Structured independent study time guided by the material in the lectures and skills developed during the classroom experience.

A course created in a blended learning model uses the classroom time for activities that benefit the most from direct interaction. Traditional education (especially at the college level) tends to place an emphasis on delivering material by way of a lecture, while in a blended learning model lectures can be videotaped ahead of time so the student can watch on their own time. The classroom time is more likely to be for structured exercises that emphasize the application of the curriculum to solve problems or work through tasks.

An individual semester of blended learning may emphasize classroom time at the beginning, then gradually increase the amount of work that students do online or during independent study. Many argue that class discussion boards, for example, are far more useful if the participants have met face-to-face first.

The "flipped" classroom, a more recent coinage, refers to classes that are structured almost exclusively around a reversal of expectations for lectures and homework. Students are expected to watch lectures online at home, and do homework while they are in class.

## Creating a Blended Learning Experience

In a blended learning approach, attention is given to the overall instructional design of the learning experience. While thoughtful planning is essential, blended learning is a fluid process whereby learning needs, moments of insight, and unique pathways evolve. Ideally, the learner is offered more choice in how the learning experience unfolds. This kind of flexibility makes it easier to differentiate instruction, satisfying the needs of a diverse population of learners. Technology is used as a tool for learning and to promote a discovery-based approach to online learning and is not necessary in all blended learning scenarios. The following questions offer additional insight into the creation of a blended experience.

1. What are the learning outcomes of this experience? I.e., what skills, knowledge, and dispositions should students develop as a result of the experience?
2. What topics and subtopics must be addressed by the entire learning experience in order to achieve the learning outcomes?
3. What are the learning events (activities) chosen to address the learning outcomes?
4. What portion of content is accessed during each learning event?
5. What is the most appropriate mode for delivering that content?
6. In what setting does the learning event occur?
7. What supports and teacher input are needed for that learning event?
8. Where should formative assessment appear relative to each learning event?
9. How does the learning event relate to previous learning events and those that follow?
10. How will learners transfer their change in understanding from one learning event to another?

## Six Forms of Blended Learning

1. Face-to-face Driver
2. Rotation
3. Flex
4. Online Lab
5. Self-Blend
6. Online Driver

## Face-to-face Driver

Face-to-face driver is a blended learning model in which teachers deliver most of the curriculum. Teachers lead the class in a lecture following an established protocol taking precedence and technology being a secondary thought. However, they also produce online resources to supplement or revise course material which students can study at home, in the classroom or in a technology lab.

## Rotation

In the Rotation model of blended learning: within a given course, a student rotates on a fixed schedule between learning online in a one-to-one, self-paced environment and sitting in a classroom with a traditional face-to-face teacher.

## Flex

Flex model of blended learning features an online platform that delivers most of the curricula. It's the model where most of the learning is done online and the face-to-face model exists to provide on-site support for a flexible and adaptive, as required basis through in-person tutoring sessions and small group sessions.

## Online Lab

Online lab is a model of blended learning that characterizes programs that rely on an online platform to deliver the entire course but in a brick-and-mortar lab environment. The entire course and teaching are done online. Teachers interact with students through pre recorded videos, audio and video conferences or discussion forums and email.

## Self Blend

The Self-Blend model is a fully individualized approach that allows students to choose to take one or more courses online to supplement their traditional school's catalog. Maximum part of the learning is done online, but the student will still attend face-to-face classes.

## Online Driver

Online Driver involves online platform as well as teachers to deliver the curricula. Students work from remote locations most of the time and come to school for optional or required face-to-face classes. Have a look at the info graphic below to know what blended learning is, what its different forms are, why it's spreading, and how it works in real and virtual class-rooms.

## Challenges of Blendeded Learning

The challenges of offering Blended Learning are:

## Managing instructional complexity

In blended learning the instructor has a wider choice of delivery mediums to combine. With wider choice also comes greater complexity and pressure on the instructor and designer. This is due to the variety of combinations of technology and possibly the lack of patterns to follow for that particular mix. These issues need to be addressed and taken into account during the design.

## Designing it

Designing a blended learning course that maximizes the potential of both the face-to-face and online components raises questions: What is the best definition of blended learning? How much of each modality should comprise a course? We argue that students and faculty should not view the face-to-face aspect of a blended course and the online element as separate components. The instructional design perspective requires a re-evaluation of teaching and learning to blend or harmonize the distinction between the two, made even more formidable by the presence of the new learners.

## Managing roles and Responsibilities

Unlike traditional classroom learning in which there usually is a single instructor, in blended learning, there are multiple individuals, each taking a role in the blend. Clarification of instructor and assistant roles is essential for success and the reduction of potential conflict and learner confusion.

## Creating a seamless learning experience

Good communications among instructors during planning is an important element in the success of blended learning. It is to be made sure that instructors and assistants communicate with one another throughout the instruction, not only just before the course. All prerequisites are to be met by the previous learning objects as different segments of the blend are designed.

## Meeting expectations

Managing expectations for instructors and learners is also important to realistically perceive the benefits during the training or course.

## Controlling costs

The cost savings of ICT introduction in blended learning still remains in theory while it seems that the greatest pedagogical advantages of ICT are the most costly: personalisation, real-time communication and other advanced functionalities lead to significant costs. Other costs may include courseware development costs, incremental capital and recurrent equipment costs, costs associated with provision of appropriate resources, infrastructure costs, maintenance, user support costs, costs of adoption, access costs, security costs, replacement costs and institutional overheads. These costs can be reduced by collaborative organizational structure and internal partnerships. Costs may be cut to significant level through sharing of e-resources among the faculty, students and instructional staff. Furthermore, initial investments will make this approach cost effective in the long run.

## Suggestions

1. At B.Ed level lesson plan can be prepared by trainees through Blended learning
2. All the Universities can be recommended to prepare modules based on blended learning
3. Students enrolled in a blended learning course ought to be techno-savvy to access online component of the course and communicate with the faculty for getting assignments checked and problems solved to make learning more effective. But most of students find it difficult to get information from web or to access online component of course or to download big files etc.

## Conclusions

Blended learning can prove a powerful strategy, if learning experiences are well designed. In spite of issues related to blend learning, it has potential to impact Indian Teacher education in a positive way by forming the underpinning of a transformational model that irrevocably holds expectations for students, faculty and administrators. The outcomes are most effective when participants share an inspiring vision, seek maximum possible involvement and bring out the best in others, celebrate accomplishments and model behaviours that facilitate collaboration.

It needs to be emphasized that transformational leadership needs to be exhibited by senior administration to fully realize the benefits and overcome the challenges associated with blended learning in Teacher education institutions. This leadership consists of three interrelated core elements; vision, interpersonal skills, and courage. These facilitative leadership components in conjunction with blended learning can create synergy for positive realignment of Teacher education. The vision for blended learning must be in the best interests of the institution and truly shared amongst the constituent members.

## Refrences

1. Bhattacharya, I. & Sharma, K. (2007). 'India in the knowledge economy–electronic Choices for Higher Education Institutions; University of Surrey, UK.
2. Hung, D. and Nichani, M. (2001). Constructivism and e-Learning: Balancing between the Individual and Social Levels of Cognition. *Educational Technology.*
3. Johnson,J. (2002). Reflections on teaching a large enrollment course using a hybrid format. *Teaching with technology today, 8*(6). Available HTTP: http://www.uwsa.edu/ttt/articles/jjohnson.htm.
4. Middlehurst, R. (2003). Competition, Collaboration and ICT: Challenges and paradigm', *International Journal of Educational Management* Vol. 21 No. 6, pp. 543-568.

# 6

# Blended Learning–An Innovative Learning Approach

## Introduction

The concept and practice of blending learning opportunities is not new, but in today's digital age what is new is the range of possible components in a blend. Blended learning, when well understood and implemented, has the potential to support deep and meaningful learning, but simply mixing information technologies with face-to-face learning is not sufficient to exploit the full potential of blended learning. Blended learning approaches have amplified the need for school leaders, teachers, students and the wider community to take advantage of learning opportunities afforded through improved personalization, collaboration, and communication enabled by learning technologies. This paper is a review of literature and current information related to blended learning to deal with several issues which includes blended learning in present situation, designing blended learning activities, impact of blended learning on teaching and learning, the role of student and the teacher in blended learning.

Learning always includes a combination of inputs such as new information blending with already existing knowledge. Learning is an inherently social process, where different strategies for effective learning can be implemented (Strobl, 2007). With the development in Information and Communication Technology (ICT) blended learning modernized and considered to be the proper combination of technologies in addition to face to face learning. The use of new technologies in teaching and learning can assist in both the enhancement of traditional teaching methods and the development of students' technical skills. Hence blended learning can be a bridge between traditional teaching and online teaching.

Many of the online learning technologies address mobility of student learning, which enables students to learn anywhere, anytime and with various devices (Herrington et al. 2012). These include learning management systems providing a virtual platform for students to access teaching resources and interact with teachers, web-based flexible learning environments, and media to encourage collaborative learning among students. In regard to developing technological skills, a wide range of technologies can be used to assist in training students.

The rapid technology change can adversely result in a shift from higher education towards training (Burtch, 2005), i.e. while trying to keep up with the new technology, more focus may be put on skill development rather than on learning theoretical principles. Therefore, a balance of the two components should always be maintained. To face this challenge, a blended learning approach, where learning education combines face to face classroom methods with computer-mediated activities (Strauss, 2012), can be used to combine technology with pedagogical principles for the benefit of student learning (Garrison and Kanuka 2004, Hoic-Bozic *et al.* 2009).

## Blended learning in present scenario

There is an increasing need and demand to respond to diverse students' needs and provide engaging and meaningful learning experiences in higher education. Compounded with new technologies beyond and within the academy, this inevitably draws information and communication technology into traditional learning environments. McGreal and Anderson's (2007) review of e-learning in Canada finds that the majority of Canadian universities have a web-based component in many courses and that this integration of technology in learning is expanding. In the USA, Allen and Seaman (2010) report that over 30% of undergraduate learners participate in some form of online/blended/technology mediated learning and over 70% of US higher educational institutions indicate that online learning is critical to their long term strategy. Further, participation in the Sloan

Consortium Blended Learning Conference has been increasing over the last eight years. Notably, the Eighth Annual Conference (2011) recognized that the incorporation of blended learning is expanding. Moreover, this growth of blended learning is based on evidence – evidence of its ability to positively impact teaching and learning, access, time to degree, and efficiency, all of which are key challenges in higher education. Sparrow (2003) listed the following reasons for developing blended learning solutions:

1. Ability to match learning styles (80%)
2. Individually tailored solutions (70%)
3. Improve the learning rate (62%)
4. Exploit the investments they've already made in re-usable training resources (59%)
5. Shortage of time to use purely classroom events (57%)

Osguthorpe (2003) suggested that pedagogical richness, access to knowledge, social interaction, personal agency, cost effectiveness and ease of revision are the reasons for blended learning.

## Designing blended learning activities

With reference to the authors of *Issues in Digital Technology in Education: Blended Learning* (Wikibooks, 2009), they have identified the following four broad principles of education design for blended learning.

1. A thoughtful integration of face-to-face and fully online instructional components
2. Innovative use of technology
3. Re-thinking the way we teach
4. Su*stained assessment and evaluation of blended learning.*

According to Bonk and Graham (2006) in their *Handbook of Blended Learning*, blended learning should be approached as a fundamental redesign of the instructional model with the following characteristics:

1. A shift from teacher-centered to student-centered instruction in which students become active and interactive learners (this shift should apply to the entire course, including face-to-face contact sessions).
2. Increase in interaction between student-teacher, student-student, student-content, and student-outside resources.
3. Integrated formative and summative assessment mechanisms for students and teachers.

The key steps involved in designing for blended learning should be considered well in advance, and include:

4. Planning for integration of blended learning principles in your unit
5. Designing the learning activities and assessment and developing them as required
6. Implementing the blended learning design
7. Evaluating the effectiveness of your blended learning designs
8. Making improvements for the next time you teach your blended unit

## Template for Designing Blended Learning

Follow these four steps to start designing your own blended pathway.

1. Identify the learning outcomes for your classroom lesson.
2. Identify the activities for student to do **in** class.
3. Identify the activities for students to do online **before** class.
4. Identify the activities for student to do **after** class

## Choosing blended learning activities

The level of learning that students' achieve is often dependent on the type of activities and assessment tasks, and whether they are aligned with the set objectives or desired learning outcomes. One useful framework for considering learning objectives and suitable activities is Bloom's Taxonomy (Bloom, 1956), a hierarchical classification of the different objectives that are typically set for students.

## Impact of blended learning on teaching and learning

According to a study conducted by Vaughan, Zimmer & Villamar (2011) at the universities, students saw the flexibility afforded by blended learning as a key advantage. They also enjoyed the increased opportunities for interacting with their classmates and the instructors through the integration of new technologies. The recent study of blended first year courses at Mount Royal demonstrated that students who perceived a higher level of active and collaborative learning in these courses were also the most successful, based on final course grades. Students who most frequently accessed the course learning management system to complete assessment tasks were also the ones with the highest final grades in these courses. It appears that the online interaction, collaboration and assessment were contributing factors to student performance – e.g., better grades.

The second advantage of blended learning is improved learning outcomes found through student surveys, formal studies, and informal feedback. University responses attributed the improved learning outcomes to the increased quality of interaction among learners, between students and instructors, and the richness of learning resources. Current research findings corroborate the responses that suggest higher learning outcomes in blended learning environments (Vaughan, 2007; Akyol & Garrison, 2011; Vaughan, Zimmer & Villamar, 2011). Internationally, blended learning research reveals similar findings. In a recent study conducted at a Spanish university with a large sample it was found that blended learning had a positive effect on reducing dropout rates and in raising exam pass rates (López-Pérez, Pérez-López & Rodríguez-Ariza, 2011). Drawing on over a decade of experience in institution-wide blended learning, Hartman (2010) reports consistently over 85% student success in blended learning course offerings. Similarly, the study authored by Collopy and Arnold (2009) shows that students in the blended courses reported significantly higher level of learning than those in the online course.

The most significant gain for the university through blended learning applications will be the change in practice through integrating face-to-face and online practices in a meaningful way (Nemiec & Otte, 2010).

Blended learning is a safer mid-point for faculty, between the familiar of face-to-face learning and the often unfamiliar online learning. Blended learning also enables and expands existing resources, particularly blending the tools and technologies available for distance learning in the classroom. Moreover, blended learning can also utilize distance education resources such as learning objects, videos etc. within the online components of blended learning classes.

## Role of teachers and students in blended learning

### *The teacher's role in the blend:*

The role of teachers has always been central to providing a structured and engaging teaching and learning environment. The classroom or face-to-face teaching component remains central to blended language learning, and the role of the teacher in the blended learning environment remains indispensable. Technology can only achieve so much, and the teacher has to be the motivating, organizing force to the integration of students' online and classroom learning. Many features of the teacher's role remain unchanged in the blended learning environment. The teacher continues to encourage and motivate, guide and monitor progress, give feedback, boost confidence, and maintain motivation. The role played by teachers in blended learning is:

1. Promoting student-centered learning in the classroom
2. Facilitating the blend
3. Creating a supportive online community
4. Managing and facilitating online interaction

***The student's role in the blend:***

It is often overlooked that students need time to adapt to and develop in a new learning environment. Supporting students through this transition is crucial. They have the following roles in blended learning.

1. Managing and planning independent study time
2. Learning independently
3. Working collaboratively online
4. Reviewing and self-correcting

## Conclusion

Blended learning provides flexibility in learning for both students and teachers. Integration of the virtual and physical landscapes enable both teachers and students to become learners but this is most effective when there is institutional support through provision of professional learning and the opportunity for redesigning courses for the most appropriate blend. Blended learning will combine traditional classroom learning with online and mobile learning in order to maximise the understanding of theoretical principles, gaining knowledge and development of technical, practical and professional skills.

## Reference

1. Akyol, Z., & Garrison, D. R. (2011). Understanding cognitive presence in an online and blended community of inquiry: Assessing outcomes and processes for deep approaches to learning. *British Journal of Educational Technology*, 42(2), 233-250.
2. Blended Learning. Education, Communication & Information, 2005. **5**(3): p. 217-220.
3. Bonk C. and Graham C. (2006) *Handbook of Blended Learning.* Jossey-Bass Inc. U.S.A.
4. Burtch, R. (2005). Surveying education and technology: Who's zooming who? *Surveying and Land Information Science*, 65(3), 135-143.

5. Collopy, R.M.B. & Arnold, J. M. (2009). To Blend or Not to Blend: Online and Blended Learning Environments in Undergraduate Teacher Education. *Issues in Teacher Education, 18(2), 85-101.*
6. Garrison, D. R. & Kanuka, H. (2004). Blended learning: Uncovering its transformative potential in higher education. *The Internet and Higher Education*, 7(2), 95-105.
7. Herrington, A., Schrape, J. & Singh, K. (2012). Engaging students with learning technologies, eScholar Program, Curtin University, Perth.
8. Hoic-Bozic, N., Mornar, V. & Boticki, I. (2009). A blended learning approach to course design and implementation. *IEEE Transactions on Education*, 52(1), 19-30.
9. Kollias, V., et al., (2005). Teachers' attitudes to and beliefs about web-based Collaborative Learning Environments in the context of an international implementation. Comput. Educ., 45 (3): p. 295-315.
10. McGreal, R., & Anderson, T. (2007). E-Learning in Canada. *Journal of Distance Education Technologies*, *5*(1), 1-6
11. Niemiec, M. & Otte, G. (2010). An Administrator's guide to the whys and hows of blended learning. *Journal of Asynchronous Learning Networks*, 13(1), 19-30.
12. Osguthorpe, R. a. G., Charles R. (2003). Blended Learning Environments: Definitions and Directions. *The Quarterly Review of Distance Education*, *4*(3), 227-233.
13. Sparrow, S. (November, 2003). Blended Learning Makes Mark. *Training Magazine.*
14. Strobl, J. (2007). Geographic learning. Geoconnexion International Magazine, 6(5). 46-47.
15. Vaughan, N. (2007). Perspectives on Blended Learning in Higher Education. *International Journal on E-Learning.* 6*(1),* 81-94.
16. Vaughan, N., Zimmer, J. & Villamar, F. (2011). Student Engagement and Interactive Technologies: What's the connection? *International Journal of Excellence in E-Learning.*
17. Wikibooks (2009) Issues in digital technology in education: Blended learning.

# 7

# Different Style of Today's Modern Learning

## Introduction

Education has been a very essential component for the success of most developed nations. The rapid technology change can adversely result in a shift from higher education towards training i.e. while trying to keep up with the new technology and more focus may be put on skill development rather than on learning theoretical principles. Therefore, a balance of the two components should always be maintained. To face this challenge, a blended learning approach, where learning education combines face to face classroom methods with computer-mediated activities can be used to combine technology with pedagogical principles for the benefit of student learning. In this paper, a blended teaching approach is mainly focused and presented using surveying education as an example. In addition to classroom learning, it includes online learning and mobile learning. Blended learning that encourages the gaining of knowledge can also be coupled with traditional information-gained skills- development learning (authentic learning).

Learning is an inherently social process, where different strategies for effective learning can be implemented. The use of new technologies in teaching and learning, e.g. e-learning, can assist in both the enhancement of traditional teaching methods and the development of students' technical skills. At present, there are several e-learning technologies available. Many of these address mobility of student learning, which enables students to learn anywhere, anytime and with various devices. These include learning management systems providing a virtual platform for students to access teaching resources and interact with teachers, web-based flexible learning environments, and media to encourage collaborative learning among students. In regard to developing technological skills, a wide range of technologies can be used to assist in training students. These can range from videos for demonstration, recording and reflective analysis purpose to simulation-based e-learning systems.

Blended Learning is an approach to learning and teaching which combines and aligns learning undertaken in face-to-face sessions with learning opportunities created online. New types of learning activities challenge our thinking as to how learning might be facilitated, creating new etiquettes of learning and teaching, and shifting the locus of control from the teacher to the learner. Blended learning is a powerful strategy for many reasons. If well designed, it addresses more learning style requirements, a wider audience and increased performance or learning results. Making the best selection of method (media) will greatly enhance these results. Blended Learning refers to a combination of online and face-to-face methods in response to learners' needs and for the achievement of instructional objectives. Considering students' learning styles in education and especially in technology enhanced education can have many benefits for students such as making students aware of their learning styles and therefore helping them to understand why learning is sometimes difficult for them.

## Approaches of Blended Learning

Blended learning is an educational approach where the traditional classroom is integrated with an online component. A web-based Learning Management System (LMS) contains curriculum and course materials, and ties the two learning environments (classroom + online) together. In a blended learning model, the teacher conducts lessons during scheduled class sessions and students are assigned independent study online. The student receives face-to-face instruction during class meetings, and then logs into the LMS for independent study (or virtual group collaboration) to continue their learning and to complete assignments. The focus is on *engaging* the learner with pre-work, classroom instruction, e-Learning before or during class, videos, etc. The focus is on keeping the learner interested and engaged with different media. Blended courses integrate online with face-to-face instruction in a planned, pedagogically valuable manner, and do not just combine but trade-off face-to-face time with online activity, or vice versa

## Characteristics of Blended Learning

1. Blended learning takes many forms. In general, it has three characteristics. It is flexibility of providing learning resources.
2. Blended learning is treated as an instructional strategy, which is developed in a networked environment. Such a strategy is usually supported by virtual learning environments (VLEs), which are a computer-based standardized learning system and are used to sustain content delivery of online learning as well as to promote online communication between an instructor and learners, Studies show that, with the medium of VLEs, the three most common uses in blended learning are providing course information, supplementing on-campus studies as well as accessing Internet resources. It can help diversify the provision of learning resources through BBS, E-mail, and other functions.
3. The second is support of learning diversity. As learners are diverse in terms of learning styles, learning proficiency, as well as learning ability, blended learning can come to the rescue by making it possible for individualized learning and self regulated learning to happen. Teachers can use combined approaches to cater for the needs of the diverse student body and to create an opportunity to make everyone's learning an equally successful experience.
4. The third is enrichment of e-learning experience on campus. From the faculty's perspective, blended learning can enable them to improve their existing teaching practices. For example, we used to ask students to submit their weekly assignments by the paper, but now we ask them to submit their work by email and then we evaluate their performance by e-Portfolios. One more specific example, we used to teach students with the typically teacher-centered approach, but now individualized learning is no longer a rarely seen phenomenon.
5. Learning systems also help teachers to reduce the burden of calculating the marks of the papers, for the systems can do the whole trick automatically. From the learners' perspective, learning has become rights of their own, which they can make own decisions

on what they do each day and what they are going to achieve by certain deadlines for the same goal and how they are going to achieve them. Moreover, learning anytime and anywhere has become a reality. From the administrators' perspective, tons of paper work has been replaced by limited e-work. Educational administration brought about by blended learning has become as easy as mouse-clicking.

## Need and Importance of Blended Learning

The three most commonly mentioned dentitions are:

1. Combining instructional modalities
2. Combining instructional methods
3. Combining online and face-to-face instruction

## Support for Development and Delivery of Blended Learning

In the course of our discussions, it became clear that any move to blended learning would be likely to present resource implications related to new or additional resources for staffing, technology, and training and support. The group suggested that such courses should become part of the resource allocation process involving the department and department head, faculty council and dean. Criteria and policies through which that support would be made accessible also need to be developed. Resource issue that surfaced includes:

### Faculty resources

Initiatives should not be allowed to get ahead of, or drive, faculty budgets and the dean therefore needs to be involved in any proposal that has resource implications for the faculty. Individuals or curriculum groups cannot design courses or programs with associated resource issues and then attempt to impose them on the dean. Conversely, if the dean of faculty seeks to promote blended learning initiatives, they need to be prepared to resource them.

At the moment, there is little consistency in practice in the Faculty, and there are at least three different models at work (i) individual initiatives, often without any formal approval or 'quality control process' and without any resource support, (ii) Faculty initiatives in which an instructor is provided release time for the course, and (iii) initiatives in which the Faculty and Extended Education collaborate to develop an online/blended course.

## Infrastructure

Equipment, facilities, and instructor support have also been handled only on a pilot basis, with some resource needs being met through individual funding applications.

## Resource issues for students

At the course level, this support includes access to a well-equipped computer and high-speed internet access as well as technical support. Resources and accessibility issues need to be investigated for all students, but with particular attention to implications for rural, northern, and First Nations communities. It is clear that we need resource policies for online/ blended course development and delivery. These might be in the form of program development funds, with funding adjudicated according to criteria relating to access, quality, costs, and priorities of the curriculum group and faculty. If blended learning initiatives are to succeed, let alone expand, we need to move beyond pilot projects to a systematic, resourced academic plan.

## Advantages of Blended Learning

1. Blended learning allows businesses and schools alike to make maximum use of the technologies and other resources that they have available to them. This means that it allows both businesses and schools to take a look at all the technologies and tools that they have and see how it can best be used to bring the greatest benefit to employee/students and the organization even as they spend as little as they possibly can and still maintain effectiveness.

2. The organization offering the course can create his/her own content.
3. The global reach of the blended approach to education and training continues to be one of its greatest advantages. Uses concerning distance are eliminated.
4. The speed with which you can reach thousands of people is unmatched by traditional methods as they can all be reach simultaneously without the restrictions of time and space.
5. Blended learning allows learners the flexibility with their time to do their lessons anytime and anyplace until a meeting with the lecturer becomes compulsory.
6. It can make it easier to deal with educational administration and communication with all students. Virtual office hours make tutors far more accessible than in a strictly face-to-face scenario.

7. Students get their learning needs and styles catered to whether they prefer online or face-to-face because it offers both in a single course.
8. For sessions held online, the communication between teacher and student is open and everyone can benefit from it because everyone can view the responses sent by the teacher.
9. Some lecturers experience an improvement in the quality of students' writing and discussion.

## Disadvantages of Blended Learning

1. Before a blended learning scenario can be considered ready for use, the lecturer has to do long, detailed and extensive work. Preparation for startup is very time consuming.
2. There can be limited contact between lecturer and students and so some of the dynamism that comes with face-to-face interaction can be lost.
3. Based on what students are used to, they often prefer the paper versions of the materials than to see them online so the face-to-face sessions in the blended programmes usually have a comparatively more successful "feel" for the students.
4. The materials developed by the lecturers cannot simply be the same set that they had developed for handouts. They have to be reformatted so that they guide the students through a process of independent study when they are not in a face-to-face session. This additional task required of the lecturers is yet to be appreciated for what it is worth.
5. Students sometimes feel that they are given more work to do when distance modalities are used.

## Conclusion

Blended Learning is a set of educational philosophies, technologies, and solutions, concerned with providing learners with increased choice, convenience, and personalization to suit the learner. In particular, blended learning provides learners with choices about where, when, and how learning occurs. Blended Learning refers to a mixing of different learning environments. The phrase has many specific meanings based upon the context in which it is used. Blended learning gives learners and teachers a potential environment to learn and teach more effectively. A blended learning approach can combine face-to-face instruction with computer-mediated instruction. It also applies science or IT activities with the assistance of educational technologies using computer, cellular or smart phones, Satellite television channels, video conference. Learners and teachers work together to improve the quality of learning and teaching, the ultimate aim of blended learning being to provide realistic practical opportunities for learners and teachers to make learning independent, useful, sustainable and ever growing. This paper has presented the successful application of blended learning in distance learning especially in terms of students' learning experience, student-student interaction and student-instructor interaction. The blended learning approach is likely to emerge as the predominant instructional model in the future.

## References

1. Alexander, S., & McKenzie, J. (1998). An Evaluation of Information Technology Projects for University Learning. Canberra, Australia: Committee for University Teaching and Staff Development and the Department of Employment, Education, Training and Youth Affairs.
2. Harel Caperton, Idit. (2012) Learning to Make Games for Impact. The Journal of Media Literacy, 59(1), 28-38
3. Martyn, Margie (2003). "The hybrid online model: Good practice.". Educause Quarterly: 18–23

# 8

# Blended Learning

Blended learning refers to a mixing of different learning environments. The phrase has many specific meanings based upon the context in which it is used. Blended learning gives learners and teachers a potential environment to learn and teach more effectively. Blended learning assumes the continued use of face-to-face teaching as a basic building block of the learning experience, enriched and enhanced by the integration of the Internet and other teaching and learning technologies into studies undertaken both in and out of the classroom. This integration should happen with the mediation and support of the teacher and, as with any materials used, should reflect and work toward the learning aims and needs of all learners.

## Blending Learning Methods, Approaches, And Strategies Are Not New

The practice of blending learning is, therefore, not a new way of teaching, nor is it a single method of learning. The term *blended learning* first appeared around 2000 and was at that time often associated with simply sup-plementing traditional classroom learning with self-study e-learning activities. More recently, the pedagogic value of providing blended learning opportuni-ties has received significant attention, and the term has evolved to encompass a much richer set of learning approaches and environments.

Today *blended learning* can refer to any combination of different methods of learning, dif-ferent learning environments, different learning styles. In short, the effective implementation of blended learning is essentially all about making the most of the learning opportunities and tools available to achieve the "optimal" learn-ing environment.

## Language Learning, the Classroom, Online Content, and web 2.0

Computers have been used in language teaching since the 1960s, and teachers have been blending face-to-face instruction with various kinds of technol-ogy-mediated language learning for decades. However, the impact of CALL (computer-assisted language learning) has been relatively modest. This has been mainly due to the absence of technology appropriate to the specific needs of lan-guage learners. This all changed with the arrival of the Internet, which provides second language learners with immediate access to the worldwide community of English language speakers, and to authentic resources through its billions of interconnected Web pages. The Internet, in particular the emergence of Web 2.0, represents a powerful medium to teach and learn foreign languages. The following strengths of blended language learning have been identified.

1. Provides a more individualized learning experience
2. Provides more personalized learning support
3. Supports and encourages independent and collaborative learning
4. Increases student engagement in learning
5. Provides a place to practice the target language beyond the classroom
6. Provides a less stressful practice environment for the target language
7. Provides flexible study, anytime or anywhere, to meet learners' needs
8. Helps students develop valuable and necessary twenty-first century learning skills

Online learning/teaching environments can provide for different ways of learning and the construction of a potentially richer learning environment that provides fresh approaches to learning, thereby allowing for different learn-ing styles, as well as greater diversification in and greater access to learning. Such learning environments should supplement or complement traditional face-to-face learning environments or, on the other hand, may provide a com-plete learning package that requires little face-to-face contact. Without a doubt, all teaching in the very near future will be suppor-ted by more or less digital- or net-based flexible solutions in the educational organization. Thus, the impor-tant question to ask ourselves now is how should we blend?

## Finding Your Blend

The starting point for establishing complementarily is to identify the learning outcomes, identify your students' needs, and identify the different, potential components available to you. At this point, you should then be able to identify how best these learning outcomes and needs can be supported by the different components available to you.

## Pedagogically Sound Learning Materials

The choice of materials is critical.

Teachers need to evaluate educational mate-rials such as software programs carefully and use only those materials that are methodologically sound. Students like to use different media. Newer technolo-gies and older media (i.e., CD-ROMs) both have a place in blended language learning where learners can choose the medium that best suits their needs. Teachers need to vary the usage of such media to accommodate student needs.

## Support

In any blended learning context in which technology supported self-study is central to the blend, learners will require support in three important ways: aca-demic, affective, and technical.

## The Teachers Role in the Blend

## Promoting Student-centered Learning In The Classroom

In student-centered teaching, we focus our planning, our teaching, and our assessment around the needs and abilities of our students. The main idea behind the practice is that learning is most meaningful when topics are relevant to the students' lives, needs, and interests and when the students themselves are actively engaged in creating, understanding, and connecting to knowledge.

## Facilitating the Blend

The teacher's role in facilitating the blend should not be unde-resti-mated. Using the technology effectively for learning often requires training and support. Students need to adopt and use learning strategies that are differ-ent from what they are used to in the more traditional, face-to-face classroom environments.

## Encouraging autonomous and collaborative learning

Blended learning allows students to decided when and where they want to study. This flexibility can present some difficulties to students who have poor time management skills and who are not used to working autonomously. It is your role as the teacher to help your students develop the skills they require to work independently, particularly if this is the first time they have learned a language in a blended learning environment.

### Managing and facilitating online interaction

Depending on the technology used, blended learning can provide opportunities for genuine interaction online. One of the simplest communication tools is a forum, or bulletin board. The teacher is to monitor this interaction and decide how best to manage it.

## The Student's Role in the Blend

### Learning independently

The online component of blended learning allows students to learn when and where they want. It offers students the complete flexibility to choose the time they study with no constraints of fixed "classroom" hours.

### Working collaboratively online

A blended language course should provide students with the tools and the opportunities to interact with their classmates, and it is important that students learn to take full advantage of the online community.

### Reviewing and self-correcting

Many online learning materials are automatically "marked," so students receive an immediate "score." Achieving the correct answers provides students with a clear sense of progress and achievement, but students also need to know what to do when they get something wrong.

## Designing Pathways For Blended Learning

### A pathway template and key principles

The pathway template is designed to provide your students with

1. an effective and efficient use of classroom time.
2. increased opportunities for using English outside of class.
3. maximum opportunities for review and recycling for improved learning.

There are three parts to the pathway template:

1. Online: prepare for class

2. In class: focus on communication
3. Online: review, extend, and consolidate

**1. *Online: Prepare for Class***

1. New vocabulary can be introduced and practiced before class.
2. Students can be prepared for "real-life" native speaker interaction.
3. Students can develop listening and reading skills in their own time and at their own pace.

**2. *In Class: Focus on Communication***

1. Students can be prepared online to actively participate in personalized pair- and group-work activities in class.
2. Student-to-student interaction is maximized in the classroom.

**3. *Online: Review, extend, and consolidate***

1. Students can review and consolidate language in their own time and at their own pace.
2. Students can be motivated and interest can be stimulated through "real-life" online interaction.
3. Students can develop writing skills in their own time and at their own pace.

## Template For Designing Blended Learning

Follow these four steps to start designing your own blended pathway.

1. Identify the learning outcomes for your classroom lesson.
2. Identify the activities for student to do in class.
3. Identify the activities for students to do online before class.
4. Identify the activities for student to do after class.

## Conclusion

The concept and practice of blending learning opportunities is not new, but in today's digital age what is new is the range of possible components in a blend. Blended learning, when well understood and implemented, has the potential to support deep and meaningful learning, but simply mixing information technologies with face-to-face learning is not sufficient to exploit the full potential of blended learning. When considering blended learning, there is no single perfect blend, nor is there a set or simple formula for making a good blend. Blended learning can help achieve the optimal language learning environment. It will examine the criteria and factors that can help you choose the appropriate blend for your students.

## References

1. Brodsky, M. May 2003. E-learning trends, today and beyond. *Learning and Training Innovations.*
2. Egbert, J. and E. Hanson-Smith. *Call Environments: Research, Practice, and Critical Issues.* Alexandria, VA: TESOL, 1999.

# 9

# Blended Learning in Education

## Introduction

In our age in which technology has been advancing, and information has been rapidly increasing and refreshing, the importance of the education has been growing accordingly. While the developments observed in science and technology in the 21st century has expanded the duties and responsibilities of the education system, they have also brought new opportunities. The fact that our world has been turning into an information-based world, the value of information increases; the acquisition of information in the right place and at the right time is of vital importance for individuals and society. Rapid and easy access to the wide dissemination of information has resulted in information access technology developments that will provide the circulation of this information.

A stronger learning environment has emerged with combining the strongest aspects of the two available approaches to remove the deficiencies of traditional learning and Web-based learning. This new learning approach is blended learning.

## Blended learning history

Technology-based training emerged as an alternative to instructor-led training in the 1960s on mainframes and mini-computers. The major advantage that blended learning offers is scale, whereas one instructor can only teach so many people. One example is PLATO (Programmed Logic for Automatic Teaching Operations), a system developed by the University of Illinois and Control Data. PLATO in particular had a long history of innovations and offered coursework from elementary to the college level. Mainframe-based training had a number of interface limitations that gave way to satellite-based live video in the 1970s. The advantage here was serving people who were not as PC-literate, the major challenge was the expense required to make this work. In the early 1980s, CD -ROMs emerged as a dominant form of providing technology-based learning as bandwidth through 56k modems weren't able to support very high quality sound and video. The limitation to CD-ROMs was tracking completion of coursework, so learning management systems emerged as a way to facilitate progress tracking. The aviation industry used this heavily to track how well one did on courses, how much time was spent, and where someone left off. AICC, Aviation Industry Computer-Based Training Committee, was formed in 1988 and companies such as Boeing used CD-ROMs to provide training for personnel. Modern blended learning is delivered online, although CD-ROMs could feasibly still be used if a learning management system meets an institution's standards. Some examples of channels through which online blending learning can be delivered include webcasting (synchronous and asynchronous) and online video (live and recorded). Solutions such as Khan Academy have been used in classrooms to serve as platforms for blended learning.

### What is Blended Learning?

Blended learning is a term increasingly used to describe the way e-learning is being combined with traditional classroom methods and independent study to create a new, hybrid teaching methodology. It represents a much greater change in basic technique than simply adding computers to classrooms. It represents in many cases, a fundamental change in the way teachers and students approach the learning experience. It has already produced an offshoot – the flipped classroom – that has quickly become a distinct approach of its own. No single, reliable definition of blended learning exists, or evens a universal agreement on the term itself. Many use terms like hybrid, mixed, or integrative to describe the same trend. But almost a decade later more than 3 million took courses that way, many of them using computers in the schools themselves.

## A learning model in three parts

There is a general consensus among education innovators that blended learning has three primary components:

1. In-person classroom activities facilitated by a trained educator.
2. Online learning materials, often including pre-recorded lectures given by that same instructor.
3. Structured independent study time guided by the material in the lectures and skills developed during the classroom experience.

A course created in a blended learning model uses the classroom time for activities that benefit the most from direct interaction. Traditional education (especially at the college level) tends to place an emphasis on delivering material by way of a lecture, while in a blended learning model lectures can be videotaped ahead of time so the student can watch on their own time. The classroom time is more likely to be for structured exercises that emphasize the application of the curriculum to solve problems or work through tasks. An individual semester of blended learning may emphasize classroom time at the beginning, then gradually increase the amount of work that students do online or during independent study. Many argue that class discussion boards, for example, are far more useful if the participants have met face-to-face first. The "flipped" classroom, a more recent coinage, refers to classes that are structured almost exclusively around a reversal of expectations for lectures and homework. Students are expected to watch lectures online at home, and do homework while they are in class.

## Blended learning redefining teaching roles

In some situations, the move to blended learning has inspired educators to redefine traditional roles. The word "facilitator" has emerged as an alternative to "teacher", bringing with it a slightly different focus. The facilitator places an emphasis on empowering students with the skills and knowledge required to make the most of the online material and independent study time, guiding students toward the most meaningful experience possible. Facilitators focus on four key areas:

1. Guiding the learning experience of individual students, and customizing material wherever possible to strengthen the learning experience.
2. Assessment and grading, not unlike the expectations for teachers within the traditional framework.

By putting an emphasis on learning through supervised activities, blended learning has proven to be very adaptable to what some corporations are calling blended training. Trainers can shift their focus from the delivery of knowledge to its application, and companies spend less flying trainers around to oversee all instruction in person.

## Blended Learning in Action

Blended or hybrid learning is a snazzy, yet relatively new tool, and not all professors use it the same way. Trends have emerged, however. For instance, most professors in blended classrooms use some version of a course management system application to connect with students online. Blackboard and Model are perhaps two of the best known CMS applications used today. Through platforms like these, students can access video of lectures, track assignments and progress, interact with teachers and peers, and review other supporting materials, like PowerPoint presentations or scholarly articles.

Even if all teachers used the same platform, however, they could each integrate them into their classrooms differently. According to a report on the subject by the Inn sight, teachers could supplement traditional coursework with online media *in* the classroom, or simply alternate between online and classroom instruction. Perhaps one of the most recent–or at least most widely covered–hybrid teaching models is what Inn sight calls the “online driver” method or as it has come to be known, “flipping.”

## Community

The Blackboard learning management system helped develop a better feel for an online community where discussions can be held to better aid students. This Virtual Learning Environment helps connect teachers with students without physically being present, thus making this a ‘Virtual Cafe’. Many schools use this online tool for online classes, class work, question & answer forums, and other school related work. Blended learning yielded positive results from the online community, such results were compared and showed similar results from that of Alcoholics Anonymous and Weight Watchers.

## Advantages of blended learning

1. Proponents of blended learning argue that by incorporating the “asynchronous Internet communication technology” into courses serves to “facilitate a simultaneous independent and collaborative

learning experience", and this incorporation is a major contributor to student satisfaction and success in such courses.

2. The use of information and communication technologies has been found to improve access to as well as student attitudes towards learning.
3. By incorporating information technology into class projects, communication between lecturers and part-time students was improved, and students were able to better evaluate their understanding of course material via the use of "computer-based qualitative and quantitative assessment modules" in a study.

## Disadvantages of blended learning

1. Blended learning has a strong dependence on the technical resources with which the blended learning experience is delivered—these tools need to be reliable, easy to use, and up to date in order for the use of the Internet to have a meaningful impact on the learning experience.
2. Additionally, IT literacy can serve as a significant barrier for students attempting to get access to the course materials, making the availability of high quality technical support paramount.
3. It has been observed that the use of lecture recording technologies can result in students falling behind on the material—in a study performed across four different universities, it was found that only half of the students watched the lecture videos on a regular basis, and nearly 40% of students watched several weeks worth of videos in one sitting.

## Conclusion

Of course, no educational model is one-size-fits-all, and some hybrid classrooms are probably more effective than others. A number of factors impact the success of hybrid learning. Teachers must be committed to and well trained in blended and hybrid education and its technologies, and students must have a clear understanding of what is expected of them in this new environment.

As blended learning becomes more common, schools and teachers will likely understand and implement it better. Yet even now, early in the game, blended education shows promise, making this an exciting time to be a student. Blended learning is a formal education program in which a student learns at least in part through online delivery of content and instruction with some element of student control over time, place, path or pace. While still attending a "brick-and-mortar" school structure, face-to-face classroom methods are combined with computer-mediated activities. Proponents of blending learning cite the opportunity for data collection and customization of instruction and assessment as two major benefits of this approach. Schools with blended learning models may also choose to reallocate resources to boost student achievement outcomes.

## References

1. "Blended Learning: A Disruptive Innovation". Knewton.
2. "Blended Learning (Staker/Horn - May 2012)" (PDF). Retrieved 2013-10-24.
3. Jump up^ Jacob, Anna M. (2011). Benefits and Barriers to the Hybridization of Schools. Journal of Education Policy, Planning and Administration, 1(1): 61-82.
4. http://www.thefreelibrary.com/Interactive Learning Centers Announces Name Change to EPIC Learning.- Jump up^ Martyn, Margie (2003). "The hybrid online model: Good practice." *Educause Quarterly*: 18–23.
5. Jumpup http://media.wiley.com/product_data/excerpt/67/07879729/0787972967.pdf
6. http://uupinfo.org/research/working/bradford.pdf

# 10

# Blended Learning

## Introduction

Blended learning is not a new concept; however, many consider it to be new. Recently, there has been a renewed focus on this learning strategy, both in the education and corporate sectors. Although the definition of blended learning is somewhat amorphous, it is generally described as an environment that includes the use of different modes of teaching and learning. Blended learning gained increasing popularity with the integration of technology in the teaching and learning environment. Blended learning holds particular promise for developing countries as it can make available to them the resources of national, regional, and international educational institutions. This could allow them to redirect the often-limited resources that they have at their disposal to other developmental needs. Some developing countries are already participating in different forms of blended learning programs. An expansion of these programs can enhance educational development in many of these nations.

The first generation of e-learning or Web-based learning programs focused on presenting physical classroom-based instructional content over the Internet. Furthermore, first-generation e-learning (digitally delivered learning) programs tended to be repetition or compilation of online versions of classroom based courses. The experience gained from the first generation of e-learning often riddled with long sequences of "page-turner" content and point-and-click quizzes, is giving rise to the realization that a single mode of instructional delivery may not provide sufficient choices, engagement, social contact, relevance, and context needed to facilitate successful learning and performance. In the second wave of e-learning, increasing numbers of learning designers are experimenting with blended learning models that combine various delivery modes. Anecdotal evidence indicated that blended learning not only offers more choices but also is more effective.

## Blended Learning History

Technology-based training emerged as an alternative to instructor-led training in the 1960s on mainframes and mini-computers. The major advantage that blended learning offers is scale, whereas one instructor can only teach so many people. One example is PLATO (Programmed Logic for Automatic Teaching Operations), a system developed by the University of Illinois and Control Data. PLATO in particular had a long history of innovations and offered coursework from elementary to the college level. Mainframe-based training had a number of interface limitations that gave way to satellite-based live video in the 1970s. The advantage here was serving people who were not as PC-literate, the major challenge was the expense required to make this work. In the early 1980s, CD-ROMs emerged as a dominant form of providing technology-based learning as bandwidth through 56k modems weren't able to support very high quality sound and video. The limitation to CD-ROMs was tracking completion of coursework, so learning management systems emerged as a way to facilitate progress tracking. The aviation industry used this heavily to track how well one did on courses, how much time was spent, and where someone left off. AICC, Aviation Industry Computer-Based Training Committee, was formed in 1988 and companies such as Boeing used CD-ROMs to provide training for personnel. Modern blended learning is delivered online, although CD-ROMs could feasibly still be used if a learning management system meets an institution's standards. Some examples of channels through which online blending learning can be delivered include web casting (synchronous and asynchronous) and online video (live and recorded). Solutions such as Khan Academy have been used in classrooms to serve as platforms for blended learning.

## Blended Learning

Blended learning combines online with face-to-face learning. The goal of blended learning is to provide the most efficient and effective instruction experience by combining delivery modalities. "The term blended learning is used to describe a solution that combines several different delivery methods, such as collaboration software, Web-based courses, EPSS, and knowledge management practices. Blended learning also is used to describe learning that mixes various event-based activities, including face-to-face classrooms, live e-learning and self-paced instruction."

## Designing Blended Learning

To design blended training, the instructional designers start by analyzing the training or course objectives and braking them down into the smallest possible pedagogically (for children) or and ragogically (for adults) appropriate chunks (learning object). After the course or training has been chunked, the best approach to deliver each segment of instruction (learning object) is identified. In some cases the best approach might be using online learning but in others it might be live instruction, for example. The course is then aggregated by grouping the instruction logically while taking into account the medium of delivery. In this way, one may require a few lessons online and some others live, for example.

## How to Manage instructional complexity:

In blended learning the instructor has a wider choice of delivery mediums to combine. With that wider choice also comes greater complexity and pressure on the instructor and designer. This is due to the variety of combinations of technology and possibly the lack of patterns to follow for that particular mix. These issues need to be addressed up front and taken into account during the design. We also need to take this into account due to its effects on the learner. It is easier to finish an online module and start another online module, for example, than it is for that second module to be videoconferencing based. Such changes require the learner to adapt. Time, guidelines, and even brief demos might need to be provided for the learner.

## Managing the roles and responsibilities

Unlike traditional classroom learning in which there usually is a single instructor, in blended learning you might have multiple individuals, each taking a modality or role in the blend. Up front clarification of instructor and assistant roles is essential for success and the reduction of potential conflict and learner confusion.

### Creating a seamless learning experience

Good communications among instructors and careful planning is another important element in the success of blended learning. Make sure that instructors and assistants communicate with one another throughout the instruction, not just before the course. Make sure that as different segments of the blend are designed, all prerequisites are met by the previous learning objects. Arrange learning objects or alter meeting times to insure each segment reinforces the previously acquired knowledge or skill and introduces new concepts seamlessly in spite of the different modality of delivery.

### Meeting expectations

As with any new technology, there are those that endorse it and there are lagers. While many perceive the lagers to be difficult, a greater challenge is posed by overly eager fast endorsers. These overly eager individuals tend to overestimate the benefits and make others develop false expectations. Manage the expectations carefully so you can meet them and have success. Management of expectations is also important for instructors and learners to realistically perceive the benefits and work to be performed during the training or course.

### Controlling costs and meet ROI goals:

Blended learning offers great flexibility and great effectiveness as it can chose the best medium for every objective; however, the challenge is to make the blend not only effective but also efficient. In cases where multiple instructors are used it is natural for each to perceive their part of the blend with disproportionate importance. As a result, without controls, ROI will suffer. From the design stage put in place cost controls that work hand in hand with quality assurance and learning effectiveness measures.

### Advantages of Blended Learning

As stated before, one obvious advantage of blended learning is its ability to maximize effectiveness by matching the best medium for each learning object (course segment). Here are some of the benefits of a few of the mediums that might be used:

**Classroom:** is good for workshops, coaching, exercises, feedback on activities and paper-based tests.

## Self-paced e-learning

Is good for simulations, online case studies, interactive learning modules, e-mail, bulletin boards interactions, online assessments, and other forms of CBT (computer based training)..Live e-Learning- is good for application exercises, online coaching, interaction between students, online feedback, assessment, chats and instant messaging.

Proponents of blended learning argue that by incorporating the "asynchronous Internet communication technology" into courses serves to "facilitate a simultaneous independent and collaborative learning experience", and this incorporation is a major contributor to student satisfaction and success in such courses. The use of information and communication technologies has been found to improve access to as well as student attitudes towards learning. By incorporating information technology into class projects, communication between lecturers and part-time students was improved, and students were able to better evaluate their understanding of course material via the use of "computer-based qualitative and quantitative assessment modules"

## Disadvantages

Blended learning has a strong dependence on the technical resources with which the blended learning experience is delivered—these tools need to be reliable, easy to use, and up to date in order for the use of the Internet to have a meaningful impact on the learning experience. Additionally, IT literacy can serve as a significant barrier for students attempting to get access to the course materials, making the availability of high quality technical support paramount.

It has been observed that the use of lecture recording technologies can result in students falling behind on the material, it was found that only half of the students watched the lecture videos on a regular basis, and nearly 40% of students watched several weeks worth of videos in one sitting.

## Community

The Blackboard learning management system helped develop a better feel for an online community where discussions can be held to better aid studentsThis Virtual Learning Environment helps connect professors with students without physically being present, thus making this a 'Virtual Cafe'. Many schools use this online tool for online classes, class work, question & answer forums, and other school related work Blended learning yielded positive results from the online community, such results were compared and showed similar results from that of Alcoholics Anonymous and Weight Watchers many educators are excited about blended learning these days, but the reality is that starting a school or district-wide program can be a long process, and does not always include the individuals that it will affect the most.

## Conclusion

To summarize, the theory is that Blended Learning has the potential of offering courses or training that, through the wise choice of the blend, can have results that are better that the sum of the parts. Blended learning is a formal education program in which a student learns at least in part through online delivery of content and instruction with some element of student control over time, place, path or pace. While still attending a "brick-and-mortar" school structure, face-to-face classroom methods are combined with computer-mediated activities. Proponents of blending learning cite the opportunity for data collection and customization of instruction and assessment as two major benefits of this approach. Schools with blended learning models may also choose to reallocate resources to boost student achievement outcomes.

# 11

# A Few Models of Teaching the Computer Era

## Introduction

The promise of e-learning, and the enabling learning technologies, is to make learning experiences in all types of settings more effective, efficient, attractive and accessible to the learners. In e-learning the Internet is used as the core medium for the delivery of information and the support of communication. Most people also think that the Internet, itself, as the key factor in the success of e-learning. However, a vast amount of research provides evidence for the proposition that it is not the medium, itself, which is accountable for the accomplishment of these promises, but the pedagogical design used in conjunction with the features of the medium. The message is that we should concentrate on the quality of the pedagogical design and its relationship to the possibilities of the Internet if we want to accomplish the promises of e-learning. Another common belief is that learning is the same as knowledge transfer. The idea which comes with it is that it is enough to make knowledge available to learners according to some pedagogical structure. However, providing adequate knowledge is not enough: it has to be learned. It is this learning process that is the process we are putting at the center when we discuss instructional design or learning design, and not the knowledge it works on. Ask yourself: 'where is the learning' in e-learning? On top of that, a lot of learning does not come from knowledge resources at all, but stems from the activities of learners solving problems, interacting with real devices, interacting in their social and work situation.

A lot of research about learning processes provides evidence for this stance that learning doesn't come from the provision of knowledge solely, but that it is the activities of the learners into the learning environment which are accountable for the learning. Learning experiences are offered mostly in chunks, like courses. These chunks (in the next paragraph we abstract them to the concept of 'units of study') are the major delivery units for e-learning. From a design perspective, the course is the aggregate containing all the necessary features to make learning successful. It is at this level that educational modelling (or instructional design/learning design) takes place; it is at this level that the pedagogical models are implemented; it is this level of aggregation that is accountable for the quality of learning. Among the various models the pedagogical Meta model and the learning model alone have been discussed here.

It is a model which models pedagogical models. This means that pedagogical models could be described in terms of the meta-model. This is of importance when you want to express semantic relationships between pedagogical entities *and* want to be pedagogical neutral. Compare this for instance with a text editor like MS-Word. MS-word is neutral to the type of text you can edit with it. It is possible to write memo's, letters, poetry and literature. That's flexibility. However, MSword has no real means of validating whether the text you have edited really is a poem or a letter, given all the varieties of poems and letters in practice. You can imagine what great help it would be when these types of tools are aware of the type of content you are editing. You could expect a lot more support in the writing process than you get now. Text writing has so many varieties in practice that a real semantic framework for texts in general is not available at the moment, and it maybe never will be. However, education is a more restricted domain with a lot of commonalities in its instances. This is mainly due to the hard work done in research into learning and instruction. There are still a lot of different stances when answering questions about learning, but there are also a lot of commonalities. These commonalities are the focus of a meta-model; the differences are made by parameterization of the meta-model. This idea has led us to the work on the meta-model behind EML.

## Content of the Meta Model

The main topics of the static structure of the pedagogical meta-model are expressed in UML diagrams here. The pedagogical semantics of EML are designed according to this model. The model is based on educational research, specifically in the field of learning psychology and instructional design. Most of these models in literature are expressed in natural language and ad hoc schemas. Most of the classes have more elaboration. Like all models this model abstracts reality. It must not be confused with the reality itself and it is not the only model possible describing learning from instruction. This is also true for learning design in general. Course designs are something different from what actually happens when courses are instantiated and used in real practice. It is not the intention of course designs to abstract all the details of the course, but its major points. Also, what I have drawn in the UML diagrams are expressions of the pedagogical models underlying units of study. It highlights the important points. In its details of implementation the models have more complexity.

## Packages in the Metamodel

There are four packages:

1. The learning model, which describes how learners learn based on commonalities in learning theories.
2. The unit of study model, which describes how units of studies which are applicable in real practice are modelled, given the learning model and given the instruction model.
3. The domain model, which describes the type of content and the organization of that content. For example, the domain of economics, law, biology, etc.
4. Theories of learning & instruction, which describe the theories, principles and models of instruction as they are described in literature or as they are conceived in the head of practitioners.

## Axioms of Learning Model

The learning model is based on the following axioms:

1. A person learns by acting in/with the external world.
2. The real world could be considered to be composed of social and personal situations, which provide the context for actions.
3. A situation is composed of a collection of things and living beings in a specific interrelationship.

4. One part of situations is communities of practice and – more specifically – learning communities.
5. There are different types of learning, the one of interest to us is learning invoked by instructional measures.
6. Learning can be considered to be a change in the cognitive or metacognitive state.
   However, changes in the connation and affection can also be considered as the result of learning. When a person has learned he or she can a) carry out new interactions or carry out interactions better or faster in similar situations, or b) carry out the same actions in another situations (transfer).
7. A person can be urged to carry out specific interactions, if:
   a. a person is willing to do so or stimulated to do so (conation / motivation factor);
   b. a person is able to do so (cognition factor);
   c. a person is in the mood to do so (affection / emotional factor);
   d. a person is in the right situation to do so (situational factor);

8. What has been set out here regarding an individual is also valid for a group of people or an organization, even though this does not have to be reducible to individuals.

The essence here is that no value judgment is made in these axioms about the following questions:

1. What does a person or group learn (knowledge, competencies, skills, insight, attitudes, intentional behavior) and in which domain?
2. What kinds of activities must be carried out to learn? For example: observing, describing, analyzing, experiencing, studying, problem solving, experimenting, predicting, practicing, exploring and answering questions.
3. How should a learning situation be arranged (context, which people, which objects) and what relationship does the situation has to the teaching-learning process?
4. To what extent are the components of the situation present externally and to what extent are they represented cognitively-internally?
5. How, precisely, do the learning and transfer processes occur?
6. How is motivation stimulated?
7. How is the learning result captured?
8. How should activities be stimulated?

The answers to precisely these questions determine the educational philosophy, the instructional model and the more practical design of the units of study. The meta-model provides the semantic framework for the units of study's notational system, alongside the structure of learning environments that was dealt with earlier. A citation from Duffy & Cunningham (1996) in this area: 'As the quote from Skinner suggests, everyone agrees that learning involves activity and a context, including the availability of information in some content domain.

Traditionally, in instruction, we have focused on the information presented or available for learning and have seen the activity of the learner as a vehicle for moving that information into the head. Hence, the activity is a matter of processing the information. The constructivists, however, view the learning as the activity in context. The situation as a whole must be examined and understood in order to understand the learning. Rather than the content domain sitting as central, with activity and the 'rest' of the context serving a supporting role, the entire gestalt is integral to what is learned.'

## Conclusion

In this article the pedagogical meta-model behind EML is presented. These were addressed and a containing framework for typed learning objects was provided. This framework ensures that the structure of the units of study used in e-learning is valid. However, this is at itself not the same as an effective, efficient and attractive pedagogical design; whether a design conforms to these criteria comes for a large part from the theories and principles of learning and instruction. These theories form the basis for the design of the meta-model behind EML. On the other hand, the designs themselves are not enough to guarantee high quality designs. They tend to be defined at too abstract a level, not providing enough details for the real structuring work that must be done when developing real units of study.

EML makes the use of pedagogical models explicit. This is one of the factors needed to enhance the quality of a pedagogical design. So the combination of good design and good structuring of the design in a notation will bring us the quality of learning we are searching for. EML provides the framework to notate and communicate the designs in a complete form, validate them on completeness in structure, makes it possible to identify the functionality of learning objects within the context of a unit of study and provides means for real interoperability and re-usability. Moreover, we think that EML can make the building of learning management systems easier and can make learning management systems more effective, because the design of the systems can take advantage of the huge body of knowledge available in educational research, based on theories, empirical findings and the experience from practitioners.

## References

1. Alessi, S.M., & Trollip, S.R. (1991). *Computer-based Instruction: Methods and Development,* Englewood Cliffs, NJ: Prentice-Hall.
2. Barrows, H.S. & Tamblyn, R.M. (1980). *Problem-based learning: an approach to medical education.* New York: Springer.
3. Berge, Z.L., & Collins, M.P. (Eds.) (1995). *Computer Mediated Communication and the Online Classroom.* Cresskill, NJ: Hampton Press.
4. Boyle, T. (1997). *Designing for multimedia learning.* London: Prentice Hall.
5. Card, S.K., Moran, T.P. & Newell, A. (1983). *The Psychology of Human-Computer Interaction.* London: Lawrence Erlbaum Associates.

# 12

# Blended Learning

Blended learning based on lecture videos and face-to-face teaching provides good opportunities for students for participation in education, regardless of time or place. The article describes a blended learning solution that is based on face-to-face teaching and the use of streaming lecture videos as it has developed in connection with master studies in mathematical information technology. The particular focus of this article is on the use of lecture videos and the impacts of blended learning on participation in education and on learning outcomes. According to the results, lecture videos have become very popular among students. Moreover the use of lecture videos increases participation activeness, and the increase in participation has a positive impact on completion of courses. However, the use of lecture videos does not seem to have any clear-cut effect on grades obtained.

## History of the term

The concept of blended learning has been around for a long time, but its terminology was not firmly established until around the beginning of the 21st century. One of the earliest references to the term appears in a press release in 1999, when the Interactive Learning Centers, an Atlanta-based education business, announced its change of name to EPIC learning. The article mentions that "The Company currently operates 220 on-line courses, but will begin offering its Internet courseware using the company's Blended Learning methodology." The meaning of blended learning widely diverged to encompass a wide variety of synthesis in learning methods until 2006, when the first Handbook of Blended Learning by Bonk and Graham was published. In this publication Graham challenged the breadth and ambiguity of the term's definition, and defined 'blended learning systems' as learning systems that "combine face-to-face instruction with computer mediated instruction." Currently, use of the term blended learning mostly involves "combining Internet and digital media with established classroom forms that require the physical co-presence of teacher and students."

## Word usage and context

The terms "blended," "hybrid," "technology-mediated instruction," "web-enhanced instruction," and "mixed-mode instruction" are often used interchangeably in current research literature. However, recent researchers in the United States tend to use the term "blended learning" with more regularity.

## Blended Learning History

Technology-based training emerged as an alternative to instructor-led training in the 1960s on mainframes and mini-computers. The major advantage that blended learning offers is scale, whereas one instructor can only teach so many people. One example is PLATO (Programmed Logic for Automatic Teaching Operations), a system developed by the University of Illinois and Control Data. PLATO in particular had a long history of innovations and offered coursework from elementary to the college level. Mainframe-based training had a number of interface limitations that gave way to satellite-based live video in the 1970s. The advantage here was serving people who were not as PC-literate, the major challenge was the expense required to make this work. In the early 1980s, CD-ROMs emerged as a dominant form of providing technology-based learning as bandwidth through 56k modems weren't able to support very high quality sound and video.

The limitation to CD-ROMs was tracking completion of coursework, so learning management systems emerged as a way to facilitate progress tracking. The aviation industry used this heavily to track how well one did on courses, how much time was spent, and where someone left off. AICC, Aviation Industry Computer-Based Training Committee, was formed in

1988 and companies such as Boeing used CD-ROMs to provide training for personnel. Modern blended learning is delivered online, although CD-ROMs could feasibly still be used if a learning management system meets an institution's standards. Some examples of channels through which online blending learning can be delivered include webcasting (synchronous and asynchronous) and online video (live and recorded). Solutions such as Khan Academy have been used in classrooms to serve as platforms for blended learning.

## Advantages

Proponents of blended learning argue that by incorporating the "asynchronous Internet communication technology" into courses serves to "facilitate a simultaneous independent and collaborative learning experience", and this incorporation is a major contributor to student satisfaction and success in such courses. The use of information and communication technologies has been found to improve access to as well as student attitudes towards learning. By incorporating information technology into class projects, communication between lecturers and part-time students was improved, and students were able to better evaluate their understanding of course material via the use of "computer-based qualitative and quantitative assessment modules" in a study by Alexander and McKenzie (1998).

## Disadvantages

Blended learning has a strong dependence on the technical resources with which the blended learning experience is delivered these tools need to be reliable, easy to use, and up to date in order for the use of the Internet to have a meaningful impact on the learning experience. Additionally, IT literacy can serve as a significant barrier for students attempting to get access to the course materials, making the availability of high quality technical support paramount. It has been observed that the use of lecture recording technologies can result in students falling behind on the material in a study performed across four different universities, it was found that only half of the students watched the lecture videos on a regular basis, and nearly 40% of students watched several weeks worth of videos in one sitting.

Blended learning is a hot phrase in the training world, and it usually refers to a mixing of traditional face-to-face classroom facilitation with computer-based modules — usually self-paced online training. Proponents of blended learning point to several benefits of the approach, including:

1. Blended learning extends training beyond a single "event."
2. Blended learning allows trainees to absorb training on their own time, leaving valuable classroom time for more skill-building activities.
3. Blended learning saves money by reducing the travel and work-stoppage costs of classroom training.

There's merit in many of these points. But there are also some holes in that logic that can't be ignored:

1. The blended learning model doesn't exactly extend training beyond an event — it simply extends the event. There's an important difference there.
2. The blended learning model allows for some lessons to be delivered online instead of in a classroom lecture. But whether any of that information is actually absorbed is another question.
3. Done right, a blended learning program can reduce can produce cost savings. But that has nothing to do with learning and performance effectiveness, only money.

## It's Blended Training, Not Blended Learning

Blended learning has really emerged as a buzzword in the last decade. In 2003, the American Society for Training and Development identified blended learning as one of its Top 10 trends to emerge in the knowledge-delivery industry.

Look again at what the ASTD describes the industry as: the "knowledge-delivery" industry. There's a big difference between knowledge delivery and learning. Amazon can deliver a book to my house, but I still have to read it to learn anything. Webster's defines learning as *the "act or experience of one that learns; knowledge of skill acquired by instruction or study; modification of a behavioral tendency by experience."* What part of that definition do you think describes how the majority of workplace learning takes place? Without question, it's the "modification of a behavioral tendency by experience." Most t real workplace learning takes place within people's work, on the job. It appends through informal sharing, observation, and coaching from peers. It's learning by actually performing. Let's return to the definition for another question: In which section of the definition do you think the work of trainers resides? I believe most of the work of trainers falls in the middle section, "knowledge of skill acquired by instruction or study." Most of what trainers do involves transferring knowledge and explaining its potential applications on the job. Explaining something isn't the same as doing it. And doing it — performing it — is how people really learn. So in reality, what we're talking about when we describe *blended learning* is just how us transferring the responsibility of "delivering content" from a person to a computer. Again, this isn't a learning strategy; it's a training strategy. If learning professionals can start focusing more on improving people's performance than on simply "delivering content," we can create a true "blended" learning model — one that gets away from the "knowledge-delivery" industry.

## Online and Classroom Isn't Enough

Most blended learning models today consist of classroom training and self-paced online courses, which are made up of information on a screen, occasional quizzes, and sometimes some student-to-student (or student-to-instructor) interactions.

As I said earlier, that's a training delivery strategy. But that's hardly the only way people learn to do their job.

People learn from one another, from job aids, Internet searches, blogs, webcasts, and countless other places. The challenge for most trainers is that these resources aren't "approved," and can't be tracked and reported on by an LMS. Approved sources and tracking learning activity are training concerns, not performance concerns. If we really want to enable workers to succeed, we need to focus more on what will really help the most. It's usually not a course, and it's usually not a knowledge-delivery system. We need to start seeing at our role as one of performance support; connecting workers with the resources they need at the time that they need them. Ironically, once we start doing that, we'll have built a true blended learning model.

## Conclusion

Blended learning is a combination of face to face teaching and learning with online teaching and learning Examples of blended learning include problem-based, project-based and authentic learning tasks Benefits of blended learning expound from an activity, subject, and course. Blended learning is a widely used and effective method of workplace training in companies with mature learning management systems. It is more effective than classroom training and meets the needs of adult learning styles. To optimize its impact it should be tied to the organization's strategic performance goals. Over time, as costs decrease and awareness of these systems increase, it is likely that blended learning will become the mainstay for workplace training.

# 13

# Learning Environment of Tomorrow

## Introduction

Every teacher wants to be a good teacher. Every student wants their teachers to be good at techniques of teaching. Traditionally followed teacher – centered methods have yielded their place today to pupil – centered techniques of classroom instruction. Many different types of technology can be used to support and enhance learning. Starting with the use of printed text books in learning, tremendous advancements have been achieved by making use of various technologies that deliver different kinds of content and serve different purposes in the classroom. For example, word processing and e-mail promote communication skills and modeling software promotes the understanding of science and math concepts. If is important to consider how these electronic technologies function as vehicles for education. This paper highlights the importance of Modern Technology in Teacher Education, exploring the charges that are taking place in the Teaching Learning process. The investigator also highlights the importance of ICT in Teacher Education and Electronic Media for Teaching and Learning.

The Modern technologies are a diverse set of tools and resources used to communicate, and to create, disseminate, store and manage information. These technologies include computers, internet, broadcasting technologies and telephony. Thus, nobody can deny that technology has revolutionized education. Educators have also dramatically adjusted their teaching methods in response to new technology over the years. They must also more toward the goal of transforming the traditional paradigm of learning.

### The traditional view of the learning process

The traditional educational paradigm is characterized by the following views of learning:

1. Learning is hard.
2. Learning is based on a deficit model of the student.
3. Learning is a process of information transfer and reception.
4. Learning is solitary process.
5. Learning is a linear process.

### Changes in views of the Learning Process

In contrast to the traditional teaching – learning paradigm, a new paradigm of the teaching – learning process is emerging.

### This encompasses the following views of the human learning process

1. Learning is a natural process.
2. Learning is a social process.
3. Learning is an active and nor a passive process.
4. Learning may either be linear or non-linear.
5. Learning is based on a strength model of student abilities, interest and culture.
6. Learning is assessed through task completion, products and real problem solving of both individual and group efforts.

### Educational Technology

Educational Technology, in its wide sense as understood today, includes the development, application and evaluation of systems and techniques involving men, machines, media and instructional materials as components, so as to improve the process of human learning and attain the educational goals".

### Teacher-Centered Technology

Gadgets that are used strictly by teachers are designed to enhance presentations, help with book-keeping or assist with outside communications. Projection devices have become more affordable and now are nearly standard in many classrooms. Interactive white boards, although still expensive, provide an instant interface between the classroom and cyberspace, allowing teachers to transform lectures into real time multimedia presentations.

### Student-centered Technology

Although providing laptors for every K-12 student in the classroom is still cost prohibitive for most school districts, wireless mobile labs can be used in group projects. These devices connect directly to the school's Internet access and the signal is relayed to laptops that can be distributed to the students.

Once technology enters the school building, dramatic revolutions usually begin. With the technological magic touch, a simple school - house turns into a systematized learning centre. Technology can be considered in two ways-technologies as things and technology as social process. So, technology is not only the 'tool' for the development of science but also the 'change' in the social process.

The Important technological aspects of teacher education are as follows

1. Programmed Instruction / Programmed Learning
2. Stimulated Teaching
3. Audio visual Aids
4. Micro Teaching
5. Mass Media
6. Information Technology
7. Teaching Machine
8. Team Teaching
9. Task Analysis
10. Instructional Designs.

These offer opportunities for unlimited sharing of ideas and feelings. Thoughtful practice and application are made possible.

### Merits of Technology in Education

Following are few advantages of using technology in education:

1. It helps to enrich and enliven the instructional process.
2. It stimulates the interest of the learners for further learning.

3. It helps the learners to easily understand what they learn and retain it for longtime.
4. It helps to win and sustain the attention of the learner.
5. It makes possible to bring to the classroom, the events or process that are inaccessible or non-amenable for accurate and rapid observation.

## Use of Information and communication Technologies

The use of new technologies like computer, internet, e-mail, CD-ROMs, DVDs, Interactive Video, Tele-conferencing, etc., enabling large number of students to get access to quality education and adopt self-learning to improve their potentials is known as teaching through ICT. In modern classrooms, electronic-media started finding their place in teaching. The use of electronic-media has changed the complexion of today's classrooms.

## Electronic Media for teaching and leering

A wide range of electronic media are available today to teachers through which they could impart instruction to students. Some of the electronic media used in the field of education are as follows.

1. Over head projector
2. E-Mail
3. E-learning
4. E-tutoring
5. Computer assisted Instruction
6. Tele-conferencing

In short we can say instruction through the electronic media will give a thrust to home-schooling.

## Reaching the Unreached

Thought there is a phenomenal expansioOn of educational institutions and India's literacy rate has gone up to seventy percent, there are millions of people who never had an opportunity to learn. These unfortunate people include nomadic tribes, landless agricultural laborers; tribal's living in hilly tracts, street children, adults and children living in remote islands and children with learning problems. These persons were tilling recently termed as unreachable. Now, with the aid of technology and enthusiastic social workers they national open school, Indira Gandhi National Open University and state Open University.

## Conclusion

The integration of modern technology in the classroom is very helpful for students learning and helps make learning more interactive. Therefore this technology is creating a new educational platform and in reconfiguring the way a student learns. The fundamental concept of this study is to empower the excellence in education through the advances in Modern Technology. Therefore the practice of learning from the utilization of technologies will emerge as a problem solving, Guided Instruction with analytical Thinking which includes self-management in a networked environment which can be accomplished in the latest development especially in the knowledge-based society through global networking.

# 14

# Similar Systems on Cloud Computing in Education

## Introduction

Cloud computing in general can be portrayed as a synonym for distributed computing over a network, with the ability to run a program or application on many connected computers at the same time. It specifically refers to a computing hardware machine or group of computing hardware machines commonly referred as a server connected through a communication network such as the Internet, an intranet, a local area network (LAN) or wide area network (WAN) and individual users or user who have permission to access the server can use the server's processing power for their individual computing needs like to run an application, store data or any other computing need. Cloud Computing is the result of evolution and adoption of existing technologies and paradigms. The goal of cloud computing is to allow users to take beneût from all of these technologies, without the need for deep knowledge about or expertise with each one of them. The cloud aims to cut costs, and help the users focus on their core business instead of being impeded by IT obstacles. The main enabling technology for cloud computing is virtualization. Virtualization generalizes the physical infrastructure, which is the most rigid component, and makes it available as a soft component that is easy to use and manage.

Cloud computing in general can be portrayed as a synonym for distributed computing over a network, with the ability to run a program or application on many connected computers at the same time. It specifically refers to a computing hardware machine or group of computing hardware machines commonly referred as a server connected through a communication network such as the Internet, an intranet, a local area network (LAN) or wide area network (WAN) and individual users or user who have permission to access the server can use the server's processing power for their individual computing needs like to run an application, store data or any other computing need.

In common usage, the term "the cloud" is essentially a metaphor for the Internet. Marketers have further popularized the phrase "in the cloud" to refer to software, platforms and infrastructure that are sold "as a service", i.e. remotely through the Internet. Typically, the seller has actual energy-consuming servers which host products and services from a remote location, so end-users don't have to; they can simply log on to the network without installing anything. The major models of cloud computing service are known as software as a service, platform as a service, and infrastructure as a service.

## Growth and Popularity

The development of the Internet from being document centric via semantic data towards more and more services was described as "dynamic web". This contribution focused in particular in the need for better meta-data able to describe not only implementation details but also conceptual details of model-based applications. The present availability of high-capacity networks, low-cost computers and storage devices as well as the widespread adoption of hardware virtualization, service-oriented architecture, and autonomic and utility computing have led to a growth in cloud computing.

## Hosted (Host) Services

The term "cloud computing" is mostly used to sell hosted services in the sense of application service provisioning that run client server software at a remote location. Such services are given popular acronyms like 'SaaS' (Software as a Service), 'PaaS' (Platform as a Service), 'IaaS' (Infrastructure as a Service), 'HaaS' (Hardware as a Service) and finally 'EaaS' (Everything as a Service). End users access cloud-based applications through a web browser, thin client or mobile app while the business software and user's data are stored on servers at a remote location. Examples include Amazon

Web Services and Google App engine, which allocate space for a user to deploy and manage software "in the cloud".

## Similar Systems and Concepts

Cloud Computing is the result of evolution and adoption of existing technologies and paradigms. The goal of cloud computing is to allow users to take beneût from all of these technologies, without the need for deep knowledge about or expertise with each one of them. The cloud aims to cut costs, and help the users focus on their core business instead of being impeded by IT obstacles.

The main enabling technology for cloud computing is virtualization. Virtualization generalizes the physical infrastructure, which is the most rigid component, and makes it available as a soft component that is easy to use and manage. By doing so, virtualization provides the agility required to speed up IT operations, and reduces cost by increasing infrastructure utilization. On the other hand, autonomic computing automates the process through which the user can provision resources on-demand. Users face difficult business problems every day. Cloud computing adopts concepts from Service-oriented Architecture (SOA) that can help the user break these problems into services that can be integrated to provide a solution. Cloud computing provides all of its resources as services, and makes use of the well-established standards and best practices gained in the domain of SOA to allow global and easy access to cloud services in a standardized way.

Cloud computing also leverages concepts from utility computing in order to provide metrics for the services used. Such metrics are at the core of the public cloud pay-per-use models. In addition, measured services are an essential part of the feedback loops in autonomic computing, allowing services to scale on-demand and to perform automatic failure recovery. Cloud computing shares characteristics with:

1. Client–server model — *Client–server computing* refers broadly to any distributed application that distinguishes between service providers (servers) and service requestors (clients).
2. Grid computing — "A form of distributed and parallel computing, whereby a 'super and virtual computer' is composed of a cluster of networked, loosely coupled computers acting in concert to perform very large tasks."

3. Mainframe computer — Powerful computers used mainly by large organizations for critical applications, typically bulk data processing such as: census; industry and consumer statistics; police and secret intelligence services; enterprise resource planning; and financial transaction processing.
4. Utility computing — The "packaging of computing resources, such as computation and storage, as a metered service similar to a traditional public utility, such as electricity.
5. Peer-to-peer — A distributed architecture without the need for central coordination. Participants are both suppliers and consumers of resources (in contrast to the traditional client–server model).
6. Cloud gaming — Also known as on-demand gaming, is a way of delivering games to computers. Gaming data is stored in the provider's server, so that gaming is independent of client computers used to play the game. One such current example would be a service by OnLive which allows users a certain space to save game data, and load games within the OnLive server.

## Service Models

Cloud computing providers offer their services according to several fundamental models: infrastructure as a service (IaaS), platform as a service (PaaS), and software as a service (SaaS) where IaaS is the most basic and each higher model abstracts from the details of the lower models. Other key components in anything as a service (XaaS) are described in a comprehensive taxonomy model published in 2009, such as Strategy-as-a-Service, Collaboration-as-a-Service, Business Process-as-a-Service, Database-as-a-Service, etc. In 2012, network as a service (NaaS) and communication as a service (CaaS) were officially included by ITU (International Telecommunication Union) as part of the basic cloud computing models, recognized service categories of a telecommunication-centric cloud ecosystem.

## Infrastructure as a service (Iaas)

In the most basic cloud-service model, providers of IaaS offer computers – physical or (more often) virtual machines – and other resources. (A hypervisor, such as OpenStack, Xen, KVM, VMware ESX/ESXi, or Hyper-V runs the virtual machines as guests. Pools of hypervisors within the cloud operational support-system can support large numbers of virtual machines and the ability to scale services up and down according to customers' varying requirements.) IaaS clouds often offer additional resources such as a virtual-machine disk image library, raw (block) and file-based storage, firewalls, load balancers, IP addresses, virtual local area networks (VLANs), and software bundles. IaaS-cloud providers supply these resources on-demand from their large pools installed in data centers. For wide-area connectivity, customers can use either the Internet or carrier clouds (dedicated virtual private networks).

To deploy their applications, cloud users install operating-system images and their application software on the cloud infrastructure. In this model, the cloud user patches and maintains the operating systems and the application software. Cloud providers typically bill IaaS services on a utility computing basis: cost reflects the amount of resources allocated and consumed.

### Platform as a service (Paas)

In the PaaS models, cloud providers deliver a computing platform, typically including operating system, programming language execution environment, database, and web server. Application developers can develop and run their software solutions on a cloud platform without the cost and complexity of buying and managing the underlying hardware and software layers. With some PaaS offers like Windows Azure, the underlying computer and storage resources scale automatically to match application demand so that the cloud user does not have to allocate resources manually.

### Software as a service (Saas)

In the business model using software as a service (SaaS), users are provided access to application software and databases. Cloud providers manage the infrastructure and platforms that run the applications. SaaS is sometimes referred to as "on-demand software" and is usually priced on a pay-per-use basis. SaaS providers generally price applications using a subscription fee. This process is transparent to the cloud user, who sees only a single access point. To accommodate a large number of cloud users, cloud applications can be *multitenant*, that is, any machine serves more than one cloud user organization. It is common to refer to special types of cloud-based application software with a similar naming convention: desktop as a service, business process as a service, test environment as a service, communication as a service.

## Security as a service (Se caas)

Security as a service (SECaaS) is a business model in which a large service provider integrates their security services into a corporate infrastructure on a subscription basis more cost effectively than most individuals or corporations can provide on their own, when total cost of ownership is considered. These security services often include authentication, anti-virus, anti-malware/spyware, intrusion detection, and security event management, among others

## Controlled cloud

Controlled cloud services are not publicly available; users are specifically authorized by services vendors. Access to the controlled cloud may be through the Internet; however, connections would be encrypted. The cloud vendor employs various techniques and technologies to prevent unauthorized access. Use of services is governed by contracts, and which specify the responsibilities of the vendor and the responsibilities of the customer with regard to data stewardship.

The services vendor discloses to customers its processes for managing customer data. Any subprocessors used in processing customer data are identified to customers. Data protection schemes, such as administrative controls, encryption methods, and other appropriate technical and organizational measures (TOMs) to protect data are described and demonstrated to customers.

The services vendor undergoes audits by an accredited independent third party using an industry standard such as the Service Organization Controls as defined by the AICPA, or achieves certification of an industry standard such as the International Standards Organization (ISO) 27001:2005 for information security or the British Standard BS 10012 for data privacy.

## Private cloud

Private cloud is cloud infrastructure operated solely for a single organization, whether managed internally or by a third-party and hosted internally or externally. Undertaking a private cloud project requires a significant level and degree of engagement to virtualize the business environment, and requires the organization to reevaluate decisions about existing resources.

### Public cloud

A cloud is called a "public cloud" when the services are rendered over a network that is open for public use. Technically there may be little or no difference between public and private cloud architecture, however, security consideration may be substantially different for services (applications, storage, and other resources) that are made available by a service provider for a public audience and when communication is effected over a non-trusted network.

### Community cloud

Community cloud shares infrastructure between several organizations from a specific community with common concerns (security, compliance, jurisdiction, etc.), whether managed internally or by a third-party and hosted internally or externally. The costs are spread over fewer users than a public cloud (but more than a private cloud), so only some of the cost savings potential of cloud computing are realized.

### Hybrid cloud

Hybrid cloud is a composition of two or more clouds (private, community or public) that remain distinct entities but are bound together, offering the benefits of multiple deployment models. Hybrid cloud can also mean the ability to connect collocation, managed and/or dedicated services with cloud resources.

### Cloud management strategies

Public clouds are managed by public cloud service providers, which include the public cloud environment's servers, storage, and networking and data center operations. Users of public cloud services can generally select from three basic categories:

1. User self-provisioning: Customers purchase cloud services directly from the provider, typically through a web form or console interface. The customer pays on a per-transaction basis.
2. Advance provisioning: Customers contract in advance a predetermined amount of resources, which are prepared in advance of service. The customer pays a flat fee or a monthly fee.
3. Dynamic provisioning: The provider allocates resources when the customer needs them, then decommissions them when they are no longer needed. The customer is charged on a pay-per-use basis.

Managing a private cloud requires software tools to help create a virtualized pool of compute resources, provide a self-service portal for end users and handle security, resource allocation, tracking and billing. Management tools for private clouds tend to be service driven, as opposed to resource driven, because cloud environments are typically highly virtualized and organized in terms of portable workloads.

## Advantages

Cloud computing relies on sharing of resources to achieve coherence and economies of scale, similar to a utility (like the electricity grid) over a network. At the foundation of cloud computing is the broader concept of converged infrastructure and shared services.

The cloud also focuses on maximizing the effectiveness of the shared resources. Cloud resources are usually not only shared by multiple users but are also dynamically reallocated per demand. This can work for allocating resources to users. For example, a cloud computer facility that serves European users during European business hours with a specific application (e.g., email) may reallocate the same resources to serve North American users during North America's business hours with a different application (e.g., a web server). This approach should maximize the use of computing power thus reducing environmental damage as well since less power, air conditioning, rackspace, etc. are required for a variety of functions. With cloud computing, multiple users can access a single server to retrieve and update their data without purchasing licenses for different applications.

## The Future

According to Gartner's Hype cycle, Cloud computing has reached a maturity that leads it into a productive phase. This means that most of the main issues with Cloud computing have been addressed to a degree that Clouds have become interesting for full commercial exploitation. In 2012 the European Commission has issued an analysis of the relevance of the open research issues for commercial stabilization in which various experts from industry and academia identify in particular the following major concerns:

1. Open interoperation across (proprietary) cloud solutions at IaaS, PaaS and SaaS levels
2. Managing multitenancy at large scale and in heterogeneous environments

3. Dynamic and seamless elasticity from in-house clouds to public clouds for unusual (scale, complexity) and/or infrequent requirements
4. Data management in a cloud environment, taking the technical and legal constraints into consideration

These findings have been refined into a research roadmap proposed by the Cloud Computing Expert Group on Research in December 2012 which tries to lay out a timeline for the identified research topics according to their commercial relevance.

## Reference

1. "Cloud computing entry". NetLingo. Retrieved 15 January 2014.
2. University of Michigan http://it.umich.edu/initiatives/cloud/content/what-cloud. Retrieved 15 January 2014. Missing or empty |title= (help)
3. http://www.crn.com/news/cloud/240150619/the-100-coolest-cloud-computing-vendors-of-2013.htm
4. "The NIST Definition of Cloud Computing". National Institute of Standards and Technology. Retrieved 24 July 2011.
5. "What is Cloud Computing?". *Amazon Web Services*. 2013-03-19. Retrieved 2013-03-20.

# 15

# System Approach in Higher Education

## Introduction

Cloud computing is the next natural step in the evolution of on-demand information technology services and products. To a large extent cloud computing will be based on virtualized resources. The idea of cloud computing is based on a very fundamental principal of 'reusability of IT capabilities. The difference that cloud computing brings compared to traditional concepts of grid computing, distributed computing , utility computing, or autonomic computing is to broaden horizons across organizational boundaries.

According to the IEEE Computer Society Cloud Computing is

*"A paradigm in which information is permanently stored in servers on the*
*Internet and cached temporarily on clients that include desktops,*
*Entertainment centers, table computers, notebooks, wall computers, handhelds, etc."*

Though many cloud computing architectures and deployments are powered by grids, based on autonomic characteristics and consumed on the basis of utilities billing, the concept of a cloud is fairly distinct and complementary to the concepts of grid, SaaS, Utility Computing etc. In theory, cloud computing promises availability of all required hardware, software, platform, applications, infrastructure and storage with an ownership of just an internet connection.

People can access the information that they need from any device with an Internet connection including mobile and handheld phones rather than being chained to the desktop. It also means lower costs, since there is no need to install software or hardware.

Cloud computing used to posting and sharing photos on orkut, instant messaging with friends maintaining and upgrading business technology.

## Concept

A powerful underlying and enabling concept is computing through service-oriented architectures (SOA) - delivery of an integrated and orchestrated suite of functions to an end-user through composition of both loosely and tightly coupled functions, or services - often network based. Related concepts are component-based system engineering, orchestration of different services through workflows, and virtualization.

## Cyber Infrastructure

Cyber infrastructure makes applications dramatically easier to develop and deploy, thus expanding the feasible scope of applications possible within budget and organizational constraints, and shifting the scientist's and engineer's effort away from information technology development and concentrating it on scientific and engineering research. Cyber infrastructure also increases efficiency, quality, and reliability by capturing commonalities among application needs, and facilitates the efficient sharing of equipment and services.

Today, almost any business or major activity uses, or relies in some form, on IT and IT services. These services need to be enabling and appliance-like, and there must be an economy of- scale for the total-cost-of-ownership to be better than it would be without cyber infrastructure. Technology needs to improve end-user productivity and reduce Technology-driven overhead

## Service-oriented Architecture

SOA is not a new concept, although it again has been receiving considerable attention in recent years [e.g., Bel08, IBM08a]. Examples of some of the first network-based service-oriented architectures are remote procedure calls (RPC), DCOM and Object Request Brokers (ORBs) based on the CORBA specifications. A more recent example is so called ¯Grid Computing architectures and solutions. In an SOA environment end-users request an IT service (or an integrated collection of such services) at the desired functional, quality and capacity level, and receive the response at the time requested or at a specified later time. Service discovery, brokering, and reliability are important .Goal of the SOA is that creating an architecture in which services are able to communicate using http protocol it is expected that in the next 10 years, service-based solutions will be a major vehicle for delivery of information and other IT assisted functions at both individual and organizational levels.

## Cloud Architecture

Cloud architecture the systems architecture of the software systems involved in the delivery of *cloud computing*, comprises hardware and software designed by a *cloud architect* who typically works for a *cloud integrator*. It typically involves multiple *cloud components* communicating with each other over application programming interfaces, usually web services.

This closely resembles the UNIX philosophy of having multiple programs doing one thing well and working together over universal interfaces. Complexity is controlled and the resulting systems are more manageable than their monolithic counterparts.

*Cloud architecture* extends to the client, where web browsers and/or software applications access *cloud applications. Cloud storage architecture* is loosely coupled, where metadata operations are centralized enabling the data nodes to scale into the hundreds, each independently delivering data to applications or users.

## Cloud Architecture

## Types Of Cloud

Public cloud
Hybrid cloud
Private cloud

## Public Cloud

Public cloud or external cloud describes cloud computing in the traditional mainstream. Public clouds are run by third parties, and applications from different customers are likely to be mixed together on the cloud's servers, storage systems, and networks. A public cloud provides services to multiple customers.

### Hybrid Cloud

Hybrid clouds combine both public and private cloud models. This is most often seen with the use of storage clouds to support Web 2.0 applications.

### Private Cloud

Private clouds are built for the exclusive use of one client, providing the utmost control over data, security, and quality of service. The company owns the infrastructure and has control over how applications are deployed on it. Private clouds can be built and managed by a company's own IT organization or by a cloud provider.

### Cloud computing products and services can be classified into 4 major categories:

They are

1. Application as service ( Aaas)
2. Platform as a Service (Paas)
3. Infrastructure as a service (Iaas)
4. Software as a Service (Saas)

### 1. Application as s service (Aaas)

These are the first kind of cloud computing services that came into being. Under this, a service is made available to an end-user. The end-user is asked to create an account with the service provider and start using the application. One of first famous application was web-based email service by hotmail started in 1996. Scores of such services are available now on the web.

### 2. Platform as a Service (Paas)

Cloud vendors are companies that offer cloud computing services and products. One of the services that they provide is called PaaS. Under this a computing platform such as operating system is provided to a customer or end user on a monthly rental basis. Some of the major cloud computing vendor is Amazon, Microsoft, Google etc.

### 3. Infrastructure as a service

The cloud computing vendors offer infrastructure as a service. One may avail hardware services such as processors, memory, networks etc on agreed basis for specific duration and price.

### 4. Software as a service (Saas)

Software package such as CRM or CAD/CAM can be accessed under cloud computing scheme. Here a customer upon registration is allowed to use software accessible through net and use it for his or his business process. The related data and work may be stored on local machines or with the service providers. SaaS services may be available on rental basis or on peruse basis.

## Components of Cloud Computing

The key to a SOA framework that supports workflows is componentization of its services, an ability to support a range of couplings among workflow building blocks, fault-tolerance in its data- and process-aware service-based delivery, and an ability to audit processes, data and results, i.e., collect and use provenance information. Component-based approach is characterized by *reusability* (elements can be re-used in other workflows), *substitutability* (alternative implementations are easy to insert, very precisely specified interfaces are available, run-time component replacement mechanisms exist, there is ability to verify and validate substitutions, etc), *extensibility and scalability (*ability to readily extend system component pool and to scale it, increase capabilities of individual components, have an extensible and scalable architecture that can automatically discover new functionalities and resources, etc),*customizability* (ability to customize generic features to the needs of a particular scientific domain and problem), and *composability* (easy construction of more complex functional solutions using basic components, reasoning about such compositions, etc.). There are other Characteristics that also are very important. Those include reliability and availability of the components and services, the cost of the services, security, total cost of ownership, economy of scale, and so on. In the context of cloud computing we distinguish many categories of components. From differentiated and undifferentiated hardware, to general-purpose and specialized software and applications, to real and virtual images, to environments, to no-root Differentiated resources, to workflow-based environments and collections of services, and soon.

## Virtualization

Virtualization is another very useful concept. It allows abstraction and isolation of lower level functionalities and underlying hardware. This enables portability of higher-level functions and sharing and/or aggregation of the physical resources. The virtualization concept has been around in some form since 1960s (e.g., in IBM mainframe systems). Since then, the concept has matured considerably and it has been applied to all aspects of computing – memory, storage, processors, software, networks, as well as services that IT offers. It is the combination of the growing needs and the recent advances in the IT architectures and solutions that is now bringing the virtualization to the true commodity level. Virtualization, through its economy of scale, and its ability to offer very advanced and complex IT services at a reasonable cost, is poised to become, along with wireless and highly distributed and pervasive computing devices, such as sensors and personal cell-based access devices, the driving technology behind the next wave in IT growth .Not surprisingly there are dozens of virtualization products, and a number of small and large companies that make them. Some examples in the operating systems and software applications space are VMware1, Xen - an open source Linux-based product developed by XenSource2, and Microsoft virtualization products, to mention a few. Major IT players have also shown a renewed interest in the technology. Classical storage players such as EMC10, NetApp11, IBM12 and Hitachi13 have not been standing still either. In addition, the network virtualization market is teeming with activity.

## Users

The most important Cloud entity, and the principal quality driver and constraining influence are, of course, the user. The value of solutions depends very much on the view it has of its end-user requirements and user categories. There four broad sets of nonexclusive user categories: System or Cyber infrastructure (CI) developers, developers (authors) of different component services and underlying applications, technology and domain personnel that integrates basic services into composite services and their orchestrations (workflows) and delivers those to end-users, and finally users of simple and composite services. User categories also include domain specific groups, and indirect users such as stakeholders, policy makers, and so on. Functional and usability requirements derive, in most part, directly from the user profiles.

## Working of Cloud Computing

Cloud computing system can be divided it into two sections: the front end and the back end. They connect to each other through a network, usually the Internet. The front end is the side the computer user, or client, sees. The back end is the "cloud" section of the system. On the back end there are various computers, servers and data storage systems that create the "cloud" of computing services. A central server administers the system, monitoring traffic and client demands to ensure everything runs smoothly. It follows a set of rules called protocols Servers and remote computers do most of the work and store the data.

## Merits and Demerits

### Merits

Cloud enabler technologies like utility computing, Grid Computing, RTI, web infrastructure and others are cloud enabled.

1. Infrastructure service providers are taking advantage of the Cloud services.
2. Information services, entertainment-oriented services such as video on demand, simple business services such as customer authentication or identity management and contextual services such as location or mapping services are positioned well by using the service.
3. Other services, such as corporate processes (for example, billing, deduction management and mortgage calculation) and transactional services (for example, fiscal transactions), would take longer to reach the cloud and the mainstream.
4. Cloud computing infrastructures allows efficient use of their IT hardware and software investments
5. A cloud infrastructure can be a cost efficient model for delivering information services, reducing IT management complexity.
6. The Cloud makes it possible to launch Web 2.0 applications quickly and to scale up applications as much as needed when needed.

### Demerits

1. Stored data might not be secure**:** With cloud computing, all our data is stored on the cloud. The unauthorized users gain access to our confidential data.
2. Dependent on internet connection: Internet connectivity isn't completely stable and reliable.

3. It's not platform agnostic: Most clouds force participants to rely on a single platform or host only one type of product.
4. Can be slow: Even on a fast connection, web based application can sometimes be slower than accessing a similar software program on our desktop PC.

## Conclusion

Cloud computing builds on decades of research in virtualization, distributed computing, utility computing, and more recently networking, web and software services. It implies a service oriented architecture, reduced information technology overhead for the end-user, great flexibility, reduced total cost of ownership, on demand services and many other things.

In today's global competitive market, companies must innovate and get the most from its resources to succeed. Cloud computing infrastructures are next generation platforms that can provide tremendous value to companies of any size. They can help companies achieve more efficient use of their IT hardware and software investments and provide a means to accelerate the adoption of innovations. Cloud computing increases profitability by improving resource utilization. Costs are driven down by delivering appropriate resources only for the time those resources are needed. Cloud computing has enabled teams and organizations to streamline lengthy procurement processes.

Cloud computing enables innovation by alleviating the need of innovators to find resources to develop, test, and make their innovations available to the user community. Innovators are free to focus on the innovation rather than the logistics of finding and managing resources that enable the innovation.

# 16

# Efficient Knowledge Shift For the Current Cohort

## Introduction

Teachers have tough jobs lots of kids and lots of responsibility and budget cuts are making things worse. They have administrators telling them to boost achievement and personalize learning, but most of them are on their own without tools. Blended learning is a shift to an online environment for at least a portion of the student day made to improve learning and improve conditions for students and teachers. Blended learning means the core for instructional delivery and it incorporates some student choice over time, location, rate. It requires that leverage talent with technology. Blended learning provides a tremendous opportunity for us all. We can be leaders in how to kick start and expand a successful program within our schools, which is a valuable, and integral role to play. The student is actively making choices about how to generate, obtain, manipulate, or display information. Technology use allows many more students to be actively thinking about information, making choices, and executing skills. As technology is used as a tool to support students in performing authentic tasks, the students are in the position of defining their goals, making design decisions , and evaluating their progress. This article explores the way of improving working conditions teaching and learning with blended learning and it stresses that Blending is the best of online and onsite learning which will be work better for students and teachers.

The purpose of this paper is to discuss the emerging trend in higher education to blend text – based asynchronous Internet technology with face - to - face learning - often referred to as simply blended learning. To begin , this paper will describe blended learning along with its capability to support meaningful learning outcomes. The real test of blended learning is the effective integration of the two main components (face – to – face and Internet technology ) such that we are not just adding on to the existing dominant approach or method. We should have solid understandings of the properties of the Internet , as well as knowledge of how to effectively integrate Internet technology with the most desirable and valued characteristics of face –to -face learning experiences, a quantum shift occurs in terms of the nature and quality of the educational experience. What makes blended learning particularly effective is its ability to facilitate a community of inquiry. Community provides the stabilizing, cohesive influence that balances the open communication and limitless access to information on the Internet. Communities also provide the condition for free and open dialogue, critical debate, negotiation and agreement - the hallmark of higher education. Blended learning has the capabilities to facilitate these conditions and adds an important reflective element with multiple forms of communication to meet specific learning requirements. A blended learning context can provide the independence and increased control essential to developing critical thinking. Along with the increased control that a blended learning context encourages is a scaffold acceptance of responsibility for constructing meaning and understanding.

## Definitions

Blended learning is an approach to learning and teaching which combines and aligns learning undertaken in face to face sessions with learning opportunities created online.

1. Blended learning is a new type of learning activities challenging our thinking as how learning must be facilitated, creating new etiquettes of learning and teaching and shifting the focus of control from the teacher to the learner.
2. Blended learning is a formal education program in which a student learns at least in part through online delivery of content and instruction with some element of student control over time, place, path or pace.

3. Blended learning refers to the use of multiple educational methodologies modalities within a unit of study. Blended learning is used to describe courses which involve both face to face and online learning component.

## Blended Learning Introductory Procedure

An instructor can begin a course with a well- structured introductory lesson in the classroom, and then proceed with follow- up materials online. Blended learning can also be applied to the integration of e- learning with a Learning Management system using computers in a physical classroom, along with face- to- face instruction. Guidance is suggested early in the process, to be used more sparingly as learners gain expertise.

## Blended Learning Continuum

**MODEL 1**: Fully online curriculum with options for face-to- face instruction.

**MODEL 2**: Mostly or fully online curriculum with some time required in either the classroom or computer lab.

**MODEL 3**: Mostly or fully online curriculum with students meeting daily in the classroom or computer lab.

**MODEL 4**: Classroom instruction with substantial required online components that extend beyond the classroom and/ or the school day.

**MODEL 5**: Classroom instruction that includes online resources, with limited or no requirements for students to be online.

## Equipments Needed to Promote Blended Learning in Schools

1. Classrooms that have some computers with digital curricula
2. Teachers who are experimenting with flipped classroom strategies.
3. Schools that have a computer lab that classes can use
4. Computer purchases that improve device access ratios.

Blended learning offers a variety of formal and informal learning assets to utilize within e- learning .

## Advantages of Blended Learning

1. Students have greater time flexibility, freedom, and convenience by working part of the time online from home due to decreased commuting and parking hassles.
2. Students are likely to interact more with the instructor and fellow students since there are numerous opportunities to do so both in class and online.

3. Students have access to unlimited up – to – date resources available via the Web.
4. Students often develop or enhance skills in time management, critical thinking, and problem solving.
5. Students enjoy increased success as measured by fewer course withdrawals and somewhat higher grades.
6. Students can participate more in class discussions since they can choose environment - online or face – to - face - in which they feel more comfortable.
7. Students have more time to reflect and refer to relevant course and other research materials when working and writing online than when responding in class.
8. Students usually receive more feedback , and more frequent feedback, from their instructors.
9. Students can acquire useful skills from using the Internet and computer technology.
10. A Blended approach can increase learner retention and greater retention leads to skills transfer and greater performance.
11. Learners also can take the responsibility for managing self paced learning, encouraging them to take full ownership of building their knowledge and skills.

## Five Ways to improve working Conditions With Blended Learning

1. Teams: Blended learning is a team sport. It allows an instructional team to work together to support hundreds of students moving at their own pace. Teaching teams can increase the support provided to new teachers. Blended learning can make learning more social and more transparent.

2. Recommendations : Smart recommendation engines and lesson sharing platforms breakdown the isolation of teaching by allowing smart tools and smart colleagues to offer recommended learning experiences for groups of students.

3. Personalized professional development PPD **:** Platforms like Bloom board ( A Web platform that facilitates educator observations and evaluations, and provides educators with a marketplace of personalized professional development (PD) and Learn Zillion ( a web-based application that helps teachers and parents meet the educational needs of every student provide a personalized learning experience for teachers .Each lesson includes a short video lesson ,downloaded resources ,a coach's commentary

to help with teacher's development). All the benefits of personalized learning that apply to students will increasingly apply to teachers with multiple ways to learn and practice. Social learning platforms like Edmodo ( a website for teachers, students, and parents. It is marketed as the Face book for schools and a power professional learning network across districts and around the world.

4. Career options : Blended learning is creating a new generation of school models that gives teachers more options of teaching environments. As more students combine online and onsite learning, teachers are increasingly able to choose from a variety of employers and working conditions. Team - based environments are creating more leadership roles in schools. Specialists are able to work from home and set their hours.

5. Earning potential : New staffing (employment) patterns , new roles , and extended learning time will allow many teachers to earn more than is typical today.

## Five ways to improve Teaching With Blended Learning

1. Diagnostics : Adaptive assessments like i-Ready (an adaptive diagnostic and both teacher led and individualized online instruction for a complete blended learning solution. It is all you need to drive student success in reading and Math for grades K - 12) and N W E A's (North West Evaluation Association ) MAP can quickly zero in on learning levels. Aided by lots of content - embedded assessment, comprehensive portable learner profiles will share information with everyone involved in promoting an individual student's growth - providing similar benefits to electronic health record in medicine.

2. Analytics : Teachers that have signed up for MangaHigh (*Mangahigh* is a comprehensive and powerful test prep math teaching resource for state standards offering more than 400 different challenges) can assign free middle grade math games as homework and review a full achievement dashboard in the morning. Students that Write to Learn get instant writing feedback and the teacher gets a standards based grade book full of evidence. In addition to extended access and more variety, the shift from print to digital curriculum will include embedded assessments and powerful dashboards that will allow teachers to more easily monitor student progress.

3. Extended reach : With the help of a team master teachers can reach twice as many students. At Carpe Diem, (PHYSICS) master teachers lead workshops for 300 secondary students. With the help of online learning,

a great physics teacher can reach hundreds, perhaps thousands of students.

4. Dynamic scheduling: At School of One (SO1) is a Middle School Mathematics program of the New York City Department of Education.. It began in 2009 and its innovative program integrates the use of technology in the development and implementation of personalized curriculum and learning as well as the use of technology in the learning environment. When students participate in small group instruction, it's the right lesson, on the right day, in the right modality for each student and that's scheduling magical. With the shift to competency – based models where more students will be moving at their own pace, scheduling software will become an important teaching tool.

5. Focus on higher order skills: At Rocket Ship Education RSED (is a charter school network . Their schools use a blended learning model with adaptive software to increase student achievement). Students spend about two hours each day doing online skill building exercises. That allows teachers to spend more class time on critical thinking and problem solving. Online writing assignment allows teachers to focus on the logic of an argument rather than grammar and word choice. Blended learning makes it easier to flip the classroom and send home a playlist of instructional resources that deliver content so that class time can be spent solving problems.

## Four ways Blended Learning is Benefiting Student Learning

1. Motivation: Students learning in different ways for different reasons. Blended learning makes it easier to provide multiple learning strategies. Some online learning curriculum make a point of teaching each concept three ways. The new developmental math courses from the National Repository of Open Content feature a variety of strategies for each sub - skill including instructional videos , tutorials, voice - over - text, and games. More engaging and more personalized content will help more kids learn difficult topics. Blended learning makes it easier to 'flip the classroom '(i.e.) students learn new content online by watching video lectures , usually at home, that deliver the content so that class time can be spent solving problems.

2. Self directed : By definition , blended learning creates some level of learner control. For many students the ability to make some choices about what to study, how to approach a topic, when and where to learn can make a difference.

3. Customization: Ed Tech enables personalized learning pathways. Visual learners and students with limited English benefit from game - based approaches like ST Math (Spatial - Temporal (ST) Math is the leader in visual math instruction and represents the highest quality and most effective blended learning math solution in k - 12 education.)

Adaptive software like Dream box (Fun and effective online elementary math help at home. When you want to help teach your child math at home, overcome math anxiety, boost math learning, erase math boredom, or just help your kids to learn to love math) and i-Ready build engaging and efficient pathways – that means more learning per hour.

4. Extended year: Blended learning can help extend the school calendar. If a school operates with two less teachers and spreads pay over the other 18 teachers, they may be able to shift to a 195 day school year. They can also extend the school calendar and add more breaks that become periods for extra academic time and / or enrichment — some of which can be provided by community based organizations. Blended learning often incorporates take home technology and that means more families connected to quality learning experiences.

We teachers are the ones that are closest to the students. We see every day what's working, what's not working, and what's inspiring our students to learn in new and better ways. Blended learning provides a tremendous opportunity for us all. We can be leaders in how to kick start and expand a successful program within our schools, which is a valuable, and integral role to play.

## Educational Benefits of Blended Learning to the Faculties and Institutions

- The ability for schools to maintain their central role in managing a student's educational process and personalizing instruction.
- Providing curriculum developers and teachers the flexibility to address standards and maintain curriculum fidelity while integrating digital content and learning experiences that better engage 21st century learners; and
- Giving teachers valuable experiences in using technology effectively in their professional development courses, preparing them to use blended models creatively and strategically as this approach becomes more and more prevalent in the classroom.

## Conclusion

Blended learning can support a variety of informal learning processes .Good blending is about establishing a balance between the instructional advantages for the learner and the learning objectives. Blended learning captures the best of both world by allowing learners to pick and choose how they want to learn and affords them greater flexibility and convenience about when they want to learn. The teacher is no longer the center of attention as the dispenser of information, but rather plays the role of facilitator, setting project goals and providing guidelines and resources, moving from student to student or group to group, providing suggestions and support for student activity. As students work on their technology supported products, the teacher rotates through the room, looking over shoulders, asking about the reasons for various design choices , and suggesting resources that might be used.

# 17

# Teaching Learning Process: Importance of the Flip Teaching

## Introduction

Flip teaching or a flipped classroom is a form of blended learning in which students learn new content online by watching video lectures, usually at home, and what used to be homework (assigned problems) is now done in class with teachers offering more personalized guidance and interaction with students, instead of lecturing. This is also known as backwards classroom, flipped classroom, reverse teaching, and the Thayer Method.

Many educators are beginning to become aware of the growing teaching method referred to as "Flipping the Classroom". Simply put... the teacher provides videos for homework, while traditional home work is done in class under teacher supervision. Unfortunately this might be just too simplistic of a definition. Possible this is why using the words "simply put" may not be the best practice in explaining anything.

The flipped classroom describes a reversal of traditional teaching where students gain first exposure to new material outside of class, usually via reading or lecture videos, and then class time is used to do the harder work of assimilating that knowledge through strategies such as problem-solving, The purpose of flipping the classroom is to shift from passive to active learning to focus on the higher order thinking skills such as Analysis, Synthesis and Evaluation (Bloom).

There are many permutations of what a flipped classroom will look like and depends on variables such as class size, resources, support and readiness to change. At UQ, several teachers across the faculties have already flipped their classrooms and their valuable evidences have been captured in the case studies section.

Learning opportunities of the flipped classroom adapted from Gerstein, Educational technologies are an important feature of the flipped classroom as they can be used to:

1. Capture key content for students to access at their own convenience and to suit their pace of learning (e.g. lecture material, readings, interactive multimedia),
2. Present learning materials in a variety of formats to suit different learner styles (e.g. text, videos, audio, multimedia),
3. Provide opportunities for discourse and interaction in and out of class (e.g. polling tools, discussion tools, content creation tools),
4. Convey timely information, updates and reminders for students (e.g. micro-blogging, announcement tools),
5. Provide immediate and anonymous feedback for teachers and students (e.g. quizzes, polls) to signal revision points,
6. Capture data about students to analyse their progress and identify the risk of the students (e.g. analytics)

In the flipped classroom, the roles and expectations of students and teachers change where:

1. students take more responsibility for their own learning and study core content either individually or in groups before class and then apply knowledge and skills to a range of activities using higher order thinking.
2. Teaching 'one-to-many' focuses more on facilitation and moderation than lecturing, though lecturing is still important. Significant learning opportunities can be gained through facilitating active learning, engaging students, guiding learning, correcting misunderstandings and providing timely feedback using a variety of pedagogical strategies,
3. There is a greater focus on concept exploration, meaning making and demonstration or application of knowledge in the face-to-face setting likely Discussions or debates.

**The traditional definition of a flipped class is:**

1. Where videos take the place of direct instruction
2. This then allows students to get individual time in class to work with their teacher on key learning activities.
3. It is called the flipped class because what used to be class work (the "lecture" is done at home via teacher-created videos and what used to be homework (assigned problems) is now done in class.

**The Flipped Classroom is Not**

1. A synonym for online videos. When most people hear about the flipped class all they think about are the videos. It is the interaction and the meaningful learning activities that occur during the face-to-face time that is most important.
2. About replacing teachers with videos.
3. An online course.
4. Students working without structure.
5. Students spending the entire class staring at a computer screen.
6. Students working in isolation.

**The Flipped Classroom is:**

1. A means to Increase interaction and personalized contact time between students and teachers.
2. An environment where students take responsibility for their own learning.
3. A classroom where the teacher is not the "sage on the stage", but the "guide on the side".
4. A blending of direct instruction with constructivist learning.
5. A classroom where students who are absent due to illness or extra-curricular activities such as athletics or field-trips, don't get left behind.
6. A class where content is permanently archived for review or remediation.
7. A class where all students are engaged in their learning.
8. A place where all students can get a personalized education.

**Five Best Practices for the Flipped Classroom:**

**(1) Need to Know**

How are you creating a need to know the content that is recorded? Just because I record something, or use a recorded material, does not mean that my students will want to watch, nor see the relevance in watching it. I mean, it is still a lecture. Also, this "need to know" is not "because it is on the test," or "because it will help you when you graduate." While that may be a reality, these reasons do not engage the students who are already struggling to find meaning and relevance in school. If the flipped classroom is truly to become innovative, then it must be paired with transparent and/or embedded reason to know the content.

### (2) Engaging Models

One of the best ways to create the "need to know" is to use a pedagogical model that demands this. Whether project-based learning (PBL), game-based learning (GBL), Understanding by Design (UBD), or authentic literacy, find an effective model to institute in your classroom. Become a master of those models first, and then use the flipped classroom to support the learning. Example: Master design, assessment, and management of PBL; and then look at how you can use the flipped classroom to support the process. Perhaps it is a great way to differentiate instruction, or support students who need another lesson in a different mode. Perhaps students present you with a "need to know," and your answer with a recorded piece to support them. This will help you to master your role as "guide on the side."

### (3) Technology

What technology do you have to support the flipped classroom? What technology gaps exist that might hinder it? Since the flipped classroom is about recorded video, then obviously students would need the technology to do this. There are many things to consider here. Will you demand that all students watch the video, or is it a way to differentiate and allow choice? Will you allow or rely on mobile learning for students to watch it? Again, these are just some of the questions to consider in terms of technology. Lack of technology doesn't necessarily close the door to the flipped classroom model, but it might require some intentional planning and differentiation.

### (4) Reflection

Every time you have students to watch a video, just like, you would with any instructional activity, you must build in reflective activities to have students to think about what they learned, how it will help them, its relevance, and more. If reflection is not a regular part of your classroom culture, then implementing the flipped classroom will not be as effective. Students need meta-cognition to connect content to objectives, whether that is progress in a GBL unit, or work towards an authentic product in at PBL project.

### (5) Time and Place

Do you have structures to support this? When and where will the learning occur? I believe it unfair to demand that students watch the video outside of the class time for various reasons. If you have a blended learning environment, that of course provides a natural time and place to watch the videos, but it will be difficult to ensure all students watch a video as homework. In addition, do not make epic videos that last hours. Keep the learning within the videos manageable for students.

## Conclusion

I know I may have "upset the apple cart" for those who love the flipped classroom. My intent is not to say that the flipped classroom is bad. Rather, it is only a start. The focus should be on teacher practice, then tools and structures. The flipped classroom is one way to help move teachers toward better teaching but does not ensure it. Like the ideas above, focus on ways to improve your instruction before choosing to use the "flipped classroom."

Flipped mastery eliminates two other out-of-class routines: daily lesson planning and grading papers. The latter happens in class and in person. Replacing lectures with group and individual activities increases in-class activity. Every student has something to do throughout the class. In some classes, students choose how to demonstrate mastery - testing, writing, speaking, debating and even designing a related game. Model provides one way to manage the testing process. It creates a different test for each student from a pool of questions. Advocates claim that its efficiency allows most students to do a year's work in much less time. Advanced students work on independent projects while slower learners get more personalized instruction. Some students might not get through the year's material, but demonstrated competence on the parts they did complete.

Flip teaching will help students not to depend to anybody. Teachers guide students to improve their creativeness. It will help young teachers to do their teaching to the future generation. As a Teacher Educator, we should make our classroom lively with flip teaching.

## Reference


1. B eesley, A., & Apthorp, H. (Eds.). (2010). Classroom instruction that works, second edition: Research report. Denver, CO: McRel.
2. Bergmann, J., & Sams, A. (2012).Flip your classroom: Reach every student in every class every day. Washington, DC: ISTE; and Alexandria, VA: ASCD.
3. Finkel, E. (2012, November). Flipping the script in K12. District Administration. Retrieved fromwww.districtadministration.com/article/flipping-script-k12
4. Flipped Learning Network. (2012). Improve student learning and teacher satisfaction with one flip of the classroom. Retrieved from author at http://flippedlearning1.files.wordpress.com/2012/07/classroom windoing for graphic 7-12.pdf
5. Greenberg, B., Medlock, L., & Stephens, D. (2011). *Blend my learning: Lessons from a blended learning pilot.* Oakland, CA: Envision Schools, Google, & Stanford University D.School. Retrieved from-blended learning -pilot4.pdfassroomwindoingforgraphic7-12.pdf
6. Hamre, B. K., & Pianta, R. C. (2005). Can instructional and emotional support in the first-grade classroom make a difference for children at risk of school failure? *Child Development, 76*(5) 949–967.
7. Hattie, J. (2008) *Visible learning: A synthesis of over 800 meta-analyses relating to achievement.* New York: Routledge.
8. Medina, J. (2008). *Brain rules: 12 principles for surviving and thriving at work, home, and school.* Seattle, WA: Pear Press.
9. Schwerdt, G., & Wupperman, A.C. (2010). Is traditional teaching really all that bad? A within-student between-subject approach. *Economics of Education Review, 30*(2), 365–379.

# 18

# Optimizing Resource Sharing in cloud Computing

## Introduction

The cloud computing is the dynamic provisioning of IT capabilities such as hardware, software or services, from third parties over a network. Resource sharing in the cloud Computing environment is the major issues that limited application of the cloud computing. The problem of enabling effective peer-to-peer resource sharing in these types of networks the availability of a wireless infrastructure and broadcast nature of wireless communication. Which bring to the notions of location awareness and MAC layer cross-layering? Through extensive packet-level simulations, I have investigated the separate effects of location awareness and MAC layer cross-layering, the performance of the P2P application. The combined protocol Optimizing Resource Sharing In Cloud Computing (ORSCC), reduces message overhead of as much as 40 per- cent with respect to the existing design, while at the same time improving the information retrieval performance. Notably, differently from the existing design, our proposed ORSCC specialization displays information retrieval performance resilient to the presence of both CBR and TCP background traffic.

The Internet is often represented as a cloud and the term "cloud computing" arises from that analogy. McKinsey [1] says that clouds are hardware-based services offering compute, network and storage capacity, where hardware management is highly abstracted from the buyer; buyers incur infrastructure costs as variable OPEX [operating expenditures]; and infrastructure capacity is highly elastic. There are three basic types of cloud computing, which are Infrastructure as a Service (IaaS), Platform as a Service (PaaS), Software as a Service (SaaS). In IaaS, CPU, grids or clusters, virtualized servers, memory, networks, storage and systems software are delivered as a service. Perhaps the best known example is "Amazon's" Elastic Compute Cloud (EC2) and Simple Storage Service (S3), but traditional IT vendors such as IBM, and telecoms providers such as "AT&T" and "Verizon" are also offering solutions. Services are typically charged by usage and can be scaled dynamically, i.e. capacity can be increased or decreased more or less on demand. PaaS provides virtualized servers on which users can run applications, or develop new ones, without having to worry about maintaining the operating systems, server hardware, load balancing or computing capacity. Well known examples include Microsoft's Azure and Sales force's Force.com. SaaS is software that is developed and hosted by the SaaS vendor and which the end user accesses over the Internet. Unlike traditional applications that users install on their computers or servers, SaaS software is owned by the vendor and runs on computers in the vendor's data center (or a co-location facility). Broadly speaking, all customers of a SaaS vendor use the same software: these are one-size- fits-all solutions. Well known examples are Salesforce.com, Google's Gmail and Apps, instant messaging from AOL, Yahoo and Google, and Voice-over Internet Protocol (VoIP) from Vonage and Skype.

## Previous Work

Lipton and Naughton [2] proposes hash table for sharing resources in the cloud based environment. A hash table or hash map is a data structure that uses a hash function to map identifying values, known as keys (e.g., a person's name), to their associated values (e.g., their telephone number). Most hash table designs assume that hash collisions the situation where different keys happen to have the same hash value are normal occurrences and must be accommodated in some way. In a well- dimensioned hash table, the average cost (number of instructions) for each lookup is independent of the number of elements stored in the table. Many hash table designs also allow arbitrary insertions and deletions of key-value pairs, at constant average, especially analysis of algorithms, amortized analysis finds the average running time per operation over a worst-case sequence of operations. Amortized analysis differs from average-case performance in that probability is not involved; amortized analysis guarantees the time per operation over worst-case performance.

Malkhi, et al [3], proposes a Distributed Hash Tables (DHT) methodology for sharing resources in the cloud based environment architecture and implementation of a distributed hash table DDS. A client in the DHT consists of service-specific software running on a client machine that communicates across the wide area with one of many service instances running in the cluster. A service is a set of cooperating software processes, each of which a service instance. Service instances communicate with wide-area clients and perform some application-level function. Services may have soft state which may be lost and recomputed if necessary, but they rely on the hash table to manage all persistent state. Ratnasamy [4] proposes Geographic Hash Table (GHT) for sharing resources in the cloud based environment. The core step in GHT is the hashing of a key k into geographic coordinates. A key-value pair is stored at a node in the vicinity of the location to which its key hashes. Choosing this node consistently is central to building a GHT. Assume a perfectly static network topology and a network routing system that can deliver packets to positions, such a GHT will cause storage requests and queries for the same k to be routed to the same node, and will distribute the storage request and query load for distinct k values evenly across the area covered by a network. The service provided by GHT is similar in character to those offered by other DHT systems. Holger Zeltwanger [5] proposes Controller Area Network (CAN) hash table for sharing resources in the cloud based environment. The CAN is a serial bus communications protocol developed by Bosch in the early 1980s. It defines a standard for efficient and reliable communication between sensor, actuator, controller, and other nodes in real-time applications. CAN is the de facto standard in a large variety of networked embedded control systems. The major pitfalls of CAN are the communication rate of a network depends on the physical distances between the nodes.

## Proposed Optimizing Resource Sharing in Cloud Computing (ORSICC)

ORSICC is based on the idea of mapping both peer (mesh router) IDs and resource IDs (keys) into the same ID space, namely, the unit ring [0,1]. Each key resides on the peer with the smallest ID larger than the key, peer p manages keys comprised between its own ID and the ID of the predecessor of p in the unit ring (denoted range (p)). Associated with each key is the IP address of the mesh client holding the corresponding resource. ORSICC maps peer and resource IDs into the unit ring using a hashing function, named Sha1, which has the property of uniformly distributing IDs in [0,1]. Indeed, IDs in ORSICC are represented through m-bit numbers, i.e., at most $2^m$ distinct (peer or resource) IDs are present in the ORSICC system.

It is a reasonable ID space for ORSCC, in which the number of shared resources is expected to be in the order of several thousands, and the number of mesh routers (peers) in the order of a few hundreds. Indeed, larger ID spaces can be easily included in the design with no modification, and with negligible impact on performance. It allows dealing with larger networks and number of shared resources, which might lead to a non-negligible probability of conflicting ID assignment with relatively low values of m. The main operation implemented by ORSICC is the lookup(x) operation, which can be invoked at any peer to find the IP address of the peer with ID =x, if x is a peer ID, or the IP address of the peer responsible of key x in case x is a resource ID. Lookup operations are used both for query resolution (Find Key operation) and for overlay maintenance. To speed up look up operations, every peer maintains a table of up to m distinct peers. The $i^{th}$ finger of peer j, with 1 d" i d" m, is the peer which has the smaller ID larger than j + ($2^{i-1}$). In order to facilitate join/leave operations, each peer maintains also the ID of its predecessor in the ORSICC ring. When a lookup (k) operation is invoked at peer p and the operation cannot be resolved locally (because k is not within range (p), a message is sent to the peer p' with largest ID <k in the finger table of node 'p'. If 'p' cannot resolve the lookup operation, it replies to peer 'p' with a message containing the ID of the peer 'p' with largest ID < k in its own finger table. Peer p then forwards the request to peer 'p', and so on, until the lookup operation can be resolved (in at most m steps). To deal with dynamic join/leaves of peers in the systems, the following procedures are implemented, When a new peer 'p' joins the network, it first needs to initialize its predecessor and finger table. This is done by sending requests to any peer currently joining the network peer 'p' is aware of (called hook peer). Then, the finger tables and predecessor pointers of currently active peers must be updated to account for the new peer joining the network.

Finally, peer 'p' must contact its successor s in the ring so that the key range previously managed by s can be split with p. In case no (active) hook peer can be found, the joint operation fails, and the peer cannot join the ORSICC overlay. When an existing peer p leaves the network, it first informs its predecessor and successor in the ring about its intention of leaving the network, so that they can change their finger tables and predecessor pointers accordingly; then, peer p transfers to its successor the key range it is responsible for. Finally, in order to deal with dynamic network conditions, each active peer in the network periodically performs a Stabilize operation, which verifies and possibly updates the content of the finger table and predecessor pointer. The period between consecutive Stabilize operations is a critical parameter in the ORSICC design: if the period is relatively short, the network is more reactive, but a higher message overhead is generated; on the other hand, a longer stabilize period reduces message overhead, at the expense of having a less reactive network. How to set the stabilize period in order to satisfactorily address this tradeoff when Basic Operation is executed in ORSCC is carefully investigated.

The first modification that proposes to the basic design concerns the function used to assign ID to peers (hash function Sha1 is still used to assign key to files/resources). The idea is to exploit locality, and to assign peers which are close in the physical network with close-by IDs in the unit ring. This choice is motivated by the observation that, according to ORSICC specifications, most of the messages are exchanged between a peer and its successor/predecessor in the unit ring.

The second contribution of the ORSCC proposal concerns the introduction of a MAC cross-layering technique. This technique aims at speeding up the lookup operations by exploiting the information that is available at the MAC layer due to the 1-hop broadcast communication occurring in wireless networks. The basic idea is that a peer u may capture packets for which it owns relevant information, even if they are not destined to 'u'. This technique is motivated by the possibility that peer 'u' that may actually be able to resolve a lookup request, is physically close to the peer invoking the lookup operation, while they are far away in the unit ring. More specifically, whenever a peer 'u' receives a packet at the MAC layer, 'u' sends it up to the application layer for further processing, even if the packet was not destined to 'u'. If the packet does not contain a lookup request, it is discarded. Otherwise, 'u' checks if it may resolve the lookup(x) operation. This occurs if x is comprised between 'u's ID and the ID of the predecessor of 'u' in the unit ring. In this case, 'u' sends a message containing its own ID to the peer that invoked the lookup(x) operation. It is important to note that, since the lookup process is invoked for both query resolution and overlay maintenance, cross-layering may improve the performance of both these operations.

Location awareness is designed to map neighboring peers to close-by IDs in the unit ring. On the other hand, cross-layering tends to be more effective when physical neighbor peers have far away ID sin the unit ring (this results in a higher likelihood of "capturing" packets). Hence, an ideal ID mapping function should, for a certain peer 'u', both 1) map pred(u)'s and succ(u)'s IDs to peers which are physical neighbors of 'u', and 2) assign the remaining u's physical neighbors faraway IDs in the unit ring. The design of a mapping function which achieves both properties 1 and 2 is a very complex combinatorial problem, which is left for future work. In this paper, we focus on property 1, and show that, even in the presence of location-aware peer ID assignment, cross-layering is indeed beneficial to the performance of the P2P application.

## Conclusion

This paper carefully investigated through packet-level simulation the performance of the ORSICC approach for peer-to-peer resource sharing in cloud computing Networking. It also proposed a specialization of the basic system approach called ORSICC, which exploits peculiar features of Cloud computing networks (location awareness and 1-hop broadcast nature of cloud computing communications) to improve performance. The main finding of the study reported in this paper is that, contrary to what happens in MANET environments [6], the basic approach can be successfully utilized for implementing file/resource sharing applications in cloud computing net- works. However, the basic ORSICC design is effective only under relatively static network conditions and in presence of modest background traffic. With respect to the basic design, our proposed ORSICC protocol achieves a considerable reduction in message overhead, and a significant improvement in information retrieval performance. This performance improvement allows an effective realization of the P2P over- lay also under very dynamic network conditions and in presence of considerable background traffic. Although our investigation has shown that ORSICC message overhead does not lead to network congestion by itself, overlay maintenance still requires the exchange of a relatively high number of messages in the network, which could induce performance degradation when other applications are executed concurrently with ORSICC. Quantifying application-layer performance degradation when several applications coexist with the P2P overlay is matter of ongoing work, as well as the problem of further reducing the message overhead induced by applications for file/resource sharing in Cloud Computing networks.

## References

1. McKinsey & Co. Report presented at Uptime Institute Symposium April 18, 2009 clearing the Air on Cloud Computing, http://uptimeinstitute.org/content/view/353/319,http://images. cxotoday.com/cxoimages/storyimages/matter101157 .pdf (accessed November 27, 2009)
2. Lipton, R.J., Naughton and J.F.: Clocked adversaries for hashing. Algorithmica 9(3), 239–252(1993)
3. Malkhi, D., Naor, M., Ratajczak, D.: Viceroy: A Scalable and Dynamic Emulation of the Butterfly. In: Proc. ACM Symp. Principles of Distributed Computing, PODC (July 2002)
4. Ratnasamy, S., Karp, B., Shenker, S., Estrin, D., Govindan, R., Yin, L., Yu, F.: Data-Centric Storage in Sensornets with GHT, a Geographic Hash Table. Mobile Networks and Applications 8(4), 427–442 (2003)
5. Zeltwanger, H.: Time-Triggered Communication on CAN. SAE Paper 2002-01-0437 (2002)
6. Sailhan, F., Issarny, V.: Scalable Service Discovery for MANET. In: Proc. IEEE Int'l Conf. Pervasive Computing and Comm, PerCom (2005)
7. Wolfson, O., Xu, B., Yin, H., Cao, H.: Search-and-Discover in Mobile P2P Network Data- bases. In: Proc. IEEE Int'l Conf. Distributed Computing Systems, ICDCS (2006).

# 19

# Ict For Promoting Teacher Education Programme

## Introduction

New advances in the internet based technology have brought challenges and opportunities as well to education and training, in particular through online instruction. The learning environments where instructional materials are transferred electronically or through the Internet or through course software with the help of computer technologies in teaching and learning environments and where the teacher and the learner are in different physical environments are known as blended learning. Blended learning is also defined both as a kind of learning which occurs through the Internet, a network or only a computer and as audible, visual and interactive synchronous or asynchronous educational activities. The most significant characteristics of blended learning are that the teacher and the learner are in different physical environments and that the communication throughout the teaching/learning process is carried out via e-mail, forums, etc. through the Internet. This paper offers new methods for teacher education based on computer and net technologies. This article explores, pioneering technological aspects like e-learning, m-learning, u-learning etc.

"Education is the complete development of individuality of the child, so that he can make his original contribution to human life according to his best capacity", opines T. P. Nunn. A child is an integral part of society. A child has to bring in him the desired changes according to the needs and demands of the ever changing society, of which he is an integral part. Thus, Education bestows upon the child immense benefits. It brings up the child as the parents do. It guides him like an affectionate father and serves him faithfully like a wife.

Education develops the individual like a flower which distributes its fragrance all over the environment. In this sense, education is that conductive process which drags a person from darkness, poverty and misery by developing his individuality in all its aspects – physical, mental, emotional and social. With this type of around development, an individual becomes a responsible, dynamic, resourceful and enterprising citizen of strong good moral character who uses all his capacities to develop his own self, his society and his nation to the highest extent by contributing his best to national honour, national glory, national culture and civilization of the nation of which he is a part, an integral part. Thus, it can be said that education is the backbone of a nation and Teacher plays an important role in the process of education.

## Role of Teachers in the Process of Education

The future of a nation is fashioned in a classroom. Education is a socially oriented activity which is associated with strong teachers having high degrees of personal control with learners. A teacher plays an important role in the process of Education. A teacher is considered to be the architect of the nation. In other words, the future of the nation lies in the hands of a teacher.

Aristotle rightly says - "Those who educate children well are more to the honoured than they who produce them; for these only gave them life, the art of living well". A teacher acts as a facility centre of information and knowledge. A teacher after gathering information from specified sources like text books, personal notes, library etc. communicates it to the students. Not only this, a teacher develops the quality of creativity in students. A teacher arises a passion for the subject among the students by getting them to look at issues in a variety of ways. A teacher instills a hunger in their students to learn more on their own which strengthens the good future of students. According to Verma (2010), a teacher plays a significant role not only in class teaching learning situation but in social engineering too. This shows the importance of a teacher in the process of education.

## Need of Teacher Education

"A good teacher is like a candle – it consumes itself to light the way for others". Very truly says Nikos Kazantzakis than – Ideal teachers are those who use themselves as bridges over which they invite their students to cross, then having facilitated their crossing, joyfully collapse, encouraging them to create bridges of their own. But a teacher becomes a good and an ideal teacher only in that condition when he/she is able to motivate students by using creative and inspirational methods of teaching. Teaching is one of the most complicated jobs today. It demands broad knowledge of subject matter; curriculum and standards; enthusiasm, a caring attitude and a love of learning; knowledge of discipline, class room management techniques and a desire to make a difference in the lives of young people.

Great teachers set high expectations for all students. Effective teachers have lesson plans that give students a clear idea of what they will be learning, what the assignments are and the grading policies. These assignments have learning goals and give students ample opportunities to practice new skills. A good teacher has empathy and positive mental attitude. A good teacher knows that his/her students are visual, auditory or kinesthetic learners and is adept at creating presentation for all three. With all these qualities of a good teacher and effective teaching approaches there is no wonder that teachers would be able to make a difference in the lives of the students.

But the teachers would be able to acquire these effective qualities of teaching and will able to become great teacher when they would be properly trained. This articles the necessity of teacher's education. Therefore, teacher education refers to the policies and procedures designed to equip prospective teachers with the knowledge, attitude, behaviors and skills they require to perform their task effectively in the classroom school and wider community. With the 'teacher education' teachers are able to become like a window through which young people will see their future.

## Information and Communication Technology

ICT stands for Information and Communication Technologies. This term is now widely used in educational research, policy, and practice. It replaces the older term, "IT", or information technology, which was most often used in reference to computers and the Internet. In the past, the "information" dimension tended to predominate in the literature, and in people's thinking, about ICT. In recent years, the "communication" dimension of ICT has assumed an equal prominence. The term "ICT" encompasses much more than just computers.

ICT can be defined as "anything which allows us to get information, to communicate with each other, or to have an effect on the environment using electronic or digital equipment". Some authors use the term learning technologies, while others simply describe it as technology. ICT is becoming a ubiquitous component of the physical and social world occupied by young children. It is an important part of the private and work lives of most people, including those who support young children's learning and development, whether as parents, family members, caregivers, or early childhood educators.

With the advancement of technology, it is possible to revolutionize the way people learn and to present the information to them. Most of the traditional instruction, students learn from the instructor-led approach. Usually in a traditional classroom setting, students have access to the experts, involved in questions and discussion, exposed to social interaction and have the opportunity to learn from others. Some students prefer an individualized or less structured environment. In other words, they need self-paced learning material. At the same time, educators are now facing with the challenges of integrating traditional and emerging technology as to balance various students learning styles.

## Enhancement of Teacher Education

Information technology has potential to gather information, store it and display it, whenever required, immediately. All this could be possible through computers. Internet has popularized it in every nook and corner of the world. Of course, at present "Internet Technology" has gained significance role in Distance Education. The following are the modern technology to enhancing the teacher education programme. They are criticized as bellow.

1. E-Learning Approach
2. B-Learning Approach
3. E-Content Approach
4. M-Learning Approach

## E-learning

E-learning can be defined as 'learning facilitated and supported through the use of information and communications technology'. E-learning involves the use of information and communication technology resources to provide novel ways to learn.

E-learning is also known as online learning. E–learning encompasses learning at all levels both formal and non-formal that uses an information network– the Internet, an intranet (LAN) or extranet (WAN). The components include e-portfolios, cyber infrastructures, digital libraries and online learning object repositories. All the above components create a digital identity of the user and connect all the stakeholders in the education. It also facilitates inter disciplinary research.

## Role of E-learning in Teacher Education

E-Learning is important in teacher education because it can improve the quality of learning experience, and extend the reach of every teacher educator

1. Individualized learning, Flexible study and personalized learning support.
2. Collaborative learning – e-learning offers a wide range of online environments to develop the cognitive and social skills of communicating and collaborating.
3. Tools for educators and teacher trainees to innovate – E-learning offers a wide range of design tools to enable educators and teacher trainees to be innovative, creating and sharing ideas, or customizing learning resources for their own use
4. Virtual learning worlds – teacher trainees can take part in active and creative learning with others through simulations, role-play, real-world tools and devices, online master classes, or collaboration with other institutions or organizations.
5. Online communities– E-Learning can bring teacher trainees, educators, specialist communities, experts, practitioners and interest groups together to share ideas and good practice, contributing to new knowledge and learning
6. Quality at scale–E-learning achieves economy of scale through wide access to digital resources and information systems, combined with quality through shared tools and resources, and common standards of design and innovation.
7. Reusability of learning objects in E-Learning- Much effort has been put into the technical reuse of electronically-based teaching materials and in particular creating or re-using Learning Objects.

## B-learning Approach

Blended learning environment integrates the advantages of blended learning method with some advantageous aspects of traditional method, such as face-to-face interaction. Blended learning brings traditional physical classes with elements of virtual education together. The integration of e-learning environment and traditional learning environment may combine ideally the useful aspects of both methods. E-learning environments ensure the flexibility and efficacy which cannot be found in a classroom environment whereas face-to-face learning environment provides the social interaction which is required for learning.

## E-content Approach

E-Content is one of the recent techniques in the educational technology. In this E-content way of instruction is learner centric. E-content as products, which are electronically recorded e.g. websites, CD/DVD-ROM. In Education 'E-content' way of instruction plays a major role. It is a web based instruction developed for individual's auto learning on any subject required by the learner. In this content is delivered via the internet, intranet/extranet, audio or video tape, satellite TV and CD-ROMs.

## M-learning

By nature the m-Learning is a form of existing d-Learning and e-Learning. Historically the distance education has more than one hundred years of experience and traditions. Its main characteristic is the distance and time separation between teacher and students. The e-Learning offers new methods for distance education based on computer and net technologies. Simultaneous to e-Learning the other forms of d-Learning still exist (for example satellite based d-Learning).

From the other side the m-Learning is part of e-Learning and therefore - part of d-Learning. In the literature there are different definitions for m-Learning. Some of them consider it as only wireless or Internet based. We think that definition of m-Learning must include the ability to learn everywhere at every time without permanent physical connection to cable networks. This can be achieved by the use of mobile and portable devices such as PDA, cell phones, portable computers and Tablet PC. They must have the ability to connect to other computer devices, to present educational information and to realize bilateral information exchange between the students and the teacher.

***Teachers can tell its good m-learning, When***

1. An m-learning approach enhances the teaching strategy or authentic context for delivery without detracting from other pedagogical considerations.
2. Learning materials support equal access to learning by providing materials in a range of formats. For example, a learner who is unable to access a mobile learning resource using a mobile phone, media player or PDA should still be able to access a version of the learning activity using a web browser or via downloadable or print based resources.
3. An m-learning approach responds to the diversity of the learner group, learning needs and styles and provides situated, relevant and flexible learning activities.
4. Figure-2 below illustrates how m-Learning works. The phone symbolizes a WAP enabled phone, Smartphone or PDA. By means of a wireless Internet / intranet connection, students can receive course content located on a remote server, student support services and other material that constitute the overall educational package. The hand-held wireless device allows for student-student and student tutor interaction. The main difference in this model compared to eLearning is that all communication is wireless. M-Learning not only breaks barriers, but also presents new challenges in the educational arena. It is with this in mind that this report has been written.

## Conclusion

Teachers should be in a position to integrate technology into teaching / learning as well as develop the art and skill of "webogogy" (i.e. to make use of Internet technology, exploring it, accessing information from it to use in teaching learning etc.). So, objectives must be set at the attainment of application and skill levels rather than just at the knowledge and understanding levels. The professional development of teachers needs to be given importance. There must be congruence between the school curriculum and teacher training curriculum. Otherwise, teachers are not ready to utilize their knowledge to effectively design teaching/learning process, project work, and assignments. In addition to offering ICT as a compulsory and special course, integrated approaches need to be studied along with methods courses. This will help student teachers to develop the concept of 'techno pedagogy' to a greater extent.

Thus, management of change in teacher education is a complex and demanding task involving comprehension, concern, caution and contemplation. Planners and administrators of teacher education hence to provide academic leadership to prepare reflective teachers who can manage the educational system efficiently at various stages of education at the pre-primary, primary, elementary, secondary, and higher secondary levels. Effective change in schools is possible only when there are corresponding changes in the management of teacher education programs.

## References

1. Aggarwal, Binod C (2005). Educational media in India, Perspectives on Distance Education: Educational media is Asia, commonwealth of learning, Vancouver,Bc, Canada.
2. Angelo, Juan Ramos, et.al. (2007).'ICT-Enabled Distance Education in Community Development in the Philippines', Journal of Distance Education Vol.28 No.2, August.
3. Bates, A.W (1995).Technology, opens learning and distance Education, Rout ledge London.
4. Ahmed, S. And Singh, M. (2010). Multimedia in Teacher Education empowering Accessible, flexible and innovative learning, Shikshak-shikha Shodh Patrika Vo. (04) No. (1) pp. 32-33.
5. Paliwal A. K. (2006). Facility development in teacher education perceptions and changing context, souvenir 7th National conference MATE pp. 10-11.
6. Takwal, R. (2003). Problems and Issues faced by Indian Education system UGC Golden Jubilee Lecture series. Pp. 5.
7. Venna S. k. (2010). Teacher Education some qualities consideration shishgak – Shiksha Shodh Patrika vol. (04) No. (1) pp. 10.
8. Casa; C. R. (2007). ICT for education and development, info ISSN: 1463-6697 Vol. 9 Issue: 4, 3-9.

# 20

# Designing Learning Environment Tomorrow

Education is the foundation of our nation. It is one of the pillars of society and a tool of building our nation. The global is changing very dramatically and quickly and it is unavoidable to produce our young generation to compete with technology world. To achicvc this we have to modernize our learning environment with new tools and strategies. Nowadays most of the percentage of our teaching – learning method is a traditional one. Even though our government takes many steps and form educational commissions to improve our teaching – learning method, there is no change or improvement in our learning methodology. Our 'sit and get' approach to learning is not an effective way to reach our goals.

There are only two basic purposes for educating children. One is, making more value to them, and the second is making more value to others. But we are failed to create valuable children. Because schools in our country is really like a factory and the faculties are the workers and the students are the products. The factory opens with the ringing bell sharply at 8.30 AM and the workers starts to produce the mark scoring machines and Xerox machines as a product and the factory closes with a long bell after 4.00 PM and over time goes for X and XII students. In the year ending the quality of the product was tested through examinations and labeled.

Another problem is Homework. When we handle it properly it will be an important tool of success. The values of homework are Responsibility, Independence, Perseverance, Time management, self reliance and resourcefulness. But what we are doing? In most of time the assignments are used as punishments. We are asking them to copy the content from the text books, in the class work note and then it in the homework note. If we were giving project work means, it is only for the parent and beneficial to stationeries shops.

The ingestion of the compulsory study leads to the production of mentally depressed and physically weak children which makes an unhealthy society and nation. Most of our children hate our school system because of its boredom traditional method. Our only goal is to get centum result and scoring centum marks. So, development life skills, moral values, social integration etc are loss, and these leads to the production of weak generation. So, to avoid this and to develop positive attitude on learning and to develop interest towards the education we have to design the tomorrows learning environment with educational technology.

Our education system need to improve the quality of education through Information technology, when it integrated into the curriculum it revolutionizes the learning process. The technology integration in the curriculum improves students learning process and their outcomes. Technology help to make ease of the students and teachers roles and relationships. Students alone take responsibility for their learning outcomes. Here the teacher acts as a guide and facilitator. The teachers have to be trained in using the technologies and implement in their teaching methods. If the students learn by using these technology based learning, they can become creators and critics instead of just consumers. The technology integrated curriculum is essential for today's students to have

1. Personal and social responsibility
2. Planning, critical thinking, reasoning and creativity
3. Strong communications skills
4. Cross – cultural understanding
5. Visualizing and decision making
6. Knowledge in using the technology

By adopting Modern Learning Methods (MLM) can facilitate the learning.

1. Collaborative learning
2. Integrated learning
3. Blended learning

4. Flipped model class room
5. Using interactive technology
6. ICT in education etc

**The suggestions for Teachers in designing the learning environment**

1. The teacher has to play new role of mentoring, coaching and helping students in their studies rather than spoon feeding in the class room.
2. The teachers can guide and coach the students to improve the ways of learning, promote their ability and skills of applying their learning in real situations
3. Developing self – learning habits at their own pace and time
4. Diagnose the learning problem of students and the teachers can prepare learning material according to them to overcome their problem
5. Students are having individual differences in their learning process. On the basis of this the teacher have to create the learning environment according to their pace and time individually
6. They can interact with individual students or a small group of students according to their learning ability. Through this they can help and facilitate students learning in an effective manner
7. The teacher while planning any lesson, should think of the method or using technology, results in making class instruction dynamic and effective
8. The teachers have to deliver their teaching with concern of students. They should avoid to deliver their lectures without any concern of students and they have to change their attitude in completing the syllabus and the aim of showing centum result by squeezing the children
9. The methods of evaluation system also have to reform. The works given for FA should be modified. The teachers have to choose the projects for the students should be appropriate to their ability. It should include realistic task that generalized the students learning and its application in new situations and not burden to parents.
10. The teachers should be the role model of the children. They should rich in good behaviour, humanism and moral values.

**The suggestions for Parents in designing the learning environment**

1. The parents should have the awareness on education. They should

know that education is not the amount of information that is put into the brain but the primary tool to achieve the power of mind. They should avoid treating the child as a miniature of adult.

2. Mostly the middle class educated parents were only comparing their children with others. They want to mould them what they wish to be. They feel proud to show that their children were engaged with extracurricular activities throughout the day, weak, month and the year. But they are forgetting to realize that they are fail in creating a physically and mentally healthy child. So, that only after their school education most of the children becomes opposite to their parents. So, the parent should give importance to their children's decisions. They should be a friend, guide and counsellor to their children.
3. They should change their attitude that the school, which makes the children engaged throughout the day i.e., giving heavy home-work, is the best school. They can avoid pulling them into the Tuition centers. They should accept their child's capacity of learning and facilitate them easy learning methods and spend at least an hour per day and chat with them about their that day's experience .
4. They should realize that the marks are not the yard sticks to measure their child's knowledge and wisdom and have to change their attitude that the centum scoring children were brilliant and others were not.
5. They should consider their child's opinions, and respect them. They should create their mind set to accept the real status of their children. This makes the children, mentally free and they can achieve what they want to be and they desire.
6. Parent should give importance to their physical and spiritual development. They should give importance in promoting the behavioural qualities humanism and they should be a role model

**The suggestions for Administration in designing the learning environment**

1. The management plays an important role in enhancing quality in education
2. The management should support and adopt the changes, suggestions and recommendations given by the government
3. Quality of education depends upon the quality of teachers and the quality of infrastructure. So, the management should introduce the modern technology inventions and discoveries which enhance the personality of the children.

4. The management should take care in creating a valuable child instead of producing the best product of their school.
5. The management should update the faculties by giving in-service training and encourage the best teachers by recognizing them and honouring with rewards and awards and this will help them to be active, innovative and work with interest.
6. The management should give importance in promoting the humanism, moral values, ethics, life skill and social skills of the children.
7. The management should consider the income of the parents, intelligence and creativity of the student and facilitate their fee structure. They can encourage the innovative children by adopting them and provide the facilities to develop their research attitude.
8. Parent should give importance to the physical and spiritual development of their children. They should give importance in promoting the behavioural qualities humanism and they should be a role model.

**The suggestions for Government in designing the learning environment**

1. The government should recognise that the teachers are the backbone of educational system and architects in designing the new nation which have to compete with this Technology Era.
2. They should begin to modernize the education system from the primary level. They should insist the school, first to change the learning environment of KGs'. All of us know that the physical development of the children is not fulfilling at the age of three. But we are compelling to read, write and to do the sums. We are breaking the fingers of the sapling by giving written works. We are stealing their childhood happiness. So, the government should restrict all these things and should limit their study hours and school hours. The infrastructure of the classrooms should be modified. They are keeping the name of Kinder Garden and are not following the Froebel's thoughts.
3. Then the study hours of primary level. Up to Third standard it is enough to develop the Reading, writing, speaking skills and doing simple maths like knowing the numerals, tables' additions, subtractions, multiplications and divisions. Along with this the basic of computer science. Instead of giving free bags, books, notebooks, writing materials ect., to them it is best to provide them desktops. Now the government is implementing the ABL method. The bitter

truth we have to accept is that there is no use of it. Most of the children at Sixth standard in government schools not able to read and write, but exceptions are there, but it is rare. They are not even known the alphabetic. So, the teaching – learning methodology should be changed and Modern Learning Method should be introduced.

4. From Fourth standard the science and social science can be introduced. The science subject should be teaches by learning and doing method. It should be alive. The social science should teach by using smart board, because we can use pen drives, modems to connect internet etc. There should be at least one spacious smart class room per primary school which can be utilised for all sections. This will reduce the burden of teaching and the children can actively take part in this. Instead of giving assignments the projects can given for them according to their individual differences. Through this method the teacher will have enough time to plan and think the method of teaching using technology which results in making class instruction dynamic and effective. Along with this we should give importance for moral education and games. Through this we can make a strong basement, and create physically and mentally healthy children.
5. For secondary and Higher secondary education the system should be completely modernized. The modern teaching techniques should be handled according to their level. Learning by doing methods, Seminars, team teaching methods can be followed. Importance should give for extra-curricular activities, life skills and research in science and technology. When the Public examination system is completely abolished mean, then automatically the production of mark scoring machines will be stopped. Yearly once compulsory exhibitions should be conducted in each and every school and prizes should be distributed for the innovations.
6. The government should reduce the burden of teachers. Nowadays the teachers in the government schools are concentrating in completing the Records and not in teaching. They are telling that their superiors are giving the first preference for the record completion. So, they have to concentrate in doing the office works. The government should minimize the non academic work of teachers.
7. Instead of conducting eligibility test for recruiting teachers, they can create quality teachers by selecting the students by conducting eligibility test for the Teachers education and to give recognition for the colleges with modernized infrastructure and well equipped

classrooms. The government should strictly follow rules and regulations without any compromise. During teaching practice the students are not taking practice in teaching but being as a teacher. The teachers were going in medical leave and in many schools due to insufficient teachers; the trainees are compelled to handle the subjects other than their major subjects and insist to complete the syllabus and to complete the official works of their Guide teacher. So, the aim of teaching practice is not achieved. The curriculum for the teacher education also should be reformed according to the school curriculum.

## Conclusion

Yesterday and today's teaching learning method is based on I hear and I see. But tomorrow's learning environment should designed as I do I understand. For this the education should integrated with technology. Technologies will increase the teaching learning process. Tomorrow will be an era of Technology. So, making the student cantered learning as a technological cantered learning we can promote our standard equal to the standard of developed countries and construct a progressive and prosperous nation.

# 21

# Edu Digital Skills

## Education

Digital skills are part and parcel of higher Education and an important part of for university students. Learning the digital skills of the $21^{St}$ century technology that surrounds us will benefit students in their purist of knowledge.Edu- Digital skills is one such vital segment that has come whole heartedly to mould the learning modules and mechanism not only in academic terms but also in other areas of practical application in live hood and empowerment. Students who have grown up in a digital environment, may be well acquainted with the on-going process of new technological innovations.

Education in its general sense is a form of learning in which the knowledge, skills, and habits of a group of people are transferred from one generation to the next through teaching, training, or research. Education frequently takes place under the guidance of others, but may also be autodidactic. Any experience that has a formative effect on the way one thinks, feels, or acts may be considered educational. Education is commonly divided into stages such as preschool, primary school, secondary school and then college, university or apprenticeship.

## Educational technology

Educational technology, sometimes termed Ed Tech, is the study and ethical practice of facilitating e-learning, which is the learning and improving performance by creating, using and managing appropriate technological processes and resources. The term educational technology is often associated with, and encompasses, instructional theory and learning theory. While instructional technology is "the theory and practice of design, development, utilization, management, and evaluation of processes and resources for learning," according to the Association for Educational Communications and Technology (AECT) Definitions and Terminology Committee, educational technology includes other systems used in the process of developing human capability. Educational technology includes, but is not limited to, software, hardware, as well as Internet applications, such as wikis and blogs, and activities.

## Technology in education

Technology in education is most simply and comfortably defined as an array of tools that might prove helpful in advancing student learning and may be measured in how and why individuals behave. Educational Technology relies on a broad definition of the word "technology." Technology can refer to material objects of use to humanity, such as machines or hardware, but it can also encompass broader themes, including systems, methods of organization, and techniques. Some modern tools include but are not limited to overhead projectors, laptop computers, and calculators. Newer tools such as smart phones and games (both online and offline) are beginning to draw serious attention for their learning potential. Media psychology is the field of study that applies theories of human behavior to educational technology.)

## Educational psychology

Educational psychology is the study of how humans learn in educational settings, the effectiveness of educational interventions, the psychology of teaching, and the social psychology of schools as organizations. Educational psychology in turn informs a wide range of specialties within educational studies, including instructional design, educational technology, curriculum development, organizational learning, special education and classroom management.

## Digitized communication

Digitized communication and networking in education started in the mid 80s and became popular by the mid -90's, in particular through the World-Wide Web (WWW), Email and Forums. There is a difference between two major forms of online learning. The earlier type, based on either Computer Based Training (CBT) or Computer-based learning (CBL), focused on the interaction between the student and computer drills plus tutorials on one hand or micro-worlds and simulations on the other. Both can be delivered today over the WWW. Today, the prevailing paradigm in the regular school system is Computer-mediated communication (CMC), where the primary form of interaction is between students and instructors, mediated by the computer. CBT/CBL usually means individualized (self-study) learning, while CMC involves teacher/tutor facilitation and requires schematization of flexible learning activities. In addition, modern ICT provides education with tools for sustaining learning communities and associated knowledge management tasks. It also provides tools for student and curriculum management.

In addition to classroom enhancement, learning technologies also play a major role in full-time distance teaching. While most quality offers still rely on paper, videos and occasional CBT/CBL materials, there is increased use of e-tutoring through forums, instant messaging, video-conferencing etc. Courses addressed to smaller groups frequently use blended or hybrid designs that mix presence courses (usually in the beginning and at the end of a module) with distance activities and use various pedagogical styles (e.g., drill & practice, exercises, projects, etc.).

## Instructional technique and technologies

"Children and adult people are growing up in a vastly changing context. No aspect of their lives is untouched by the digital era which is transforming how they live, relate and learn. Some examples of these changes in the classroom include: Problem Based Learning, Project-based Learning, and Inquiry-based learning. Together they are active learning educational technologies used to facilitate learning. Technology which includes physical and process applied science can be incorporated into project, problem, inquiry-based learning as they all have a similar educational philosophy. All three are student centered, ideally involving real-world scenarios in which students are actively engaged in critical thinking activities. The process that students are encouraged to employ (as long as it is based on empirical research) is considered to be a technology. Classic examples of technologies used by teachers and Educational Technologists include Bloom's Taxonomy and Instructional Design.

## Benefits of Educational Technology

Educational technology is intended to improve education for the 21st century learner. Students today are considered "Digital Natives" who were born and raised in a digital environment and inherently think different because of this exposure to technology. Some of the claimed benefits of incorporating technology into the classroom are listed below:

1. **Easy-to-access course materials**. Teacher can post their course material or important information on a course website, which means students can study at a time and location they prefer and can obtain the study material very quickly.
2. **Student motivation**. According to James Kulik, who studies the effectiveness of computers used for instruction, students usually learn more in less time when receiving computer-based instruction and they like classes more and develop more positive attitudes toward computers in computer-based classes. Teachers must be aware of their students' motivators in order to successfully implement technology into the classroom.
3. **More opportunities for extended learning**. According to study completed in 2010, 70.3% of American family households have access to the internet. According to Canadian Radio Television and Telecommunications Commission Canada, 79% of homes have access to the internet. This allows students to access course material at home and engage with the numerous online resources available to them. Students can use their home computers and internet to conduct research, participate in social media, email, play educational games and stream videos.

## Open Course Ware

In recent years, Open Course Ware (OCW), an academic initiative that gives the public access to much of the same information used in undergraduate and graduate programs at institutions of higher education, has greatly improved the quality of educational material available for free on the Internet. The idea of Open Course Ware gained prevalence in 2002 when MIT began distributing academic material from courses to the public for free. Through the early 2000s, this idea began to gain popularity with other colleges and universities. As of 2008, there were close to 150 collegiate institutions that had operational Open Course Ware programs, or were in the process of planning such programs. These institutions include Harvard, Princeton, Stanford, University of Pennsylvania, and University of Michigan. Such programs are an example of how technology can allow more people to have access to information and resources that have originally only been accessible to students at prestigious universities.

## Over-the-Counter Data

Advancements in the design of education technology tools that present data to education stakeholders, such as the student data system, have had a significant impact on education and students. For example, data systems' capacity to assist data analysis is unprecedented and it is inadvisable to use data without the assistance of a data system. To improve the accuracy of data analyses performed with the use of Edtech, it is recommended these Edtech tools adhere to a design approach called over-the-counter data (OTCD), which involves embedding labels, supplemental documentation, and a help system and making key package/display and content decisions.

## Digital Skills Students Need for the Future

Every single teacher is concerned about her teaching practices and the skills involved in this process. It is amazing how technology has changed the whole world giving rise to new forms of education. students are more digitally focused than any time before. They spend more time interacting with their mobile devices than they do with their parents or close relatives. Admittedly, this digital boom has both positive and negative impact on our students. Lack of concentration, short attention span, distraction, visual stimulus overload, identity theft, lack of real world socializing, privacy issues, depression, and many more are but a direct result of the growing exposure to this technology. Studies have even proved that multitasking, which some educational technology experts brag about in relation to the use of today's technology, reduces the power of our concentration to the half. There are actually several pluses for the use of technology in Education.

While digital natives, people who were born in the digital age, will have no trouble obtaining digital literacy, for the rest of us, the digital immigrants, a more conscious effort is needed to become competent digital citizens, capable of coping with and making the most out of our daily, web-centric practices. Technology will become even more intuitive and ingrained in our daily life, and this leads to one important conclusion: the better equipped we are to handle this technological shift, the better our adjustment to it. Some digital skills are no-brainers; for example, today's 5- and 6-year-old children know how to type and surf the web, a skill that adults might require a bit of studying and effort to fully master.

## The 21st century teacher should be able to:

1. Create and edit digital audio
2. Use social bookmarking to share resources with and between learners

3. Use blogs and wikis to create online platforms for students
4. Exploit digital images for classroom use
5. Use video content to engage students
6. Use info graphics to visually stimulate students
7. Use Social networking sites to connect with colleagues and grow professionally
8. Create and deliver asynchronous presentations and training sessions
9. Compile a digital e-portfolio for their own development
10. Have knowledge about online security
11. Be able to detect plagiarized works in student's assignments
12. Create screen capture videos and tutorials
13. Curate web content for classroom learning
14. Use and provide students with task management tools to organize their work and plan their learning
15. Use polling software to create a real-time survey in class
16. Understand issues related to copyright and fair use of online materials
17. Use digital tools for time management purposes

## Technology in the classroom

There are various types of technologies currently used in traditional classrooms. Among these are:

1. **Computer in the classroom:** Having a computer in the classroom is an asset to any teacher. With a computer in the classroom, teachers are able to demonstrate a new lesson, present new material, illustrate how to use new programs, and show new websites.
2. **Class website:** An easy way to display the student's work is to create a web page designed for their class. Once a web page is designed, teachers can post homework assignments, student work, famous quotes, trivia games, and so much more.
3. **Class blogs and wikis:** There are a variety of Web 2.0 tools that are currently being implemented in the classroom. Blogs allow for students to maintain a running dialogue. They work a tool for maintaining a journal of thoughts, ideas, and assignments, as well as encourage student comment and reflection. Wikis are more group focused to allow multiple members of the group to edit a single document and create a truly collaborative and carefully edited finished product. Blogs allow the student to express their knowledge of the information learned in a way that they like. Blogging is

something that students do for fun sometimes, so when they are assigned an assignment to do a blog they are eager to do it!

**Wireless classroom microphones:** Noisy classrooms are a daily occurrence, and with the help of microphones, students are able to hear their teachers more clearly. Children learn better when they hear the teacher clearly. The benefit for teachers is that they no longer lose their voices at the end of the day.

**Mobile devices**: Mobile devices such as clickers or Smartphone can be used to enhance the experience in the classroom by providing the possibility for professors to get feedback.

**Interactive Whiteboards**: An interactive whiteboard that provides touch control of computer applications. These enhance the experience in the classroom by showing anything that can be on a computer screen. This not only aids in visual learning, but it is interactive so the students can draw, write, or manipulate images on the interactive whiteboard.

1. **Digital video-on-demand:** Replacement of hard copy videos (DVD, VHS) with digital video accessed from a central server (e.g. SAFARI Montage). Digital video eliminates the need for in-classroom hardware (players) and allows teachers and students to access video clips immediately by not utilizing the public Internet.
2. **Online media:** Streamed video websites can be used to enhance a classroom lesson (e.g. United Streaming, Teacher Tube, etc.)
3. **Online study tools**: Tools that motivate studying by making studying more fun or individualized for the student (e.g. Study Cocoa)
4. **Digital Games:** The field of educational games and serious games has been growing significantly over the last few years. The digital games are being provided as tools for the classroom and have a lot of positive feedback including higher motivation for students.

There are many other tools being used depending on the local school board and funds available. These may include: digital cameras, video cameras, interactive whiteboard tools, document cameras, or LCD projectors.

**Podcasts:** Pod-casting is a relatively new invention that allows anybody to publish files to the Internet where individuals can subscribe and receive new files from people by a subscription. The primary benefit of pod-casting for educators is quite simple. It enables teachers to reach students through a medium that is both "cool" and a part of their daily lives. For a technology that only requires a computer, microphone and internet connection, pod-casting has the capacity of advancing a student's education beyond the classroom. When students listen to the pod-casts of other students as well as their own, they can quickly demonstrate their capacities to identify and define "quality." This can be a great tool for learning and developing literacy inside and outside the classroom. Pod-casting can help sharpen students' vocabulary, writing, editing, public speaking, and presentation skills. Students will also learn skills that will be valuable in the working world, such as communication, time management, and problem-solving.

## Conclusion

Teachers must be aware of their students' motivators in order to successfully implement technology into the classroom. Students are more motivated to learn when they are interested in the subject matter, which can be enhanced by using technologies in the classroom and targeting the need for screens and digital material that they have been stimulated by outside of the classroom. The types of students we teach today are completely different from last century's. We definitely, need to look at some of the skills we, as teachers, need to equip ourselves with to better live up to the challenge. Among all the challenges we would have in education, is digital skills. Finally saying by means of Edu-digital skills make the students to better communication, collaboration, critical thinking and problem solving, creativity and invention, global awareness Information and Technology literacy, self direction.

## References

1. Dewey, John (1916/1944). Democracy and Education. The Free Press. pp. 1–4. ISBN 0-684-83631-9.
2. Domain. New York: David McKay Co Inc. for Individual Learning? Journal of e-learning, 2004.
3. Jump up^ Geer, R., & Sweeney, T. (2012). Students' voices about learning with technology. Journal of social sciences, 8 (2). 294-303
4. "Computer-managed instruction: an alternative teaching strategy." US National Library of Medicine National Institutes of Health Jump Shurville, S., Browne, T., & Whitaker, M. (2009). Accommodating
5. The newfound strategic importance of educational technologists within higher education: A critical literature review. Campus-Wide Information Systems, 26 (3), 201-231 B. S. (1956). Blooms Taxonomy of Educational Objectives,

# 22

# Innovative Strategies and System For Effective Higher Education

## Introduction

The Indian higher education system is facing an unprecedented transformation in the coming decade. This transformation is being driven by economic and demographic change: by 2020, India will be the world's third largest economy, with a correspondingly rapid growth in the size of its middle classes.

Higher Education in India is undergoing a paradigm shift with many innovative changes being introduced. Some changes are called for due to the changing environment like anti-ragging and sexual harassment policies, changing perception of the younger generation ; while some changes are thought of as an essence to innovation and redefining strategies like changes in teaching pedagogy and assessment and evaluation mechanism.

The paper also explores the issue of assessment. This has always been a very debatable issue of higher education since it is subjective and often involves unethical practices. Also the objections and doubts raised by students on the validity of the process puts a question mark on how authentic the process is. The hypothesis made by the authors in this respect is that the present system is far from being full-proof and needs drastic changes so that it is accepted by the teachers and students alike. While these suggestions are being made they are subject to lot more debate and discussion, since individual thoughts and perceptions would still differ. The authors have used a questionnaire to seek answers to these debatable issues and arrived at their conclusions based on the response received to the questionnaire.

A look at the educational system across the globe indicates that most universities and institutions deliver their programs using a structured mechanism. The structured mechanism involves attending scheduled classes followed by well-defined assessment structures. Even if for some reason students decide to remain outside the class, they are expected to spend that time engaging in reading and assignment related work as the assessment structure requires so. The assessment structure forms the basis of eventually determining the overall grade/marks of the students.

Before we proceed further with the research, we need to understand how the system actually works. Universities and institutions across the globe were using face-to-face classroom teaching till 1980's. With the advent of IT, universities have started using a lot of on-line teaching. If we look at the scenario in India, one finds a lot of face-to-face learning happening. One very important aspect of classroom pedagogy is attendance gets weight age in the assessment criteria and ensures students come to class regularly.

While institutions in developed countries use the on-line platform for delivery of courses, one finds that the on-line teaching platforms are being used as a substitute and not complementary to the classroom-based delivery. While the advocates of web-based and on-line teaching talk strongly in favour of these systems, one finds that even these platforms have a very negative impact on the overall performance. Instead of using the so called convenient platforms for learning, students show casualness and the attendance and performance falls. In spite of the popularity of the web-based systems, India education system stills follow the traditional face-to-face system. Keeping in mind the Indian education system, the paper focuses on face-to-face learning where attendance and assessment criteria's are critical.

## Definition

**(a) Face-to-face Learning** is a method wherein the students attend regular classes and there is interaction between the facilitator and the students. Face-to-face learning happens in the form of lectures, tutorials, guest lectures and other co-curricular activities.

(b) **Attendance** is a process of recording the physical presence of the student in the learning process.

(c) **Assessment** is a process of evaluating the student's understanding of the subject and ascertaining the overall impact of the learning process.

## Literature Review

Attendance and Assessment has always caught the fancy of the educationists who feel these are two important areas of the system. Students, on the other hand want to spend less time on campus because of their occasional casual behaviour, personal commitments, medical reasons, etc. This constant tug of war between the two stakeholders raises a question whether on line self assessment opportunities can ease the negative impact of lower attendance rates.

In view of this, researchers have often tried to ascertain the reasons for poor attendance as they feel it is a very complex and sensitive issue. While it is a general belief that poor attendance could be the result of lack of motivation, there are no concrete evidences on the same and the same is not a global phenomenon. Teachers often argue that a student should be made to realize the importance of attendance. For this they recommend that their performance should be assessed given equal weight age to attendance and academics. While it sounds good but may not be a practical suggestion. So it is suggested that one should take into account the circumstances at the start of the semester, the rhythm established during the term itself, the continuous learning of the student over the term and the preparation for the final exams at the end of the semester.

To prove the point we have gone through the research papers/articles already published. These include:

(a) International Students: Do attendance and performance correlate? In this research paper David Hamilton, Leone Hinton and David Qain suggest that students should be actively encouraged to attend classes from the outset if they are to optimize their chances of success. They also suggest that counselling the students about the risk of missing classes, engaging them in class, attendance links and assessment tasks may help.

(b) Optional Formative Assessment and Class Attendance: Their impact on student performance. In this research paper the authors Peter Collett, Nikole Gyles and Sue Hrasky suggest that well-designed courses, delivered exclusively on-line are able to provide students with rewarding learning experience. They further suggest that on-line formative self-assessment opportunities enhance student performance. They also conclude that on-line activities cannot compensate for poor attendance.

(c) Intervening Early: Attendance and Performance Monitoring as a Trigger for First Year Support in the Biosciences. This research article by Debbie Bevitt, Chris Baldwin and Jane Calvert states that early signs of absence and poor performance trigger immediate intervention by academic staff, with the aim of providing support for students at risk of failure or withdrawal. Difficulties associated with monitoring attendance in large lecture classes are avoided by monitoring attendance only at 'high stakes' classes, namely practical's and seminars. Level of attendance at non-lecture classes was a predictor of academic achievement and the early intervention strategy was associated with improvements in attendance. Student perceptions of attendance monitoring were evaluated and found to be positive. Meeting with absent and underperforming students at the earliest possible opportunity has proved an effective way of promoting dialogue between staff and students who are experiencing difficulties.

(d) Who Maximizes What? A Study in Student Time Allocation. The State University carried out a survey of the impact of attendance on student classroom success and the results were published in AMERICAN ECONOMIC REVIEW, May, 1983, pp. 23-28. In this survey the author measured the impact of time commitments by students to various course activities on the students' performance in the given class. The results were revealing. By far, the most valuable and important time commitment in a course was the time actually spent in the classroom. That time was the most important determinant of student success and each unit of time in the class itself provided, among all the class related activities, the greatest improvement in student performance. The next most important time spent on a class was any time spent in discussion sections that accompanied the lectures. Third in importance was any time spent studying outside of class preparing for the class session itself. Perhaps most surprising was the result that the least significant time commitment in improving student performance in a particular class was the time spent studying for the final exam. Thus the study concluded that the most productive time in any course is the time actually spent in the classroom. That time had the greatest positive impact on overall student performance. The hour or two spent in class each day (for a particular course) did the most to improve the student's grade.

(e) Student Self-Evaluation: What Research says and what practice shows? This research article by Carol Rolheiser and John A. Ross focuses on teachers experimenting with assessment alternatives to traditional tests. Performance assessment, portfolio collections, classroom observation, peer assessment and self-evaluation are being increasingly used along with unit test and the final exam. This increase in assessment tools ensures that an over-reliance on testing does not seriously distort instruction or impede important school improvement efforts. Also, the programs are being based on a range of assessment approaches, which is helping students and improving their learning experience. The article further states that teachers who include authentic assessment in their repertoires are driven by a belief that curriculum-assessment experiences should prepare students for life in the real world.

(f) Alternative Approaches to Assessing Student Engagement Rates

This research article by Elaine Chapman provides a broad overview of methods used in assessing learning task engagement on a class wide basis. The paper was designed to provide options for teachers who wish to develop relevant assessment protocols that incorporate a combination of indices across the cognitive, affective, and behavioural domains. In addition to these data, a comprehensive protocol may include measures that address the question of why students do, or do not, engage with particular types of tasks. The latter information can greatly facilitate the interpretation of the overall level indices. Within each of these domain areas, using a range of methods can also strengthen the validity of findings and provide alternative perspectives on the results. Clearly, however, final decisions on protocol components must also take into account any practical constraints within the given context.

(g) Podcasts and Mobile Assessment Enhance Student Learning Experience and Academic Performance

This research article by Neil P Morris is based on the study where the author tried testing use of Podcasts and Mobile Assessment strategies to assess the effect on examination performance. Students ($n = 100$) on a final year, research-led, module were randomly divided into equal sized control and trial groups. The trial group was given access to podcasts / mobile formative assessments for lectures on the module. Towards the end of the module, all students on the module completed a 'mock' examination on the material in the lectures. Students in the trial group who listened to podcasts of the lectures and completed mobile assessments ($n = 31$) performed significantly better in the formative assessment ($58.1 \pm 1$, mean $\pm$ S.E.M; $P<0.05$,

Student's t-test) than other students on the module (52.2 ± 2; n = 54). Students accessed the podcasts via iTunes (or similar software; 38%), from the institutional virtual learning environment (31%), or using a combination of the two (31%). Interestingly, only around 21% of students listened to the majority of their podcasts away from a computer. The results of this study indicate that providing supporting resources does have a positive impact on student performance.

While these are some research papers, a lot of interest is seen in the areas of attendance and assessment and lot of studies are been initiated to understand the impact of these two variables on student performance.

## Objectives of the Study

The study aims at attaining the following objectives:

1. To understand the importance of attendance in face-to-face learning.
2. To ascertain the assessment criteria commonly used
3. To ascertain whether the assessment norms change with attendance compulsion
4. To understand the linkages between attendance and performance

## Methodology

The methodology followed in the paper includes the use of both primary and secondary tools. The secondary tools include research articles published on the subject. The objective was to understand the conclusions drawn by researchers doing similar study.

The primary too, on the other hand, involves use of two specially designed questionnaire viz. questionnaire for faculty and questionnaire for students. The sample size for the questionnaire is 96 students and 50 faculty members. The objective of this questionnaire is to ascertain what the two important stakeholders of the education system think on the sensitive areas of attendance and assessment.

## Hypothesis

The study is based on the following hypothesis:

**Null Hypothesis1**: Monitoring the attendance is critical to improving the performance of the students and promotes effectiveness in teaching and learning.

**Alternate Hypothesis1**: Monitoring the attendance is not critical to improving the performance of the students and does not promote effectiveness in teaching and learning.

**Null Hypothesis2**: The prevailing assessment criteria and pedagogy are accepted standards in the present education system in India and stakeholders would not like a change in the same inspite of the prevailing drawbacks and weaknesses.

**Alternate Hypothesis2**: The prevailing assessment criteria and pedagogy do not represent accepted standards in the present education system in India and stakeholders would be willing to change same to make them more effective and acceptable.

## Analysis

The study has been completed with the help of two types of questionnaires viz. one for the Faculty and the other for the students. While the questions were more or less common, the intention was to ascertain how the same variables are perceived by the respondents. While initiating the study we had assumed that the responses shall be different.

## Implications for Stakeholders

The study presents a good insight into the issues that have been critical all-throughout but nobody is trying to debate these at open forums. While nobody questions their importance in the education system, there remain issues that are to be discussed informally. It is time that we start looking at these issues more seriously and initiates a national debate to bring about changes that everyone feels are long due. While changes are desired in these, the consent of the stakeholders should be taken before introducing the same. Also one could consider the following options while deciding on the issues viz. (a) use of SMART Technology to make recording of sessions realistic and convenient so that students can refer the same at their convenience and (b) On-line and Web Based Learning have become a reality and represent an important alternative to attendance.

## Limitations of the Study

The study has given a good insight into the issues of attendance and assessment, but it suffers from the following limitations:

1. The sample size selected has been very small considering that India has a very huge population that is undergoing education.

2. The study was restricted to the city of Mumbai only and amongst under-graduate students alone. Studying the other stakeholders and in other cities could change the results.

3. The element of subjectivity and peer influence in the responses cannot be ruled out.

4. Parents and Administrators also need to be included in the study since they constitute important stakeholders.

5. There is a need to increase the awareness levels of the Faculty and Students on these issue and they should be made parties to the process, especially assessments.

## Future Research

The future research could focus on the same topic and should try to investigate the antecedents and consequences of these variables. While we very often observe suicidal tendencies amongst students, one needs to investigate whether these are due to faulty attendance and assessment systems. Similarly the sample should focus on parents and administrators also, so that wider perspectives to the issues are available. One could either use the same questionnaire or modify it while undertaking any further study. But care should be taken that the study covers a cross-section of the stakeholders across cities and the sample size should cover a huge population undergoing or active in the field of education. Future research can be made more interesting by studying the impact of this variable on the students and one could approach people who have completed their studies but still feel that the systems prevalent was not fair to them. These are areas which require continuous research so that the education sector can face the paradigm shift facing it with greater readiness and confidence. While the 21st century has put before us a lot of challenges, reforming the education system remains to be a major challenge that requires our immediate attention. Future research would give direction to the initiatives required and measures needed for the change.

## Conclusion

To conclude, one can say that attendance and assessment have been two of the most critical aspects of our education system and continue to impact the way education is imparted. If we have to make our education system current and useful, we need to introduce lighting reforms and not dwell on issues that work in favour of quantity and not quality of education.

## References

1. Browne, N. M., J. Hoag, M. V. Wheeler, and N. Boudreau, 1991, The Impact of Teachers in Economic Classrooms, Journal of Economics (Vol. 42) 25-30.
2. Buchanan, T. 1998. Using the World Wide Web for Formative Assessment, Journal of Educational Technology Systems (Vol. 27, No. 1) 71-79.
3. Durden, G., and L. Ellis. 1995. The Effects of Attendance on Student Learning in Principles of Economics, The American Economic Review (Vol. 85, No. 2) 343-346.
4. McAlpine, M. 2002. Principles of Assessment, Blue paper Number 1 (Glasgow: Robert Clark Centre for Technological Education).
5. Romer, D. 1993. Do Students Go to Class? Should they? Journal of Economic Perspectives (Vol. 7, No. 3) 167-74.
6. Schmidt, R. 1983. Who Maximizes What? A Study in Student Time Allocation, AEA Papers and Proceedings (Vol 73, No. 2) 23-28.
7. St. Clair, K. L. 1999. A Case against Compulsory Attendance Policies in Higher Education, Innovative Higher Education (Vol. 23, No. 3) 171-180.
8. Yorke M. 2001. Formative Assessment and Its Relevance to Retention, Higher Education Research and Development (Vol. 20, No. 2) 115-126.

# 23

# Techniques of Educational Innovation In Web-based Learning

## Introduction

Most educational organizations have to address the imperative for change. The circumstances that have unfolded over the last decade, including the use of new computer and communication technologies together with a variety of social, demographic and economic changes, challenge educationalists to reflect upon traditional methods of teaching. The theory that effective web-based learning environments can promote learning is embryonic, perhaps futuristic. The real challenge of designing web-based learning environments lies in harnessing its huge potential as a realistic tool for improving learning. If educationalists are interested in discovering in whether web-based learning really works, then this might be done scientifically using a problem-solving approach carried out in a piecemeal way. This involves the formulation of testable hypotheses, experimentation and attempts at refutation. This I would argue is an important heuristic than may guide a realistic inquiry into the effectiveness of innovation in teaching.

Swann and Pratt (1999) present a popperian account of knowledge in which a methodological similarity is drawn between the growth of science by conjecture and refutation, and the creation and testing of educational theory in practice. This is the fallibilist position in which the quest for certainty is abandoned, yet not the quest for the truth, and where competing ideas are evaluated and criticized in the hope of improving understanding. Relentless innovation in computer and information science and the products that emerge from this innovation present educationalists with new and almost revolutionary ideas for creating teaching and learning environments. Such concepts as 'Virtual learning', even 'Virtual Universities', and e-learning radically challenge notion of how teaching can be carried out and where learning is achieved.

## The fallibility of knowledge

The role of the scientist is to make progress by actively engaging in a trial and error exercise which involves creating new or modified ideas or theories and eliminating bad ones. Bad ideas or theories are those which do not check with reality. Popper makes the assumption that most ideas are error prone, that is, they contain some falsity, as well as, some truth. He sees scientists as fallible constructors of theories that aim at the truth. Science progresses by paring off falsity (Popper 1991).

Popper's approach is hypothesis driven. This is in stark contrast to the more data driven approach, inductivism that is popularly thought to characterize the method of science. Inductivism is a justificatory approach that pursues and supports its claim for the truth by a method of confirmation.

An in-depth discussion of Popper's philosophy and technology is given in Levinson (1982) who gives much credit to Popper for his theory of the fallibility of knowledge and its insight into problem of human/technology interaction. The analogy is one that views technologies as physical embodiments of theoretical ideas. Technologies themselves and the theories that underpin human/technological interaction, theories of improved efficiencies and synergism, are fallible and profit most when experiences challenge rather than conform to expectations.

## A methodological approach to integrating web-based learning into traditional teaching

New computer and communications technologies present, in Popperian terms, opportunities to create bold new ideas concerning the problem of how to improve student learning. In less than a decade, the facility for the storage and rapid communication of knowledge and ideas plus the potential for mass assessment to these has improved almost beyond expectation.

This potentiality is now being applied to problems of inclusiveness, and Life Long Learning. New technologies are applied and pedagogic strategies invented that encompass the term, e-Learning. (Molyneux 2000 ).

One analogy is that of the ecological niche. A new niche has opened up to allow educationalists and learners to achieve their ends. The conjecture is that bold new approaches to learning mediated via computers and communication technologies can improve learning by removing impediments. For this conjecture to be tested it must be capable of being falsified. If the conjecture is falsified, as difficult as it may be, then the logic compels the enquirer to look for alternative hypotheses to improve learning.

A methodology that can be most appropriately adopted is Popper's problem solving approach. Below I have attempted to list a number of questions for consideration when examining new theories and ideas. The questions are based upon ideas about the process of discovery in Popper (1972,265) and Polya (1973).

1. Are you clear about the problem?
2. Are you clear about the theories you hold? What are they ?
3. Are you holding some theories unconsciously or taking them for granted?
4. Might any of them be false theories?
5. Have you made several attempts to formulate your theories - for instance by writing them out of discussing them and then tried to criticise them?
6. Try to construct alternative theories; this may help you understand your current theory more clearly.
7. If an experiment or observation appears to support a theory, remember this may mean it really weakens some alternative theory -perhaps one you may not have thought of before.
8. Attempt to refute your own theories; it is better than defending then and leaving it to others to refute them.

Actions taken may change the situation to bring the situation nearer to the goals. For instance, it may be speculated that by employing web-based learning several problems are avoided such as:

1. The lack of access to intellectual material relevant to the learning situation
2. The lack of durability and adaptability of the current learning situations i.e. university scheduled lectures and seminars

3. Over dependence on lecturers
4. The lack of use of new technologies
5. A lack of active learning and motivation.

At the moment, these conjectures remain as somewhat fuzzy, yet interesting, speculations. They need much tighter formulation and testing.

## The method of case studies- dealing with proto-scientific ideas in education

A brief word can be said about the methodological value of case studies. A method is needed for the description and evaluation of unique situations. In biological and social disciplines even quasi-experimental conditions are difficult to produce, even if they are ethically defensible. When case studies are employed, it is possible to focus on specific processes or phenomena. Further inquiry can result in discovery and investigation rather than a collaboration or refutation of a hypothesis, although the logic of Popper's ideas inevitably takes us down that path. Case studies can aim at testing clarifying, amending, evaluating examples and making recommendations.

## Web based learning: new technologies with different pedagogies

One of the strongest arguments for adopting a web-based learning approach springs from Popper's idea that as learners we create ideas before we test or evaluate them: according to E.H. Gombrich, learners 'make and match'. A learner may grasp a problem and suggest a solution. The solution may or may not be a realist one. The World Wide Web improves access to information and ideas and is becoming an important learning resource which is potentially accessible to most people in the western world.

H.J. Perkinson has considered how the lessons of Popper's philosophy of science may be applied to the classroom or lecture theatre (Levinson 1982). In a series of books, Perkinson (1971, 1980, 1984) shows how the popperian approach to learning, the system of conjectures and refutations and problem-solving, can be fashioned into a non-inductive model of education. This approach views the teacher not as someone who injects knowledge into passive minds by a process of transmission, but as one who elicits students responses, creates environments in which ideas are criticized freely and mistakes are made without humiliation and corrected. The student is an active creator of ideas and solver of problems.

The role of the teacher or lecturer shifts away from a more orthodox one involving the effective transmission of ideas, facts and figures to a role that encourages learners to actively and critically engage with and, perhaps, improve new and old ideas. Active engagement by the learners is compelled by the logic of the fallibility of knowledge. The posing of ideas and questioning is more familiarly known as the Socratic approach.

## Technology in the classroom

There are various types of technologies currently used in traditional classrooms. Among these are:

1. **Computer in the classroom:** Having a computer in the classroom is an asset to any teacher. With a computer in the classroom, teachers are able to demonstrate a new lesson, present new material, illustrate how to use new programs, and show new websites.
2. **Class website:** An easy way to display your student's work is to create a web page designed for your class. Once a web page is designed, teachers can post homework assignments, student work, famous quotes, trivia games, and so much more. In today's society, children should know how to use the computer to navigate their way through a website, so why not give them one where they can be a published author? Just be careful, as most districts maintain strong policies to manage official websites for a school or classroom. Also, most school districts provide teacher WebPages that can easily be viewed through the school district's website.
3. **Class blogs and wikis:** There are a variety of Web 2.0 tools that are currently being implemented in the classroom. Blogs allow for students to maintain a running dialogue. They work a tool for maintaining a journal of thoughts, ideas, and assignments, as well as encourage student comment and reflection. Wikis are more group focused to allow multiple members of the group to edit a single document and create a truly collaborative and carefully edited finished product.
4. **Wireless classroom microphones:** Noisy classrooms are a daily occurrence, and with the help of microphones, students are able to hear their teachers more clearly. Children learn better when they hear the teacher clearly. The benefit for teachers is that they no longer lose their voices at the end of the day.
5. **Interactive Whiteboards:** An interactive whiteboard that provides touch control of computer applications. These enhance the experience in the classroom by showing anything that can be on a computer screen. This not only aids in visual learning, but it is interactive so the students can draw, write, or manipulate images on the interactive whiteboard.

6. **Digital video-on-demand:** Replacement of hard copy videos (DVD, VHS) with digital video accessed from a central server (e.g. SAFARI Montage). Digital video eliminates the need for in-classroom hardware (players) and allows teachers and students to access video clips immediately by not utilizing the public Internet.
7. **Online media:** Streamed video websites can be used to enhance a classroom lesson (e.g. United Streaming, Teacher Tube, etc.)
8. **Online study tools:** Tools that motivate studying by making studying more fun or individualized for the student (e.g. Study Cocoa)
9. **Digital Games:** The field of educational games and serious games has been growing significantly over the last few years. The digital games are being provided as tools for the classroom and have a lot of positive feedback including higher motivation for students
10. **Podcasts:** Pod-casting is a relatively new invention that allows anybody to publish files to the Internet where individuals can subscribe and receive new files from people by a subscription. The primary benefit of pod-casting for educators is quite simple. It enables teachers to reach students through a medium that is both "cool" and a part of their daily lives. For a technology that only requires a computer, microphone and internet connection, pod-casting has the capacity of advancing a student's education beyond the classroom. Students will also learn skills that will be valuable in the working world, such as communication, time management, and problem-solving.

## Conclusion

The case study might be the only methodological option to begin with, even though its major weakness is bias. So although there are no general theories for precise predictions, it is possible to accomplish practical tasks, rough generalizations, lower level theories and possibly some level of control. Using this method, it is possible to report upon exemplars as a focus for debate, and test out ideas by uncovering flaws and, also, to formulate hypotheses despite uncertainty and grossly imperfect evidence. More systematic and more organized studies may ensue as more crucial details are revealed. Of course, we should make the tightest possible case for our ideas, and give our critical preference for the approaches that guide action, yet these should be formulated in such as a way that they can openly criticized in theory and practice and capable of refutation and improvement by ourselves or others. Students will also learn skills that will be valuable in the working world, such as communication, time management, and problem-solving.

## References

1. Chamberlain, T.C. (1965) The method of multiple working hypotheses. Science 148, 754-759.
2. Evans, T.D. and Nation, D. (2000) Changing University Teaching: Reflections on Creating Educational Technologies. London: Kogan Page
3. Laurillard, D. (1998) Computers and the Emancipation of Students: Giving Control to the Learner. In: P. Ramsden (ed.) Improving Learning: New Perspectives. Kogan Page.
4. Levinson, P. (1982)What technology can teach philosophy: ruminations along Kantian/Popperian lines. In: Pursuit of the Truth.
5. Musciano, C. and Kennedy, B. (1998) HTML: the definitive guide. O'Reilly. Third Edition.
6. Faludi, A. (1986) Critical Rationalism and Planning Methodology. Pion.
7. Medawar, P. (1991) The Threat and the Glory: Reflections on Science and Scientists. Oxford University Press.
8. Miller, D. (1994) Critical rationalism: a restatement and defence. Chicago: Open Court, 1994 Miller, D. (1983) Editor's Introduction. In: Popper, K.R. (1983) A Pocket Popper. Fontana Press.
9. Perkinson, H.J. (1984) Learning from our Mistakes: A Reinterpretation of Twentieth-Century Educational Theory. Westport, CAT: Greenwood Press.
10. Perkinson, H.J. (1993) Teachers without Goals/Students without Purposes. New York: McGraw-Hill.
11. Popper, K.R. (1991) Objective Knowledge: an evolutionary approach. Oxford: Clarendon Press.
12. Shredder-Frechette, K.S. and McCoy, E.D.(1993) Method in Ecology: strategies for conservation. Cambridge: Cambridge University Press. Swann, J. and Pratt, J. (1999) Improving education: realist approaches to method and research. London: Cassel.

# 24

# Edu–Digital Skills

## Introduction

The rapid development and adoption of digital technologies is changing the way we work and communicate. Firms have recognized the need to embrace technology in order to remain competitive in the global marketplace; artistic creators have embraced digital technologies to enhance their art; and individuals have recognized the value of technology to become effectively connected. Creating the right conditions for a world-class digital economy will require digital skills for all. Arguably the backbone of the digital economy is a strong, globally competitive information and communications technology sector. For a strong ICT sector, it is essential to have a sufficient quantity of qualified ICT workers across occupations and geographical regions. But, ICT workers are not alone in grappling with the effects of advances in digital technologies. The entire workforce, from highly skilled scientists to production line workers, is increasingly affected by rapid changes in the use of digital technology in the workplace.

The advances in technology are having profound impacts on the learning system, both how we teach and how we learn. The Internet, social media and virtual realities have opened up new channels for learning. But, there are concerns that a digital skills divide is emerging, where some groups have less access to new technology and are falling behind in their adoption of digital skills. This is of particular concern because effective participation in the labour market is increasingly linked to digital competence.

## Digital Literacy

Digital literacy is one component of being a digital citizen - a person who is responsible for how they utilize technology to interact with the world around them. Digital technology allows people to interact and communicate with family and friends on a regular basis due to the "busy constraints" of today's world. Not only do white-collar jobs require digital literacy in the use of media to present, record and analyze data, but so do blue-collar jobs that are looking for way to increase productivity and analyze market trends, along with increase job safety.

## Digital Skills

While there is no standard or agreed upon definition, digital skills can be understood as the ability to locate, organize, understand, evaluate, create and share information using digital technology.* It involves knowledge of current communications technology and an understanding of how it can be used. Digital skills are a suite of skills that help to connect in today's world and function in the labour market of today and tomorrow.

## Some of the digital skills

1. **Life-long Learning:** the ability to self-teach new concepts in a quickly changing work environment.
2. **Understanding Copyrights:** know the difference between 'fair use', plagiarism, creative commons and other copy-right related topics.
3. **Time Management:** know the online digital tools that can aid in time management and planning.
4. **Graphic Design**: ability to edit and resize images for online presentations and exhibit.
5. **Audio recording:** ability to create, edit and publish audio recordings.
6. **Web 2.0**: understand the appropriate uses of Web 2.0, both in the classroom and on the job. Know the limits and dangers of Web 2.0 in these contexts as well.
7. **Screen capture/video:** know how to edit and create screen captures and videos for educational and/or work needs.
8. **ePortfolios:** know how to create, edit and manage an online e-Portfolio, for educational or professional exhibit.
9. **Online Talks**: know how to create, edit, and managed online webinars, trainings, or presentations.

10. **Mobile Learning**: know how to exploit mobile technologies for education and work related needs.
11. **Collaboration:** know how to use a variety of online office tools and file sharing components for virtual collaboration.

## The 21st Century Brain

Students in this modern world need to utilize all of the higher order thinking skills taught to students in previous times. Students for centuries have been taught and encouraged to evaluate, apply, analyze and synthesize knowledge. Today's students are able to use the internet to research and find text sources, videos, pod casts and presentations related to anything they would like to learn about. The big catch is, can this "Google, yahoo" part of the brain begin to differentiate what resources they consume online are valid or not. Can this "Google, yahoo" part of the brain create new meaning from the authentic sources they read? Will this "Google, yahoo" part of the brain lead to great innovations and discoveries that help humans understand their place in the world and make life easier for all our world's citizens? Technology is a lovely asset to any classroom, but in a global community, will students transfer their learning beyond their community? Educators around the globe will be tuned in to find the answers to these questions in the years ahead.

## Technology is an advantage in the classroom for the following reasons

1. Motivates students in their learning due to their enjoyment and ease of use with various technological mediums.
2. Reaches students of various learning styles. Technology use applies to and compliments Gardner's Multiple Intelligences.
3. Allows students to create and design their own unique products reflective of their personalities and learning needs/styles.
4. Encourages students to manipulate media to construct their own meaning.
5. Enables students to easy share their learning with teachers, families and peers.
6. Gives students the chance to explore technological mediums which in inevitable increase job skills that employers look for in the workforce.
7. Just like text has different genres, technology too requires that students be able to think critically about different types of media to evaluate purpose and to construct their own meaning.

8. The various Digital-Age Literacy's apply to the more traditional academic disciplines of reading, writing, mathematics, sciences, social studies, history and the humanities.
9. The goal of all teachers is to promote higher order thinking skills in their students. Incorporating Digital -Age Literacy's and technology into lessons and activities is a sure way for teachers to facilitate their student's construction of knowledge and meaning.

## Recent technology developments within education include

1. Young people and their parents increasingly expect to find information, carry out transactions and connect to other people and services when and where they need to. How should education develop within an increasingly digital and connected world?
2. Classroom assessment tools which enable teachers to understand in real time what children can and can't understand. Teachers can be immediately aware of gaps in understanding for specific pupils, tailoring their teaching accordingly and delivering greater personalization.
3. Sophisticated data analysis and management tools that offer the potential for greater tailoring of learning and feedback, and better management information for school leaders.
4. Lesson videos and clips online, which enable teachers to learn more about the successful techniques and approaches of others, and offer pupils access to excellent teaching beyond the classroom.
5. A variety of rich media resources, and other ways of accessing knowledge such as online subject communities, experts and other educators.
6. Games and interactive software, developed with rigour, to help pupils acquire skills and knowledge in an engaging and effective way.
7. Online learning and virtual schooling is beginning to play an important role alongside traditional approaches. These approaches can support flexibility and choice in the curriculum and extend learning beyond the school environment.

## What does this mean for schools?

1. Consider how technology can help when making decisions about how to deliver excellent teaching, effective school management and improved accountability.
2. Think about the scope of the knowledge and resources available to pupils beyond the bounds of the classroom and the textbook, to the very best online lessons, digital resources and tools.

3. Consider the scope of professional tools in the hands of teachers, so they can carry out assessment, record and access data easily when they need to.
4. Ensure teachers are equipped with the skills to integrate digital technologies and new approaches successfully into their teaching, and set a clear expectation that no teacher should ignore the importance of technology in learning.
5. Deliver an ICT curriculum that engages pupils and equips them with the skills and knowledge needed for further study and the 21st century workplace.
6. Manage technology infrastructure and services professionally, offering access to tools and resources anywhere, anytime and achieving best value when purchasing technology.

## Online Provisions on Digital Skills

### 1- Vocaroo

This is basically a free service that allows you to record short audio message without having to install any software or register for any account. All you need to have is a built-in microphone and head over to its main page and click on record then grant access to Vocaroo and start talking. Once finished you can either publish your audio message or scrap and start over. Vocaroo also gives you the option to download your recording or embed it in your blog or website.

### 2- Audio Pal

This is another awesome tool where you can record audio message and share them with others. Here are some of its features:

1. It is free
2. It is easy to use
3. It lets you record your audio messages by phone or computer
4. You can also upload your audio message if you want
5. There is a limit of 60 seconds on each audio message

### 3- Voki

It has some kind of animation in it. What Voki really does is it allows you to create animated audio avatars that you can embed into your blog, wiki, or website.

### 4- Record MP3

It allows users to easily and instantly record short audio messages to share with others. It does not require any sign up just head over to its homepage and start recording and once done a link will be generated for you to email or post it to others to listen to your recording.

## Some plusses of using mind mapping tools in education:

The following are some of the advantages of using mind mapping tools in education: Mind mapping enables teachers to manipulate ideas and concepts with great ease and flexibility,

1. It helps present information in a visually attracting and comprehensive way
2. Its organizational structure helps students understand and communicate their knowledge effectively
3. Teachers can use it to manage their classes and activities
4. It helps teachers summarize, organize, and present lecture information
5. It can be used by both teachers and students to create tutorials and explain difficult concepts
6. Visual maps gets students attention and focus
7. It promotes active note taking, thinking, and learning skills
8. It fosters inquiry and problem solving

## Free mind mapping tools for teachers

1. SpiderScribe: This is a great mind mapping tool that allows users to easily visualize their ideas by connecting various pieces of information together and create free style maps. It also combines elements like text, images, files, calendar events and geographic locations.
2. Edistorm is a great web2.0 tool for educators. It allows you to work on your ideas during a structured brainstorming and organize them into sticky notes for others to see. It has two plans one is free and limited and the other is paid.
3. Wridea is an idea management service and a brainstorming tool. It allows its users to create new idea entries in seconds, update details, discuss in depth with your friends and organize your data under different categories. Wridea can be a very useful tool for teachers and students.
4. Bubbl.us is another great mind mapping and brainstorming web2.0 tool. It allows its users to create concept maps in such an easy way with the minimum tools possible.
5. Wise Mapping is a free online mind maps editor that allows you to create and share your mind maps with others. It also lets its

users create and edit colorful and complex mind maps using just mouse and keyword.

6. Lucid Chart is a flowcharts and mind map making tool. It uses simple drag and drop technique to draw charts and even lets users upload their images into diagrams. It has both free and pro plans. Free as you know is always limited.
7. Text 2 Mind Map is a cool website. It is an application that converts texts to mind maps.
8. Spicynodes allows its users to create visually attractive nodes for their blogs, websites or wikis. Nodes are visually displayed pieces of information that helps visitors easily navigate the content of your site so that they find what they are looking for with the minimum time possible.

## Conclusion

Thus, the Edu-Digital Skills are inevitable part of the modern technological world. Digital Skills and Innovations are basic not only to the student community but also to the teaching community at the Global Level. Today we find an ever growing mountain of information which necessitates both the educators and the students to acquire the knowledge as to how to use technology in education and learn critically to assess the mammoth information at our disposal.

# 25

# Effectiveness of Blended Mode in Teaching and Learning of English

## Introduction

Teaching English as a second language is, of course, a great deal because there is a possibility of getting denied by the learner due to its anonymity. In recent years the proficiency of English determines the future of a student. Being an English teacher, he/she should encourage English conversations both inside and outside the classrooms so that a student involves himself with English. There are numerous job opportunities for the English teachers in India because of the craze of Indians in learning English as a second language and they are also interested to become familiar in English as the native speakers speak. Collegiate education consists of literature and technical usage of English whereas school education deals to nurture English language with prose, poetry, grammar and composition. The transitional period from the school level to the higher education level should be taken into account. Since the right method will be helpful to improve the basic knowledge on English among school students we need to adopt the finest method according to the standard of learners. Communicative approach is wide popular nowadays. The teacher becomes a facilitator at the time of using blended methodology and the latest technical equipment render team spirit and problem solving ability among learners. A teacher can concentrate on apt technology for qualitative and quantitative development. Blended learning concept is specially made to observe the new perspectives in ELT (English Language Teaching) field.

Nowadays teaching of English has become a challenge for the teachers since it needs innovative methods which invoke the learners to high standard of education. Teaching English as a second language is, of course, a great deal because there is a possibility of getting denied by the learner due to its anonymity. It paves a way to pursue higher studies for the learners. This is the right time to think of a novel method, Blended learning in which the traditional teaching method and modern technique of teaching are to be combined. Blended learning gives the same essence of tradition in addition to originality. The teaching society found a new era of educating in which the learner centered system is predominant. E-learning has been already implemented and its success demands the elevated levels of tools. Teaching English is now a curious activity by applying fresh ideas and blooming views.

## English

English is the most familiar language all over the world. Its familiarity might be due to its versatility but, simply we can say that it is the first language in many countries. It is originated in Europe and now it is wide spread throughout the world. It is a language with numerous dialects and it also has a quality of adapting new vocabulary from almost all languages. Since the language is helpful in continuing higher studies and research works it is also called as library language or reference language. However it is decided by the academicians as an International language. It evolves with LSRW skills through which Listening, Speaking, Reading and Writing are developed. In recent years the proficiency of English determines the future of a student. A survey says, about 470 million people speak English and it is the official language for 45 countries. A learner is expected to gain mastery of the language so that the language can conquer his ability of translation to mother tongue.

## English Teacher

A good English teacher should be able to make the students to understand his/her teaching concepts. In particular they should have proficiency in English, a good personality, good body language, organizational behavior, friendly attitude, fine pronunciation, vocabulary fluency and speech techniques and so on. A teacher should possess caring attitude and a good sense of humor through which a student observe a flexible situation in learning. Unbiased environment regarding culture will lead to a comfortable atmosphere. In addition to the cultural balance an English teacher should hold the strategies of teaching a second language. Being an English teacher, he/she should encourage English conversations both inside and outside the classrooms so that a student involves himself with English. This association helps him to learn the language fast. It is very common that a learner tries to express his views in the language in which he/she learns. This interest keeps him close with the teacher. It paves a way that the teacher can understand the need of the student. Among all he/she should be able to mingle with the entire community without any hesitation thereby the relationship gets improved.

## Ongoing Research Work in Blended Mode in Teaching & Learning of English

It is as great opportunity to look up the trend of blended mode in teaching and learning of English. Being a Ph. D Research Scholar, one should concentrate on the available sources. It may be a single or more groups for sample. In order to know about the impact of blended mode in Teaching and Learning of English this study is carried out. Because of the curiosity of knowing about the situation in the class rooms when blended mode is used this study will be taken into account. The response of the students and the feedback of the teacher are to be registered. The samples can be taken as the college students since the study is going to be associated with the higher education.

## Teaching of English in India

After the advent of British, Indians realized the importance of English in India. Since the system of education in India was regularized by Macaulay the need of English education was taken as an indispensable one. This leads to the awareness of learning a foreign language and the wide opportunities of getting employment through the knowledge of a foreign language. Nowadays the government of India gives importance to the English medium of instruction due to the interest of parents and students. There are numerous job opportunities for the English teachers in India because of the craze of Indians in learning English as a second language and they are also interested to become familiar in English as the native speakers speak. In particular the corporate sector started giving importance to people who speaks English fluently and they keep their other talents aside in recruitment. The young Indians wished to be trendy by speaking

English wherever they go. As a result of universalization Indians realize the necessity of English and the demand for the English teachers is growing every day. However the English teachers find difficulty in teaching a foreign language to Indians, non-native speakers because we are lacking modern methods of teaching.

## Visible research outputs on Blended Mode in Teaching and Learning of English

CR Graham explains in his blended Learning systems that "The term blended learning is being used with increased frequency in both academic and corporate circles. In 2003, the American Society for Training and Development identified blended learning as one of the top ten trends to emerge in the knowledge delivery industry."

In Blended Learning: Let's get beyond the hype, Margaret Driscoll says that "The Blended Learning is to combine or mix modes of web-based technology to accomplish an educational goal and to combine various pedagogical approaches to produce an optimal learning outcome with or without instructional technology. It is also to combine any form of instructional technology with face-to-face instructor-led training. In particular it is to mix or combine instructional technology with actual job tasks in order to create a harmonious effect of learning and working.

CR Graham again handles this blended learning in his Emerging Practice and research in Blended Learning and expresses that blending learning (BL) is appearing with increased frequency in both the scholarly literature and the popular press. Although BL is often described in terms of blending the physical attributes of online and face-to-face instruction, the psycho-social relationships are the issues at the core of blended learning research and design. Because education is a design-oriented field like engineering or architecture, it must be concerned with tradeoffs involving cost, efficiency, and effectiveness.

## Teaching of English in India at different levels

Elementary education in medium of English is quite easy when compared to the higher education because the learner will be able to understand the vocabulary and its usage aptly. But in the case of middle classes the student fix his/her mind prepared for the mother tongue and still feels difficulty in learning a new language. If it is the medium of instruction there will be a possibility of hating entire education system. Here we need new strategies to make the students to feel acquaintance with English. Collegiate education consists of literature and technical usage of English whereas school education deals to nurture English language with prose, poetry, grammar and composition. However, for the teachers, primary education is always safer than higher education. Because student will be in a urge that he should be fit for the employment after the higher education. He will be interested in knowing things technically and he will not concentrate on the language education.

## Merits and Demerits of teaching and learning through English medium

As the higher education is going to determine the future of the student, he / she are urged to consider the medium of instruction also. The reason is very simple that the knowledge of another language will work out well during their career development. When the student was forced to take their native language as a medium of instruction he / she will realize the importance of the knowledge of a foreign language to propagate his personality. This thought is a usual one and everybody lies between these two phases only. The transitional period from the school level to the higher education level should be taken into account. Finally the students should know the interference of second language and the importance of their mother tongue. A student should possess interest in learning a foreign language, involvement in what he is learning, personal attitude towards the new language, environmental factors which make him to invite the new vocabulary and it should support him to practice, internal motivation to face troubles during the learning process. The recorded lectures are not preferred by many numbers of students all over the world.

## Different methods of teaching English at school level

Due to the transition from elementary level to secondary school, higher secondary to college level the student needs to adopt a new trend in which he/she can realize the importance of English. This new method may be modified according to the learners. The various methods are,

1. Grammar Translation Method, in which each and every word is translated in the mother tongue.
2. Bilingual Method, in which the instructional language will be both English and mother tongue.
3. Direct Method, in which teacher and learner must use only English.

Since the right method will be helpful to improve the basic knowledge on English among school students we need to adopt the finest method according to the standard of learners. The capability of occupying new vocabulary and knowing grammar will facilitate the frequency of language practice.

## Different methods of Teaching English at higher education level

In the higher education level students could not be handled only with the proficiency of prose they should be treated with the fluency of vocabulary. This idea can be practiced through conducting

1. GROUP DISCUSSION – a group will be formed to discuss on a common topic where all the participants will express their views on that theme.

2. DEBATES – the argumentative task where two or more number of team members will support their side and oppose the other team by revealing points.

3. ROLE PLAYS – a character will be assigned to the learner and he/ she should involve in that character and deliver dialogues for that character.

4. CALL (Computer Assisted Language Learning) – it is quite impossible for a learner to learn a language in a short period without the help of computer. It is indispensable for the present learner to use recent technology through advanced methods of websites.

5. INDIVIDUAL PRESENTATION – through which the participant is given opportunity to speak spontaneously by conveying his /her opinions on the given subject.

Communicative approach is wide popular nowadays. Other than the above said methods we are following Lecture method, Assignment, Seminars, Workshops, Conferences, Brain Storming discussions, Case Study. These strategies help the students to well verse in English language and they get confidence to converse without any inhibition. Here, the eye contact, voice audibility, pronunciation, intonation, subject knowledge and body language are checked for the better results.

## English and Technology

English can be taught effectively with the use of recent scientific inventions. Use of technology has made the teaching learning process easier than ever. English teachers are expected to be experts in handling internet sources. The learner needs to be a constant searcher of technical tools in order to access several exercises which are available in the internet.

Students need to be specialists in verbal and nonverbal presentations where they prove their critical analytic thinking in addition to LSRW skills. Classroom teaching is altered by blended learning in which mere teacher's participation occurs. The learner actively involves in self-assessment exercises because he/she evokes original curiosity about their potentiality. Smart classes are appealing prominent in the current scenario. At present abundant number of language games are offered in teaching websites. The following are some of the scientific junctions useful for teaching as well as learning.

1. Google Drive – a free online storage cloud.
2. Edmodo – a free social learning platform for students.
3. Screen Casting–ScreenR and Explain Everything are there for students at cheap rate.
4. YouTube –the video clips can help the student to know more.
5. Blogging – Word Press and Blogger are the most popular blogging platforms.

## Techniques in teaching English

"Tell me, I forgot.

Show me, I remember.

Involve me, I understand." This is a great example for the use of repetitive exercises in English Language Teaching using blended method. Audio visual aids with music are also helping in multimedia coaching through blended learning method. Teachers are presently using real life models and pictures to ease the concepts and to promote better understanding. Students highly believe that they can exhibit their talents when they made to be in a group. Consequently they like peer tutoring policy. School level teaching can be managed with giving drama concepts and the college level students should be given GDs, Role Plays, Debates and oral presentations.

## Blended mode in teaching and learning of English

It enhances creative thinking of a student. At the same time it enables the reproductive skill in which the speaker replies for the statement of the opponent. The promotion of thinking takes place in this situation and so the learner grabs the chance of expressing his views without any embarrassment. The teacher becomes a facilitator at the time of using blended methodology and the latest technical equipment render team spirit and problem solving ability among learners. Information and Communication Technology (ICT) persuades a fine, successful objective through the Outcome Based Learning. It exactly opens an arena where the teacher and the learner will be independently associated with their work. Though a teacher is constantly telling that his/her prime duty is to make the student to speak in English in public without nervousness learner should have the spirit to converse in English. Blended method provides the strength of facing situations individually and to come out of it.

## Effectiveness of blended mode in teaching and learning of English

In order to satisfy the needs of the corporate world English should be handled as a language rather than a subject. Blended Learning in English will help the teachers to ease the concepts and make the teaching and learning process an effective one. This idea will also help in selecting methodology along with the content competency. Besides, this notion will make the optimum utility of the subject. Through this study a teacher can make the students comfortable with the subject and the selection and preparation of the blended learning material will also be possible. A teacher can concentrate on apt technology for qualitative and quantitative development. Every student in the class should speak on the given concept at least for few minutes to wipe out their fear so that they could be able to involve in public speaking situations. This practice can be possible only with the help of videos on GDs, oral Presentations, Role Plays, Lectures, Standard Speeches and Debates. Use of multimedia tools helps in language teaching in a wide range. Influence of communication devices is also a major component in language learning.

## Uses of blended mode

The use of technology in blended learning has created a true awareness on language learning. It also created a sort of interest in knowing new corners by using online websites. The online modules and tests are more popular among the student community. The students are not interested to cope up with traditional chalk and talk method whereas the growing trend related the subject with technology. When a teacher held up with the ancient type of teaching the outcome will not be fruitful. As the learner has been already stacked with numerous sets of creative exercises in the leading websites the monotonous classroom teaching is not encouraged. The outdated approaches make the learner very dull and classes become vague. The student is involved to participate in almost all the activities of the learning segments. Hence the blended learning technique is a precious gift to the field of teaching English.

## Significance of blended mode in teaching and learning of English

Blended learning in English helps the teachers to ease the concepts and make the teaching-learning process an effective one. For a teacher content competency over the subject alone is not sufficient. He / She should be good in selecting the teaching methodology also. Teaching a subject is not only for its outcome but also for its optimum utility. It's a teacher's responsibility to make the students to feel comfortable with the subject. But the selection and preparation of blended learning material is his/her choice. Apt technology for quantitative and qualitative development helps a teacher to give the best out of his/her knowledge.

## Conclusion

Most of our teachers are concentrating only on Reading and Writing skills but not on Listening and Speaking skills. This affects the overall proficiency of a student and so he needs extra coaching classes for updating his knowledge. Since during his school days the hours are wasted by the drilling of exercises in grammar he could not flourish in the higher education field. To change this scenario, all the language skills are to be concentrated equally and student's participation is to be increased. Blended learning concept is specially made to observe the new perspectives in ELT (English Language Teaching) field. Teachers and students can use this tool for finding better results. Learners will feel comfort in language class rooms when they use educational technology tools for learning. It is just a step thinking ahead a well-developed environment of teaching and learning process.

## Reference

1. Clarke, S., Lindsay, K., McKenna, C. & New, S. (2004) Inquire: A case study evaluating the potential of online MCQ tests in a discursive subject. *ALT-J, Research in Learning Technology.* 12 (3), 249-260.
2. Laurillard, D. (2001) *Rethinking university teaching-a framework for the effective use of educational technology.* New York: Routledge.
3. Graham, C.R., &Dziuban, C.D. (2008). Core research and issues related to blended learning environments. In J.M. Spector, M.D. Merrill, J.J.G. Van Merrienboer, & M.P. Driscoll Eds., *Handbook of research on educational communications and technology* (3rd ed.). Mahwah, NJ: Lawrence Earlbaum Associates.

4. Vaughan, N. & Garrison, D.R (2005).Creating cognitive presence in a blended faculty development community. *Internet and Higher Education, 8(1)*, 1-12.
5. Smith, Judith M. Ph.D. (2001). "Blended Learning: An Old Friend Gets a New Name." Executive Update, Online. Retrieved Sept 25, 2005 from http://www.gwsae.org/Executiveupdate/2001/March/blended.htm.
6. Garnham, C., &Kaleta, R. (March 20, 2002). Introduction to hybrid courses. *Teaching with Technology Today, 8* (6). Retrieved May 13, 2011, from http://www.uwsa.edu/ttt/articles/garnham.htm
7. King, K. P. (2002). Identifying success in online teacher education and professional development.[Electronic version].*Internet and Higher Education, 5* (2002), 231-246.
8. Christensen, T. K. (2003). Finding the balance: Constructivist pedagogy in a blended course. *Quarterly Review of Distance Education, 4(3)*, 235-243.

# 26

# Flipped Classrooms

## Introduction

Flipped Classrooms are shifting the way teachers provide instruction by inverting traditional teaching methods to engage students in the learning process. Using technology, lectures are moved out of the classroom and delivered online as a means to free up class time for interaction and collaboration. In order to effectively implement a Flipped Classroom, teachers must possess a set of requisite technical skills, conceptual knowledge and pedagogical expertise. Through this study, a web-based instructional module was developed to provide this information to prospective teachers interested in implementing a Flipped Classroom.

Flipped Classroom is a form of blended learning in which students learn new content online by watching video lectures, usually at home, and what used to be homework (assigned problems) is now done in class with teachers offering more personalized guidance and interaction with students, instead of lecturing. This is also known as backwards classroom, Flipped classroom, reverse teaching, and the Thayer Method.

## Flipped Classrooms

The Flipped classroom is a teaching strategy that allows instructors to more actively engage with students in the classroom. In the Flipped

Classroom, instructors typically assign recorded video lectures as homework, and use class time for active learning exercises and direct engagement with students. As Mung Chiang from Princeton said, "class time is for two-way interactions." Flipped Classrooms help make these two-way interactions possible. Derek Bruff from Vanderbilt contributed his own flipped overview to the Coursera Partners' Portal forums along with the following diagrams highlighting the differences between the traditional and Flipped Classroom Model:Traditional vs Flipped Classroom

The traditional pattern of teaching has been to assign students to read textbooks and work on problem sets outside school, while listening to lectures and taking tests in class. In flip teaching, the students first study the topic by themselves, typically using video lessons prepared by the teacher or third parties. In class students apply the knowledge by solving problems and doing practical work. The teacher tutors the students when they become stuck, rather than imparting the initial lesson in person. Complementary techniques include differentiated instruction and project-based learning. Teachers are blending the advantages of flipped learning with traditional in-class lecturing through tools like education that keep students accountable to video lessons at home through time-embedded formative assessments. Flipped Classrooms free class time for hands-on work. Students learn by doing and asking questions. Students can also help each other, a process that benefits both the advanced and less advanced learners.

Flipping also changes the allocation of teacher time. Traditionally, the teacher engages with the students who ask questions — but those who don't ask tend to need the most attention. "We refer to 'silent failers,' " said one teacher, claiming that flipping allows her to target those who need the most help rather than the most confident. Flipping changes teachers from "sage on the stage" to "guide on the side", allowing them to work with individuals or groups of students throughout the session.

## Advantages of Flipped Classrooms

The traditional classroom is frequently organized as a place where the teacher presents and explains content whilst students listen to and note down all the information provided. The class is usually teacher centered, though one can have a more dialogic approach with the students, depending on one's own perspective. Routinely, in the classroom, all students have to do the same activities, based on the resources available in the classroom and following the same pace and the one established by the teacher.

Sometimes, the teacher provides some homework tasks, or asks for exercises to be completed outside the classroom, to reinforce knowledge or elicit further questions.

In the Flipped Classroom model, the teacher provides in advance materials created or selected by him/herself (short videos, screen casts or podcasts), for the students self learning activities, out of the classroom. These activities can be performed when and where the student feels most comfortable, taking into account his/her own learning rhythm. In this model, the student studies the materials and the resources pointed out by the teacher, he/she also identifies his/her difficulties and topics he/she wishes to be cleared. Students also look for extra information and follow their own learning rhythm and can review the learning materials whenever they need to. Classroom time is used for questioning and to deepen the knowledge, in a more personalized learning environment where students can learn side-by-side, in small groups, and the teacher helps them to clear misunderstanding.

In this model the teacher provides resources and plans learning opportunities for the students, proposes specific questions that can direct the learning process. The teacher can anticipate where students need the most help and as a consequence offer activities and experiences in the classroom that adapt to their difficulties and doubts, establishing a logic of questioning and learning valued by several researchers e.g. Rupert Wegerif (Wegerif and Yang, 2011; Wegerif, 2013).

Instead of using classroom time to present information, the teacher has time to clarify doubts, provide extra resources, create activities in the classroom that might be felt as necessary and evaluate immediately the students' performance within the classroom. This way, it promotes the improvement of the quality of learning. This classroom organization model inverts the traditional lecturing classroom concept, creating classes where students are highly engaged in an active and participatory learning.

Kathleen Fulton (2012) listed the following advantages of the Flipped Classroom: (i) students move at their own pace; (ii) doing "homework" in class gives teachers better insight into student difficulties and learning styles; (iii) teachers can more easily customize and update the curriculum and provide it to students 24/7; (iv) classroom time can be used more effectively and creatively; (v) teachers using the method report seeing increased levels of student achievement, interest, and engagement; (vi) learning theory supports the new approaches; and (vii) the use of technology is flexible and appropriate for "21st Century Learning."

## Benefits of Flipped Classrooms

The Flipped Classroom experience makes optimal use of instructor and student time, provides increased access to the instructor's expertise and enables better scalability of instructional resources to support high-enrolment demands. From the instructor's perspective, key beneûts of the Flipped Classroom include:

1. Increased classroom time to present content, discuss complex topics and work with students — either individually or in small groups;
2. Reduced time spent answering basic and repetitive questions — due to students' ability to review lectures online;
3. The ability to use recorded lectures in multiple course sections — year over year, with easy tools for updating content; and
4. Quick adaptation of lecture content to respond to new learning needs.

## Conclusion

The Flipped Classroom is a strategic direction that helps higher education meet the expectations of today's students while optimizing teaching and classroom resources. The blended learning approach of the Flipped Classroom can be leveraged for both individual courses and on an organizational level to improve instructional delivery and enhance student achievement and satisfaction.

## Reference

1. Wegerif, R. (2013). *Dialogic: Education for the Internet Age.* London: Routledge.
2. Wegerif, R. and Yang, Y. (2011). *Technology and Dialogic Space: Lessons from History and from the 'Argunaut' and 'Metafora' Projects.* In H. Spada, G. Stahl, N. Miyake and N. Law (Eds.), Connecting Computer-Supported Collaborative Learning to Policy and Practice: CSCL2011 Conference Proceedings. Volume I — Long Papers (pp. 312-318). Hong Kong, China: International Society of the Learning Sciences.

# 27

# Flipped Classroom

The flipped classroom describes a reversal of traditional teaching where students gain first exposure to new material outside of class, usually via reading or lecture videos, and then class time is used to do the harder work of assimilating that knowledge through strategies such as problem-solving, discussion or debates. Flip teaching is a form of blended learning in which students learn new content online by watching video lectures, usually at home, and what used to be homework is now done in class with teacher offering more personalized guidance and interaction with students, instead of lecturing. In essence, "flipping the classroom" means that students gain first exposure to new material outside of class, usually via reading or lecture videos, and then use class time to do the harder work of assimilating that knowledge, perhaps through problem-solving, discussion, or debates.

In terms of Bloom's revised taxonomy (2001), this means that students are doing the lower levels of cognitive work (gaining knowledge and comprehension) outside of class, and focusing on the higher forms of cognitive work (application, analysis, synthesis, and/or evaluation) in class, where they have the support of their peers and instructor. This model contrasts from the traditional model in which "first exposure" occurs via lecture in class, with students assimilating knowledge through homework; thus the term "flipped classroom."

## Flipped Classroom

The flipped classroom approach has been used for years in some disciplines, notably within the humanities. Barbara Walvoord and Virginia Johnson Anderson promoted the use of this approach in their book Effective Grading (1998). They propose a model in which students gain first-exposure learning prior to class and focus on the processing part of learning in class.

To ensure that students do the preparation necessary for productive class time, Walvoord and Anderson propose an assignment-based model in which students produce work (writing, problems, etc.) prior to class. The students receive productive feedback through the processing activities that occur during class, reducing the need for the instructor to provide extensive written feedback on the students' work. Walvoord and Anderson describe examples of how this approach has been implemented in history, physics, and biology classes, suggesting its broad applicability.

## Inverted Classroom

The traditional lecture format is incompatible with some learning styles. To make their course more compatible with their students' varied learning styles, they designed an inverted classroom in which they provided students with a variety of tools to gain first exposure to material outside of class: textbook readings, lecture videos, Power point presentations with voice-over, and printable Power point slides.

To help ensure student preparation for class, students were expected to complete worksheets that were periodically but randomly collected and graded. Class time was then spent on activities that encouraged students to process and apply economics principles, ranging from mini-lectures in response to student questions to economic experiments to small group discussions of application problems. Both student and instructor response to the approach was positive, with instructors noting that students appeared more motivated than when the course was taught in a traditional format.

## Peer Instruction

The peer instruction (PI) model requires that students gain first exposure prior to class, and uses assignments (in this case, quizzes) to help ensure that students come to class prepared. Class time is structured around alternating mini-lectures and conceptual questions. Importantly, the conceptual questions are not posed informally and answered by student volunteers as in traditional lectures; instead, all students must answer the conceptual question, often via "clickers", or handheld personal response systems, that allow students to answer anonymously and that allow the instructor to see (and display) the class data immediately. If a large fraction of the class (usually between 30 and 65%) answers incorrectly, then students reconsider the question in small groups while instructors circulate to promote productive discussions. After discussion, students answer the conceptual question again. The instructor provides feedback, explaining the correct answer and following up with related questions if appropriate. The cycle is then repeated with another topic, with each cycle typically taking 13-15 minutes.

## The key elements of the flipped classroom

In all the examples cited above, students completed a task associated with their preparation and that task was associated with points. The assignment can vary; the examples above used tasks that ranged from online quizzes to worksheets to short writing assignments, but in each case the task provided an incentive for students to come to class prepared by speaking the common language of undergraduates: points. In many cases, grading for completion rather than effort can be sufficient, particularly if class activities will provide students with the kind of feedback that grading for accuracy usually provides.

## Provide a mechanism to assess student understanding

The pre-class assignments that students complete as evidence of their preparation can also help both the instructor and the student assess understanding. Pre-class online quizzes can allow the instructor to practice Just-in-Time Teaching, which basically means that the instructor tailors class activities to focus on the elements with which students are struggling. If automatically graded, the quizzes can also help students pinpoint areas where they need help. Pre-class worksheets can also help focus student attention on areas with which they're struggling, and can be a departure point for class activities, while pre-class writing assignments help students clarify their thinking about a subject, thereby producing richer in-class discussions. Importantly, much of the feedback students need is provided in class, reducing the need for instructors to provide extensive commentary outside of class (Walvoord and Anderson, 1998). In addition, many of the activities used during class time (e.g., clicker questions or debates) can serve as informal checks of student understanding.

## Provide in-class activities that focus on higher level cognitive activities

If the students gained basic knowledge outside of class, then they need to spend class time to promote deeper learning. Again, the activity will depend on the learning goals of the class and the culture of the discipline. For example, Lage, Platt, and Treglia described experiments students did in class to illustrate economic principles (2000), while Mazur and colleagues focused on student discussion of conceptual "clicker" questions and quantitative problems focused on physical principles (2001). In other contexts, students may spend time in class engaged in debates, data analysis, or synthesis activities. The key is that students are using class time to deepen their understanding and increase their skills at using their new knowledge.

## The Advantages

Many of the advantages of the flipped classroom have been covered throughout the blogosphere and elsewhere. There are many things to praise about the concept of the flipped classroom. With positive results from many teachers and school districts throughout the country, there's no denying that the approach can be successful in certain cases. Students are able to approach material and take it in at their own speed. By covering lecture material at home and from a video-based platform, students can privately view the material. This allows them to approach things at their own pace without worry of peers noticing them moving slower or faster. Students can stop, pause, rewind, and fast forward material so that they can examine things in their own way.

By taking the lecture portion of the classroom home with them, students are able to utilize their teachers' one-on-one attention more successfully in the classroom. Students sit through lecture, gather questions, and prepare themselves for the day with the teacher to tackle "homework". Because the actual exercises are done in the classroom rather than at home with this model, students have their teacher available for questions with problems when they occur.

The flipped classroom also allows teaching to adapt more easily to the different teaching styles that individual students may be most successful with. By putting lectures in a video format, students can listen to the lesson and watch the video illustrate the lesson. Of course, this largely depends on how successful the actual video lecture is. You want a lecture (like the Khan videos) that explains concepts verbally, but also draws them out in images and pictures. This provides adequate learning opportunities for verbal learners and for visual learners. With in-classroom lecturing, the visual aspect of lecturing can be significantly more difficult to accomplish.

## The Disadvantages

Of course, as with anything, there are going to be some disadvantages to the flipped structure of learning as well. Just as classroom lecturing works better for some and doesn't work for others, the flipped classroom method is not going to accommodate every individual perfectly. The biggest setback today to the flipped classroom method is that not all students and schools have access to technologies that can really work for this method.

Students from lower income areas and lower income families may not have access to the computers and internet technologies that the flipped classroom requires. The structure really hinges on every student having personal access to his or her own personal device. This simply is not the case for every student and every school district. Students who do not have personal home computers or access to the internet would be forced to use public computers at a library or at the school. This, to some degree, eliminates the personal and private experience of taking in the lecture. What makes having lectures as homework so powerful is that students can do it on their own time and in their own way. At a library computer or school computer time limits typically exist and access can be limited if it is busy.

Another downside to the idea of the flipped classroom that many people bring up is the fact that students would be spending all of their "homework time" plugged-in in front of a computer screen. Not only do not all students do well with learning from a screen, but this also adds to a student's time in front of a screen and sitting sedentary. While this concern isn't singular to the flipped classroom, the teaching concept doesn't help our young students to get up and get away from their computers, televisions, and ipods.

The purpose of flipping the classroom is to shift from passive to active learning to focus on the higher order thinking skills such as analysis, synthesis and evaluation (Bloom). As explained in this short video, flipping the Classroom: Simply Speaking (Penn State), students access key content individually (or in small groups) prior to class time and then meet face-to-face in the larger group to explore content through active learning and engagement strategies.

There are many permutations of what a flipped classroom will look like and depends on variables such as class size, resources, support and readiness to change. At UQ, several teachers across the faculties have already flipped their classrooms and their valuable experiences have been captured in the Case Studies section.

In the flipped classroom, the roles and expectations of students and teachers change where: students take more responsibility for their own learning and study core content either individually or in groups before class and then apply knowledge and skills to a range of activities using higher order thinking, teaching 'one-to-many' focuses more on facilitation and moderation than lecturing, though lecturing is still important. Significant learning opportunities can be gained through facilitating active learning, engaging students, guiding learning, correcting misunderstandings and providing timely feedback using a variety of pedagogical strategies, there is a greater focus on concept exploration, meaning making and demonstration or application of knowledge in the face-to-face setting.

## Conclusion

Students to access at their own convenience and to suit their pace of learning (e.g. lecture material, readings, interactive multimedia),present learning materials in a variety of formats to suit different learner styles (e.g. text, videos, audio, multimedia),provide opportunities for discourse and interaction in and out of class (e.g. polling tools, discussion tools, content creation tools),convey timely information, updates and reminders for students (e.g micro-blogging, announcement tools),provide immediate and anonymous feedback for teachers and students (e.g. quizzes, polls) to signal revision points, capture data about students to analyse their progress and identify 'at risk' students.

The flipped classroom constitutes a role change for instructors, who give up their front-of-the-class position in favor of a more collaborative and cooperative contribution to the teaching process. There is a concomitant change in the role of students, many of whom are used to being cast as passive participants in the education process, where instruction is served to them. The flipped model puts more of the responsibility for learning on the shoulders of students while giving them greater impetus to experiment. Activities can be student-led, and communication among students can become the determining dynamic of a session devoted to learning through hands-on work. What the flip does particularly well is to bring about a distinctive shift in priorities— from merely covering material to working toward mastery of it.

# 28

# Flipped Classroom

## Introduction

First, what is a flipped or inverted classroom? You can find a wide range of definitions, but typically an instructor "flips" by replacing lectures with more active forms of student engagement in the classroom - students watch video lectures outside of class. This mode of instruction is not so different from the kind of instruction people in the humanities have using for years: read/watch materials outside of class and then discuss ideas in class.

While the three of us were satisfied with our interactive, lecture-driven courses, we started studying flipped classrooms to explore ways we could use class time (when students and instructor are in the same space simultaneously) to the best advantage. Flipping allows students to engage in hands-on activities, discussions, writing exercises, or other tasks. Their instructor can assess whether students are learning by watching them engage in tasks that make use of what they have supposedly absorbed.

## Need for flipped classroom

We set out to measure whether students would learn more in flipped classrooms than in our usual interactive lecture courses. We are in the middle of a multiyear study across three disciplines (chemistry, engineering, and mathematics), and our preliminary study results have not shown any appreciable differences in student learning between traditional and flipped courses. But even if our longer study shows the same result, it doesn't mean that flipped classrooms would necessarily be good, bad, or neutral in other situations. To understand the results of an educational study, it is important to pay attention to the learning environment.

Students spend a lot of time in groups working together both in and out of classes. They generally have confidence in their skills and ability to learn, and have positive attitudes about learning science and mathematics. It could be a different story in another environment. For instance, say you attend a college whose students mostly have full-time jobs, live far from campus, and don't have time or proximity to engage in group work outside of class.

## Developing the Flipped Classroom

A flipped class might increase student opportunities for group interaction, which could not only improve your learning but also provide experience working in teams. If you have difficulty focusing during long lectures, you might enjoy having the chance to rewind parts of a video and spending class time discussing ideas with your peers. On the other hand, if you are a person who needs plenty of quiet processing time before you begin a task with other learners, you may find the flipped classroom scene challenging.

Should every classroom be flipped? Most teachers would happily (if not easily) stand on their heads if it would help their students learn. But schools should not mandate flipped classrooms, or any other educational trend, just to be on the cutting edge. Rather, they should encourage innovation and give instructors freedom and resources to experiment with different teaching strategies. We need more educational research to examine different modes of instruction, the effects these instructional methods have on students, and the contexts in which the instruction takes place. Research results can inform and improve teaching practices.

But we must be careful not to over generalize or oversimplify the results of these studies. Just as no flavor of yoga will suit everyone, no universal solution will improve learning for all students in every situation. When you think back to your school days, or even if you are still in school, you likely sat through numerous lectures then went home and worked on math or science problems on your own.

Now some teachers such as High School are turning the traditional notion of schoolwork and homework on its head by "flipping the classroom."As the school bell rings signaling the start of class, the students get settled into their seats. Not to hear a lecture about the class — but to work out problems in class."And then when they come in to class, what used to be their homework assignment, which in physics is mostly problems, they used to go home and do those at home on their own. Now when they come into school, they get into groups, and they are able to work on what used to be their homework — but now it's class work."

## Role of Teachers and Students

The way this is designed now, the teacher said to help them," "They don't have that take home homework anymore. They come into class, and they work with me, like they will ask me the questions and they will l get all of their questions answered during class when teacher there to help them."The students themselves, overall, say they like the flipped classroom, though some say it does take getting used to."During the lecture part of the class where the teacher explaining something, there are rarely any questions, and if they would have a question now that they are at home listening to lectures, they can always ask at the beginning of class the next day.

## Benefits of Flipped the Classroom

"Some students that normally would have dropped the class because they just could not do the work, they are now able to take the class, "Some of the kids will say, 'I have to watch those two or three times. I see more students are succeeding. It's also been good for students' emotional health.

## Conclusion

Now a days the technology was very improved and effectiveness. The flipped classroom model was developed in the 1990s and as technology has improved so has the delivery. As a long-time educator have made an impact. As we have changed through the years, different things came about and better than this. Like with the overhead projector and then the LCD, or teach from the back of the classroom using this changed everything!' But not all classrooms and schools can take advantage; students at high school have access that many larger districts do not. Each student is supplied with one school-issued laptop he or she can take home each night.

## Reference

1. Berrett D (2012). How 'flipping' the classroom can improve the traditional lecture. *The Chronicle of Higher Education*, Feb. 19, 2012.
2. Anderson LW and Krathwohl D (2001). *A taxonomy for learning, teaching, and assessing: a revision of Bloom's taxonomy of educational objectives.* New York: Longman.
3. Bransford JD, Brown AL, and Cocking RR (2000). *How people learn: Brain, mind, experience, and school.* Washington, D.C.: National Academy Press.
4. Crouch CH and Mazur E (2001). Peer instruction: Ten years of experience and results. *American Journal of Physics* 69: 970-977.
5. DesLauriers L, Schelew E, and Wieman C (2011). Improved learning in a large-enrollment physics class. *Science*332: 862-864.
6. Fitzpatrick M (2012). Classroom lectures go digital. *The New York Times*, June 24, 2012.
7. Hake R (1998). Interactive-engagement versus traditional methods: A six-thousand-student survey of mechanics test data for introductory physics courses. *American Journal of Physics* 66: 64-74.
8. Lage MJ, Platt GJ, and Treglia M (2000). Inverting the classroom: A gateway to creating an inclusive learning environment. *The Journal of Economic Education* 31: 30-43.
9. Mazur E (2009). Farewell, Lecture? *Science* 323: 50-51.
10. Novak G, Patterson ET, Gavrin AD, and Christian W (1999). *Just-in-Time Teaching: Blending Active Learning with Web Technology.* Upper Saddle River, NJ: Prentice Hall.
11. Pashler H, McDaniel M, Rohrer D, and Bjork R (2008). Learning styles: Concepts and evidence. Psychological Science in the Public Interest 9: 103-119.
12. Walvoord BE, and Anderson VJ (1998). *Effective grading: A tool for learning and assessment.* San Francisco: Jossey-Bass.

# 29

# The Art of Learning in the Contemporary Scenario

The ability to obtain, assimilate and apply the right knowledge effectively will become a key skill in the century. Our ability will no longer be judged solely by qualifications gained in the past, but will also be assessed by our capacity to learn and adapt in the future.

Learning is not just about economic success, however. It is the key to achieving our full potential. Human beings are uniquely adapted to learn and have the ability to do so throughout our lives. Teaching professional needs good understanding of the general characteristics of learning in order to apply them in a learning situation. lf learning is a change in behavior as a result of experience, then instruction must include a careful and systematic creation of those experiences that promote learning. This process can be quite complex because, among other things, an individual's background strongly influences the way that person learns. To be effective, the learning situation also should be purposeful, based on experience, multifaceted, and involve an active process.

## Introduction

Learning is the act of acquiring new, or modifying and reinforcing, existing knowledge, behaviors, skills, values, or preferences and may involve synthesizing different types of information. The ability to learn is possessed by humans, animals and some machines. Progress over time tends to follow learning curves. Learning is not compulsory; it is contextual. It does not happen all at once, but builds upon and is shaped by what people already know. To that end, learning may be viewed as a process, rather than a collection of factual and procedural knowledge. Learning depends very much on the context: age, place (school, work, job, etc.), time, previous learning, role models, motivation, alone or with other people, level of knowledge, know-how, experience, etc.

1. Learning as a quantitative increase in knowledge. Learning is acquiring information or 'knowing a lot'.
2. Learning as memorising. Learning is storing information that can be reproduced.
3. Learning as acquiring facts, skills, and methods that can be retained and used as necessary.
4. Learning as making sense or abstracting meaning. Learning involves relating parts of the subject matter to each other and to the real world.
5. Learning as interpreting and understanding reality in a different way. Learning involves comprehending the world by reinterpreting knowledge.

Learning has the power to transform people into more successful person at home and with our families, at work and at large in our local community. Learning leads to three outcomes as is able to know, be able to do and be able to explain to others

| Generic outcome | Specific outcome | Examples |
|---|---|---|
| **1. Be able to know** | • knowledge<br>• know-how<br>• skills | • - e.g. history, the rules-<br>• how to cook, recipes<br>• presentation, negotiation, speak English, etc. |
| **2. Be able to apply** | • practices<br>• applications | • driving a car -<br>- developing a business plan, creating a business plan.<br>solving problems, building an engine, repairing a car |
| **3. Be able to explain to others** (master) | • teaching<br>• coaching<br>• facilitating<br>• mentoring | |

## Evolution of Learning

There are two ways in which animals can gain knowledge. The first of these two ways is learning. This is when an animal gathers information about its surrounding environment and then proceeds to use this information. For example, if an animal eats something that hurts its stomach, it may learn not to eat this again. The second way that an animal can acquire knowledge is through innate knowledge. This knowledge is genetically inherited. The animal automatically knows it without any prior experience. An example of this is when a horse is born and can immediately walk. The horse has not learned this behavior; it simply knows how to do it. In some scenarios, innate knowledge is more beneficial than learned knowledge. However, in other scenarios the opposite is true - animals must learn certain behaviors when it is disadvantageous to have a specific innate behavior. In these situations, learning evolves in the species.

## The importance of learning

People live and work in a changing world. New laws are introduced that lead to the introduction of new policies. New ideas and approaches emerge. New problems arise and new solutions are sought. The world of work is therefore a constantly moving and evolving one. What this means, then, is that, if people are not constantly learning as we go about our day-to-day business, then each day people are getting further and further out of touch with the demands of the modern working world. It can be dangerous to get into a rut whereby continue to carry out the duties in much the same way as we have done in the past. Expectations change over time and, if we do not adapt to the new circumstances, then we will be steadily more out of tune with what is required for all. It is therefore important that people enter into a process of what is known as 'continuous learning process'.

## Purposes for Learning

**Access:** To gain access to information and resources so that adults can orient themselves in the world.

**Voice:** To Express Ideas And Opinions With The Confidence They Will Be Heard And Taken Into Account.

**Action:** To Solve Problems And Make Decisions Without Having To Rely On Others To Mediate The World For Them.

**Bridge To The Future:** Learning to learn so that adults can be prepared to keep up with the world as it changes.

## Types of learning

1. **Rote learning:** Rote learning is memorizing information so that it can be recalled by the learner exactly the way it was read or heard. The major technique used for rote learning is learning by repetition, based on the idea that a learner can recall the material exactly, if the information is repeatedly processed. Rote learning is used in diverse areas, from mathematics to music to religion. Although it has been criticized by some educators, rote learning is a necessary precursor to meaningful learning.
2. **Meaningful learning:** Meaningful learning is the concept that learned knowledge is fully understood to the extent that it relates to other knowledge. To this end, meaningful contrasts with rote learning in which information is acquired without regard to understanding. Meaningful learning, on the other hand, implies there is a comprehensive knowledge of the context of the facts learned.
3. **Informal learning:** Informal learning occurs through the experience of day-to-day situations (for example, one would learn to look ahead while walking because of the danger inherent in not paying attention to where one is going). It is learning from life, during a meal at table with parents, play, exploring, etc.
4. **Formal learning:** Formal learning is learning that takes place within a teacher-student relationship, such as in a school system. The term formal learning has nothing to do with the formality of the learning, but rather the way it is directed and organized. In formal learning, the learning or training departments set out the goals and objectives of the learning.
5. **Non-formal learning:** Non-formal learning is organized learning outside the formal learning system. For example: learning by coming together with people with similar interests and exchanging viewpoints, in clubs or in international youth organizations, workshops.

## A Model of the Relationship between Learning and Teaching

1. Learning is at the center of the diagram which point out, learning can occur without deliberate teaching – as is the case in people's participation in the activities that make up family and community life and in many work situations.
2. In most countries, however, it is considered important to make provision in schools and colleges for the more systematic, guided

learning that is required to master the various disciplines that underpin activities in technologically advanced societies.

3. In such formal educational contexts, where learning is an intended outcome of activity, teaching has two major functions: the first is to select and introduce the overall topic of inquiry, provide access to the necessary resources, and negotiate with the learners the challenges they will take on; the second is to monitor the progress of individuals and groups and to provide guidance and assistance as appropriate. This latter responsibility includes engaging individuals and the whole class in "met cognitively" reviewing the products and the processes of their learning in order that they may take greater control over, and responsibility for, their efforts to achieve understanding.

## Factors Affecting Learning

There are a whole range of factors that can help or hinder in learning. It include factors within each of such as motivation, preferred learning styles as well as external factors such as the opportunities that exist to learn and the other demands that life makes on time and resources.

The key factors affecting learning include:

1. Their resources
2. Their image of learning
3. The rewards associated with any learning activity
4. The availability of information about learning opportunities
5. The availability of appropriate learning environments
6. The climate in which learning takes place, especially that created by government and employers.

In terms of environments, it is acknowledged that learn best in a high-challenge, low-threat environment. Much thinking has gone into how that environment can be created. Often it is an individual teacher's enthusiasm and ability that influences how to learn. Most of them remember a good teacher or a strong role model from when we were young; someone who got excited about their subject by teaching in an interesting way. Equally, many barriers to learning exist which prevent people from getting started on learning or make it impossible to continue however strong that person's determination. Some of the most commonly recognized barriers to learning include:

1. Shortage of money for course fees and related expenses
2. Lack of confidence

3. Lack of provision
4. Lack of tutorial support when studying
5. Lack of personal support
6. Courses organized at inappropriate times and inaccessible places

## Conclusion

Learning is not just important to ensure that, keep up-to-date with developments in the particular field. It is also an important source of motivation, stimulation and job satisfaction. Learning should be seen as something positive and worthwhile in its own right, not just something that we have to do to meet other people's expectations. Most people have fairly definite ideas about what they want to do and achieve. Their goals sometimes are short term, involving a matter of days or weeks. On the other hand, their goals may be carefully planned for a career or a lifetime. Each student has specific intentions and goals. Some may be shared by other students. Students learn from any activity that tends to further their goals. Their individual needs and attitudes may determine what they learn as much as what the instructor is trying to get them to learn. In the process of learning, the student's goals are of paramount significance. To be effective, teaching professionals need to find ways to relate new learning to the student's goals.

## References

1. Case, R. (1996). Changing views of knowledge and their impact on educational research and practice. The handbook of education and human development. D.R.Olson and N.Torrance. Cambridge, M.A., Blackwell: 75-99.
2. Cole, M. (2006). The Fifth Dimension: An after-school program built on diversity New York, Russell Sage Foundation.
3. Olson, D. R. and J. S. Bruner (1996). Folk psychology and folk pedagogy. The handbook of education and human development. D. R. Olson and N. Torrance. Cambridge, MA, Blackwell. 9-27.
4. http://www.campaign-for-earning.org.uk/cfl/yourlearning/why_is_learning_important.asp
5. http://livingjoyfully.ca/blog/2013/04/learning-is-learning/
6. http://www.citehr.com/18695-importance-learning-must-read.html#ixzz30UBV0kYW
7. http://www.dynamicflight.com/avcfibook/learning process/

# 30

# Past, Present and Future of Creative Educative Environment

## Introduction

The widespread adoption and availability of digital learning technologies has led to increased levels of integration of computer-mediated instructional elements into the traditional face-to-face learning experience. From the distributed learning perspective, we see evidence of the convergence in face-to-face residency requirements and limited face-to-face events, such as orientations and final presentation. In addition, there is greater emphasis on person-to-person interaction, and increasing use of synchronous and high-fidelity technologies to mediate those interactions. The intersection of the distributed learning environments and its convergence with face-to-face learning environments gives way to blended learning systems. Although it is impossible to see entirely what the future holds, we can be pretty certain that the trend toward blended learning systems will increase. It may even become so ubiquitous that we will eventually drop the word *blended* and just call it learning, as both.

## Definition of blended learning

Blended learning combines online with face-to-face learning. The goal of blended learning is to provide the most efficient and effective instruction experience by combining delivery modalities.

## Need for Blended Learning

Speedier performance was detected on real world tasks by those who learned through blended strategies as opposed to those that learned via e-learning along Adults don't just "learn" in one way. Likewise, associations should not make the mistake of providing just one way for adult learners to receive their educational content.

## Method of designing Blended Learning

To design blended training, the instructional designers start by analyzing the training or course objectives and braking them down into the smallest possible pedagogically (for children) or andragogically (for adults) appropriate chunks (learning object). After the course or training has been chunked, the best approach to deliver each segment of instruction (learning object) is identified. In some cases the best approach might be using online learning but in others it might be live instruction, For example.

The course is then aggregated by grouping the instruction logically while taking into account the medium of delivery.

## Challenges of Blended Learning

1. How to manage instructional complexity
2. How to design it.
3. How to manage the roles and responsibilities.

**How to manage instructional complexity:** In blended learning the instructor has a wider choice of delivery mediums to combine. With that wider choice also comes greater complexity and pressure on the instructor and designer. This is due to the variety of combinations of technology and possibly the lack of patterns to follow for that particular mix. These issues need to be addressed up front and taken into account during the design. We also need to take this into account due to its effects on the learner. It is easier to finish an online module and start another online module, for example, than it is for that second module to be videoconferencing based. Such changes require the learner to adapt. Time, guidelines, and even brief demos might need to be provided for the learner.

**How to manage the roles and responsibilities:** Unlike traditional classroom learning in which there usually is a single instructor, in blended learning you might have multiple individuals, each taking a modality or role in the blend. Up front clarification of instructor and assistant roles is essential for success and the reduction of potential conflict and learner confusion.

**How to create a seamless learning experience:** Good communications among instructors and careful planning is another important element in the success of blended learning. Make sure that instructors and assistants communicate with one another throughout the instruction, not just before the course. Make sure that as different segments of the blend are designed, all prerequisites are met by the previous learning objects. Arrange learning objects or alter meeting times to insure each segment reinforces the previously acquired knowledge or skill and introduces new concepts seamlessly in spite of the different modality of delivery.

## Advantages

Proponents of blended learning argue that by incorporating the "asynchronous Internet communication technology" into courses serves to "facilitate a simultaneous independent and collaborative learning experience", and this incorporation is a major contributor to student satisfaction and success in such courses. The use of information and communication technologies has been found to improve access to as well as student attitudes towards learning. By incorporating information technology into class projects, communication between lecturers and part-time students was improved, and students were able to better evaluate their understanding of course material via the use of "computer-based qualitative and quantitative assessment modules" in a study by Alexander and McKenzie (1998).

## Disadvantages

Blended learning has a strong dependence on the technical resources with which the blended learning experience is delivered—these tools need to be reliable, easy to use, and up to date in order for the use of the Internet to have a meaningful impact on the learning experience. Additionally, IT literacy can serve as a significant barrier for students attempting to get access to the course materials, making the availability of high quality technical support paramount. It has been observed that the use of lecture recording technologies can result in students falling behind on the material—in a study performed across four different universities, it was found that only half of the students watched the lecture videos on a regular basis, and nearly 40% of students watched several weeks worth of videos in one sitting.

## Conclusion

Blended Learning is part of the ongoing convergence of two archetypal learning environments. On the one hand, we have the traditional face-to-face learning environment that has been around for centuries. On the other hand, we have distributed learning environments that have begun to grow and expand in exponential ways as new technologies have expanded the possibilities for distributed communication and interaction. In the past, these two learning environments have remained largely separate because they have used different media and method combinations and have addressed the needs of different audiences . For example, traditional face-to-face learning typically occurred in a teacher-directed environment with person-to-person interaction in a live synchronous, high-fidelity environment. On the other hand, distance learning systems emphasized self-paced learning and learning materials interactions that typically occurred in an asynchronous, low-fidelity (text only) environment.

## Reference

1. Waddoups, G., & Howell, S. (2002). Bringing online learning to campus: The hybridization of teaching and learning at Brigham Young University.
2. Thomson, I. (2002). *Thomson job impact study: The next generation of corporate learning.* Retrieved July 7, 2003, from http://www .netg.com/DemosAndDownloads/Downloads/ JobImpact.pdf.

# 31

# New Approache For Present and Future Generation

## Introduction

To achieve human goals one of the prerequisite is education. From various researches it is clear that the human welfare developments are associated with Information and Communication Technologies commonly known as ICT. A relevant education is more important today than ever, because today's Networked World demands a workforce that understands how to use technology as a tool to increase productivity and creativity. With the demand for the needs of infrastructure, software and platform the need for a technology is required by the institution.

The word "cloud" in cloud computing arises as the Internet is represented inside the cloud in networks. Computing in the Internet is called as "Cloud Computing". Cloud has hundreds and hundreds of servers and computers which are linked together by the Internet. To use cloud computing, you should have computer with the internet connection. As you have connected with the cloud, all you do is based on the web, rather than tied with a single computer processes. Wherever the persons are residing, as they are connected in cloud, they can use and share the files, whenever needed.

You might be surprised, if I tell most of you are processing in the cloud computing often, unknowingly. How??? Here is the answer. If you are using Google's Gmail or Microsoft's hotmail, then you are in the cloud. Hope you understood you are connected with the cloud.

## How to use the Cloud?

In the cloud, all the applications are available. For example, if you need to run Linux OS or Windows OS, you no need to install in your computer. Instead you need to connect into the cloud and can even use both the OS without installing in your computer.

For using cloud you should be the authorized member by registering. You need to pay only for the usage and no need to pay for owning the software or hardware. The cloud process is "Pay as you go". Some of the cloud services are even free to use. The user tries to enter into the cloud by logging in using some authentication process, which is normally username and password. The cloud verifies and allows entering into cloud if it matches correctly. Then the user selects for any applications or documents or services. The request is accepted and searches for the resources. The selected work is caught from the cloud data center and provided to the user. The user is charged from that moment for using alone. The user uses and can store their data in the cloud itself.

## Cloud Storage

The stored data in the cloud is present in the servers of third parties. If that third party moves out of the cloud or if that server gets crashed, then whole of your data will not be getting back. Oops! Then what will be your situation, if not getting back your long day works?

No problem when you are in the cloud. The cloud stores your data in multiple third party servers. That is, it makes duplicates of your data in more than one server. The data storage location will be varying from time-to-time, as the cloud data center servers need to utilize the memory at the maximum. Even it changes its location of your original data, your data's duplicate copy is also relocated somewhere in the cloud. Thus you can get your long day works from the cloud even if any third party moves out or crashed.

If two users sharing the files and modifying simultaneously, the modifications done by one user gets the updated or reflected to the other user onscreen.

## Types of Cloud

The cloud is of three types. They are:

1. Public Cloud – It can be used by anyone who is connected with the cloud,
2. Private Cloud–It is owned by the private organizations. The institutions or organizations that need their data to be more confidential and secure, can have private cloud. Here you need to invest to have a private cloud.
3. Hybrid Cloud–It has both types private and public cloud usage.

## Types of Cloud Services

The cloud is scalable. The cloud offers different types of services to give easier access according to your needs.

1. Software as a Service (SaaS): Based on the requirement of the user the application is given as a service.
2. Platform as a Service (PaaS): The environment for developing your application is given as service.
3. Infrastructure as a Service (IaaS): The user can get a whole infrastructure as a service. It will be useful for organizations.

## Advantages of the Cloud

Some of the advantages are listed below:

1. All the applications run in the cloud rather than on your computer, hence no need of high powered computers.
2. To own any software or hardware to run your data, you need to pay a huge sum of money. In the cloud, you need to pay only for the usage of the softwares and hardwares.
3. The cost for maintenance is reduced greatly.
4. You can have the latest versions instead of running back with the older versions.
5. You can work fast as the memory speed is tremendous.
6. You can store any size of data and it is also secured.
7. You can get universal access and can collaborate easily in the group for sharing documents, pictures, videos, projects.
8. You no need to install or get license or update.

## Collaborating in the Cloud

Collaboration can be done in the cloud for schedules, purchasing lists, to-do lists, budgets and contact lists, photos, creating broachers and flyers, presentations, projects, reports, selling the materials, purchasing the materials, financial statements.

## Cloud in Education

Now-a-days the cloud entered in most of the human activities. One of the vital entrances of the cloud is in the educational system. Every educational institution has different slogans but their aim is same, which is to provide education.

The traditional method of using chalks, markers and boards is getting out dated. Most of the schools and colleges are using projectors or even providing individual computer systems to the students. The teacher or the lecturer provides the soft copy of the material to the students that they have downloaded or prepared. Instead of hearing and imagining the process the students can get a clear view on seeing the materials. He or she can view it till they are inside the organization. But if the student moves out of the organization they can have a copy in their secondary storage devices like CD's, DVD's or pen drives or in their e-mails.

Imagine if your teacher or lecturer have prepared in the latest version and given to you. It cannot be opened with the older version. Then you need to get and install the latest version which consumes much of the time, energy and also your computer's memory which may slow down the speed of your system.

1. How can the resources reach the students easily?
2. How to make the resources accessible to all?
3. How to make the resources accessible at anytime?
4. How to make the resources accessible from anywhere?

The teacher or lecturer can store the materials in the cloud. Then what ever may be the version, size or operating system you can use it easily at anytime from anywhere.

Through cloud, the standard of the educational services getting improved. It makes easier to collaborate in the classrooms across the world. The students have a wide range of opportunities to improve their skills and shine in the digitized world. It zaps the barriers in education by which everyone can have an equal education. This educational service through cloud is with the softwares and it can be accessible at any-time and from any-where, provided the computer with internet.

## Benefits

### 1. To students

The students can view their assignments, assessments, home-works and reports even when they are outside the organization. They can do their works and submit in the cloud through e-mail. If the students have doubts while studying they can clarify with the teachers by connecting in the cloud.

Some of the applications that can be used by students:

1. **Prints Selection** – It prints only the content what you need with one click! Select what you want to print on the web page and click 'Print Selection' in context menu.
2. **Remind101** – a service that provides a safe way for teachers to text message or email students and parents.
3. **Sound Note** for iPod is great for classes and meetings — lets you take notes, record audio, and share both via email.
4. **Google calendar** – it is used to create shared calendars and personal calendars, through which the students can have their time tables for assignment, reports and other activities. It has 4 types: public, personal, friends and holiday calendars.

### 2. To parents

Parents can view their wards attendance, performances in the test and exams, fees details. They can also contact the teachers and head of the institution in live chat through cloud. Parents can save their time and travelling expenses.

Some of the applications that can be used by parents:

1. **Zoho Meeting** – it shares application and desktop files, can chat and also have Skype integration. Parents can contact the institution members to know about their wards in the school.
2. **Skyward** – it is the student administration system that we use to track student grades, attendance, and discipline. This information is available to parents/guardians via the web.
3. **School Stickers** - site enables pupils to log their sticker rewards, creating an online album of their achievements throughout their school career. It contacts a parent who had been invited by their own child to sign up to the rewards portal.

### 3. To teachers

The teachers can have their lesson plans, time tables and the study materials. They can also upgrade themselves by using latest versions and different softwares. They can prepare their materials comfortably as easily as the students can understand. They can also intimate the performances, mischief activities for the students to their parents.

Some of the applications that can be used by teachers:

1. **Too Noisy** — an application to control the noise levels in the classroom.
2. **Drop box** — help you keep track of notes and plans by synching with your computer or cloud.
3. **Class Dojo** — is a classroom tool designed to help teachers improve student behaviour. It allows you to save, analyze and print reports on the class.
4. **Edmodo** — increasingly popular with teachers who want to collaborate with their students outside of the classroom. Edmodo provides a secure network for teachers and their students to collaborate and share content.
5. **Ever note - it is** an effective way to lesson plan. It is a note taking app that allows you to create notes that include text, photos, video and audio.
6. **Teacher Kit** — an application that covers most teachers' classroom administration. It manages everything from attendance records and grades through to seating charts. Through Teacher kit, a teacher can keep track of all your students and can also reduce the paper-work.
7. **Prep Up Hindi** - provides comprehensive study material for Hindi Language for primary school students.

### 4. To head of the institution/owners

The head of the institution can have a clear schedule of the staffs. The overall idea about the events in the schools can be known from their place. Performance of the school can be looked up. They can also have details about the valuable materials in the school.

Some of the cloud applications for head of the educational institutions:

1. **High-rise** – it is used to store the contacts with basic details like name, e-mail, address. It can also have notes, file attachments, images, and links to video and audio files.
2. **People Matrix** – apart from contact management, you can send mass e-mails about events, job announcements and others.

## 5. To the institution

The institution gets relief from carrying huge size cupboards and lockers with bundles of papers to have the students and staffs record. The space can be utilized usefully in the institution. The cloud saves the institution from large amount expenses. The educational institutions have the opportunity to offer a good quality of education to the students at the low cost.

Some of the cloud applications for educational institutions:

1. **Google Apps Education Edition**
2. **MicrosoftLive@edu**
3. **Nias**—College administration software with modules for admissions, registration, grading, billing, degree audit, G/L, and A/P.
4. **Academia**—School/College software covering all functions - student record management, examination marks and back office management.
5. **Aesop**—School absence management software that serves over 3,000 school districts.
6. **Diamond D**—Automate financial aid, placement, accreditation reporting, lead tracking and academics.

## Conclusion

Using cloud, one can sit a place and wander around the world. But some are using it unknowingly, some are not known about the cloud. According to the analysis done by various researcher school and educational services uses the cloud by only 4%. According to another analysis only 12% of respondents are familiar with the use of cloud computing in education while 88% of them would agree that cloud computing should be implemented in the education sector. It is everyone's responsibility to educate about the usage of the cloud and its benefits to upgrade our country.

## References

1. "Cloud computing in education" - policy brief by UNESCO Institute for Information Technologies in Education
2. Mallikharjuna Rao, N., Sasidhar, C., Satyendra Kumar, V(2010), *Cloud Computing Through Mobile Larning, International Journal of Advanced Computer Science and Applications, Vol.1, No. 6, December 2010.*

3. Srinivasa rao V, Nageswara rao N K, E kusuma kumara (2009)"*Cloud computing: an overview" by in Journal of Theoretical and Applied Information Technology © 2005 – 2009 JATIT*
4. Sakshi Dhingra, Vinod Goyal, Vinay Malik (2014*)"Necessity of cloud computing in education system: A Study" by, in International Journal of Latest Trends in Engineering and Technology (IJLTET), Vol. 3 Issue 3 January 2014.*

# 32

# Designing Learning Environment For Tommorow

## Introduction

As Mark W. Boyer said, " The best help we can offer the youth of today is to prepare them for tomorrow", Research has shown that the appropriate use of ICTs can catalyst the paradigm shift in both content and pedagogy that is the heart of education reform.But today the classrooms are same with the students still in a classroom, doing the same things just with simple and affordable technology e.g. smart boards. Because technology is rapidly changing and affects student's lives in and out of the classroom, it is important that the integration of technology be carefully implemented at a reasonable pace. To encourage far higher levels of active student engagement, where knowledge is obtained by sharing, problem – solving and creating, rather than by passive listening to lectures we are going to design classrooms that enables both active engagement and equal access, the existing pedagogical practices can be transferred into computer supported learning environment bringing added value for both the teacher and the learner. Innovative learning environmental designs helps educators to use digital technology and methods to teach whole classes while personalizing each student's instruction. It is therefore wireless technology and portable laptop and tablet devices bring the internet not just too every student's dorm room, but also to every desk in the classroom. Professor Steve Higgins said, "Technology like this has enormous potential for teaching as it can help teacher and to manage to orchestrate the learning of individuals and groups of learners to ensure they are both challenged and supported so that they can learn effectively". It is true technology driven, practice oriented, and theory - based approaches, if used appropriately, the use of technology and new media has great potential for enhancing learning.

"Good educational use of technology has to help students make the transition from being consumers of knowledge to contributors and, eventually, producers," said Michael Marder, the executive director of the U Teach science program. Technology is swiftly assuming a dominant role in classrooms, and in student's lives. For the 'net generation', technology choices are an aspect of lifestyle and identity and it is the real innovation hub for the region and beyond. A key challenge for schools and educational institutions facing the digital and creative sector is to maximise its competitive advantage by not just keeping pace with technological and other innovations but leading them to satisfy their consumers' expectations.

## Building Innovation

We live in a fast-changing 'runaway world' where the social, economic, cultural and political foundations of society are being redefined on a continual basis (Giddens, 2000). Teaching in a way that communicates respect and understanding for all students and creating an environment in which all students feel valued and an integral part of the classroom community can be especially challenging when teaching large classes with diversified learners. As Moyle says "Now schools can be considered more as environments that consist of physical, online or simulated learning spaces or they can be environments that consist of any combination of these environments." It is true digital technologies are essential to our workplaces and social spaces, and to foster creativity, self directed and lifelong learning. Thus ICT and www have made learning more vibrant, interactive, collaborative, constructive and effective by providing variety of opportunities through internet.

## Generating Employability

Harvey (2004) suggests that employability is an ongoing developmental process that does not stop once the graduate is employed. It is much more than the acquisition of key skills or getting a job; it is about developing graduates as critical and empowered learners. Employability then is not just about having knowledge and being able to slot into a niche. It is the utmost duty of all educational institutions to provide application of information technology basic IT skills, including familiarity with word processing, spreadsheets, file management and use of internet search engines are the essential qualities that are required for immediate employment.

The ability to access information and the knowledge of basic computer literacy, use of internet search engines can function as a potential stepping stone out of poverty by qualifying them to get employability. Further they need to foster the following qualities for better adjustment.

1. Self-management – readiness to accept responsibility, flexibility, time management.
2. Readiness to improve own performance.
3. Team-working respecting others, co-operating, negotiating/ persuading, contributing to discussions.
4. Problem solving – analysing facts and circumstances and applying creative thinking to develop appropriate solutions.

If the above said minimum requirements are provided it is sure that even low-income students those who have no access to computers at home, by the integration of new technology into all aspects of school and college life ensures that they have greater opportunities going forward.

## Interactive Learning Environments

The following figure shows some of the interactive learning environment that could be provided for tomorrow.

## Flipped Classrooms

A flipped classroom is where students receive the key instructional elements at home. Then in the classroom, they apply the knowledge. Instruction can be provided through videos, podcasts, websites, DVDs, CDs, or any other form that provides a clear instructional message. In the classroom, students work together under the guidance of the teacher in applying the instruction to complex problems. (Wikipedia)

## Cloud Computing

Cloud computing in general can be portrayed as a synonym for distributed computing over a network, with the ability to run a program or application on many connected computers at the same time. It specifically refers to a computing hardware machine or group of computing hardware machines commonly referred as a server connected through a communication network such as the Internet, an intranet, a local area network (LAN) or wide area network (WAN) and individual users or user who have permission to access the server can use the server's processing power for their individual computing needs like to run an application, store data or any other computing need.

### Future Learning Environment (Fle3)

Future Learning Environment (Fle3) is software for computer supported collaborative learning (CSCL). Fle3 is a web based learning environment, which can be used with standard web-browsers. Fle3 is designed to support learner and group centered work that concentrates on creating and developing expressions of knowledge. This way Fle3 can be installed at a classroom, school, school district, and communal centre, at national or international level depending on what kind of learning, design or development projects it will be used for. (Teemu Leinonen and Helsinki Giedre Kligyte)

### Administration and Organizational Environment

The simultaneous enhanced interaction between the student and the teacher, on the one hand, and the physical environment, on the other, optimises new information flows (Lehtinen, 1997). The same concept is depicted as a flow chart which has been given below.

1. Provide in-class activities that focus on higher level cognitive activities. (Internet connected through cloud computing)
2. Provide an opportunity for students to gain first exposure prior to class (flipped classroom)
3. Provide a mechanism to assess student understanding (Evaluation)
4. Provide all teachers with appropriate training, to encourage teachers to make real use of digital technology in their lessons. (Training and competency development).

### Recommendation and Suggestions

1. To present the information via video lecture, content-rich websites and simulations and online text/readings, the classrooms should contain computer networking and have facilities for video conferencing.

2. Rooms may have wheelchair-friendly with wide, unobstructed passageways and low handles and switches.
3. The classroom of the future could resemble a television studio with monitors, cameras, and related equipments.
4. The television cameras could be directed at students and the teacher, or could focus on visual aids used in teacher presentations. This type of classroom would include bright overhead spotlights to enhance the quality of video transmission.
5. A setup that includes an audio room with music-mixing software and podcasting equipment for better animation with sound in digital effect.
6. Acoustics, Electrical Settings, Modular Designs for network proposed and comfortable, energy-efficient designs are recommended.
7. Coupled with projectors, microphones, and video cameras, the entire classroom experience is fully connected to the internet and portable laptop and tablet devices to every desk in the classroom.
8. The VGo, a computer-operated robot with a camera display with a Wi-Fi connection and a webcam could be recommended for future learning environment though it is costly. (Rackley and Viruru, 2013).

## Technology in Teaching

1. Lecture videos
2. Audio lectures
3. Websites related to content
4. Personalized projects
5. Creative presentations

All the above said activities are teacher made for the students, with the following objectives.

1. To *structure and organize a series of experiences* which positively influence each individual's potential and also tailored to individual's needs and requirements.
2. To engage in Virtual Learning Environment (VLE), access to Skype and social networks on arrival, upgraded software in labs, online assessment submission system and
3. To actively involved in identifying advantages, disadvantages, limitations, and potentials of interactive learning models and concentrating on online communication, collaboration, and visualization technology that play role in the behavioral, cognitive, constructivist, and social dimensions of learning.

These are some of the teacher's responsibility in designing learning environments for digital learners.

## Technology in Learning

1. Games
2. Simulations
3. Interactive sessions
4. Taking projects, Assignments
5. Taking online tests with online software like polleverywhere.com.

Attending lectures, recording and reflecting on their progress, receiving feedback and discussing with their peer group about the topic being covered through written blogs or verbal-based audio or video recordings are some of the student activities.

## Barriers to the Innovative Design

1. Reluctance to embrace change, being fixed to stereotypes.
2. Lack of funds to use the potential of the internet to provide online teaching and learning resources.
3. Learning how to use the technology as well as learning with the technology is a challenge for many students. (Bennet, 1999).
4. Persons learning style is affected by individual traits such as personality, cognitive styles, temperaments, sensory processes and age. (Kolb, 1984, Kiersey, 2000, Fleming, 2001, Honey, 2002).
5. Lack of time for flow in the teaching and learning schedule, would lead to monotonous environment.

## Conclusion

User-based innovative processes should be at the heart of designing the physical learning environment of tomorrow's classrooms. "It's about being literate for the modern world, it's about functioning fully as a professional, as an academic but also as a human being" as said by Senior Librarian, Oxford Brookes University. Wireless technology is likely the best answer to ensure a state of the art network infrastructure to promote innovation, and to create knowledge society where everyone will have the capacity to create access, evaluate, utilize, share and disseminate information and to pursue their interests and talents, improve their quality of life, and to achieve their full potential. Digital media, content and other technologies have the power to reshape social bonds and to foster a greater sense of community. Though new technologies and revised theories of teaching could make the best-laid plans obsolete, it should not make them intellectual lazy. And keeping parents informed and engaged by using permission forms for classroom activities should eliminate concerns about technology abuse (Kolb, Technology in School: A Better Perspective, 2011). Definitely technology is no substitute for an inspiring teacher. In a freedom learning situation where the personalized instruction dominates, it is the responsibility of both the teacher and the student for the powerful outcomes since freedom means responsibility.

## References

1. Future Learning Environment for Collaborative Knowledge Building and Design Paper submitted to the "Development by Design": 2nd International Conference on Open Collaborative Design of Sustainable Innovation. December 1-2, Bangalore, India. Teemu Leinonen UIAH Media Lab University of Art and Design Helsinki Giedre Kligyte UIAH Media Lab University of Art and Design Helsinki.
2. The eLearning Action Plan Designing tomorrow's education Brussels, 28.3.2001COM (2001)172 final.
3. Supporting Learners in a Digital Age Briefing paper September 2011 JISC
4. Giddens, A (2000). Runaway World: How Globalisation is shaping our Lives. London: Rout ledge.
5. Beyond the digital divide, Rethinking digital inclusion for the 21st century Neil Selwyn and Keri Facer Future lab 2007.
6. Harvey, L. (2004) on employability. York: Higher Education Academy. Available from: http://78.158.56.101/archive/palatine/files/emp/1236.pdf [accessed 26 April 2013].
7. Employability in Psychology: a guide for departments. Peter Reddy, Caprice Lantz and Julie Hulme.
8. How Jackie Craven.About.com .Architecture tomorrow's schools. How will architects design tomorrow's schools? By Jackie craven.
9. http://www.udlcenter.org/advocacy/state/report
10. en.wikipedia.org
11. User-*Generated Education, June, 2011) phet.colorado.edu.*
12. http://www.redorbit.com/news/technology//next-generation-school-desk.
13. Andreas Schratzenstaller, Department of Psychology, University of Munich
14. The benefit and danger of Education Technology, by Jesse Langley, October 8,2011

15. Bennet Frederick PhD., (1999). Computers as Tutors, USA
16. Fleming, Neil, (2001) "VARK"-Multimodal Study Strategies.
17. Peter Honey.Com, "The Learning Series" (2002).
18. Kirby, Patricia (ed), (1979) Cognitive Style, Learning Style and Transfer Skill Acquisition. USA: The National centre for Research in Vocational Education. The Ohio State University.
19. Kolb, David A., (1984) Experiential Learning. New Jersey, USA: Prentice Hall.

# 33

# Flipped Classroom

## Introduction

The traditional pattern of teaching has been to assign students to read textbooks and work on problem sets outside school, while listening to lectures and taking tests in class. In flip teaching, the students first study the topic by themselves, typically using video lessons prepared by the teacher or third parties. In class students apply the knowledge by solving problems and doing practical work. The teacher tutors the students when they become stuck, rather than imparting the initial lesson in person. Complementary techniques include differentiated instruction and project-based learning. Teachers are blending the advantages of flipped learning with traditional in-class lecturing through tools like eduCanon that keep students accountable to video lessons at home through time-embedded formative assessments. Flipped classrooms free class time for hands-on work. Students learn by doing and asking questions. Students can also help each other, a process that benefits both the advanced and less advanced learners. Flipping also changes the allocation of teacher time. Traditionally, the teacher engages with the students who ask questions — but those who don't ask tend to need the most attention. "We refer to 'silent failers,' " said one teacher, claiming that flipping allows her to target those who need the most help rather than the most confident. Flipping changes teachers from "sage on the stage" to "guide on the side", allowing them to work with individuals or groups of students throughout the session.

"Flipping the classroom" has become something of a buzzword in the last several years, driven in part by high profile publications in *The New York Times* (Fitzpatrick, 2012); *The Chronicle of Higher Education* (Berrett, 2012); and *Science* (Mazur, 2009); In essence, "flipping the classroom" means that students gain first exposure to new material outside of class, usually via reading or lecture videos, and then use class time to do the harder work of assimilating that knowledge, perhaps through problem-solving, discussion, or debates.

In terms of Bloom's revised taxonomy (2001), this means that students are doing the lower levels of cognitive work (gaining knowledge and comprehension) outside of class, and focusing on the higher forms of cognitive work (application, analysis, synthesis, and/or evaluation) in class, where they have the support of their peers and instructor. This model contrasts from the traditional model in which "first exposure" occurs via lecture in class, with students assimilating knowledge through homework; thus the term "flipped classroom."

***flipped classroom*** *or* ***Flip teaching*** *is a form of blended learning in which students learn new content online by watching video lectures, usually at home, and what used to be homework (assigned problems) is now done in class with teachers offering more personalized guidance and interaction with students, instead of lecturing.*

## What is Flipped Class room?

The flipped classroom describes a reversal of traditional teaching where students gain first exposure to new material outside of class, usually via reading or lecture videos, and then class time is used to do the harder work of assimilating that knowledge through strategies such as problem-solving, discussion or debates.

The purpose of flipping the classroom is to shift from passive to active learning to focus on the higher order thinking skills such as analysis, synthesis and evaluation (Bloom). As Flipping the Classroom: Simply Speaking students access key content individually (or in small groups) prior to class time and then meet face-to-face in the larger group to explore content through active learning and engagement strategies.

## How does Flipped Classroom work?

There is no single model for the flipped classroom—the term is widely used to describe almost any class structure that provides prerecorded lectures followed by in-class exercises. In one common model, students might view multiple lectures of five to seven minutes each. Online quizzes or activities can be interspersed to test what students have learned. Immediate quiz feedback and the ability to rerun lecture segments may help clarify points of confusion. Instructors might lead in-class discussions or turn the classroom into a studio where students create, collaborate, and put into practice what they learned from the lectures they view outside class. As on-site experts, instructors suggest various approaches, clarify content, and monitor progress. They might organize students into an ad hoc workgroup to solve a problem that several are struggling to understand. Because this approach represents a comprehensive change in the class dynamic, some instructors have chosen to implement only a few elements of the flipped model or to flip only a few selected class sessions during a term.

## Who's doing it?

A growing number of higher education individual faculties have begun using the flipped model in their courses. At Algonquin College, a video production class has been using this model to explain the workings of editing software, a procedure that is notoriously difficult to explain in a standard lecture. Short tutorial video lectures let students move at their own pace, rewind to review portions, and skip through sections they already understand meaning. Students come to class able to use the software and prepared to do creative projects with their peers. A particularly successful example of a blended and flipped class in accounting at Penn State accommodates 1,300 students. In-class time is used for open discussion, a featured guest speaker, or hands-on problem solving where instructor support is supplemented by student assistants. At Harvard University, one physics professor not only employs the flipped model but has also developed a correlative site, Learning Catalytic that provides instructors with free interactive software enabling students to discuss, apply, and get feedback from what they hear in lecture

## Where is it going?

As the flipped class becomes more popular, new tools may emerge to support the out-of-class portion of the curriculum. In particular, the ongoing development of powerful mobile devices will put a wider range of rich, educational resources into the hands of students, at times and places that are most convenient for them. Greater numbers of courses will likely employ elements of the flipped classroom, supplementing traditional out-of-class work with video presentations and supporting project-based and lab-style efforts during regular class times. At a certain level of adoption, colleges and universities may need to take a hard look at class spaces to ensure they support the kinds of active and collaborative work common in flipped classes.

## Steps followed in flipped Classroom

### Beginning of Class

(i) Instructor prepares lecture.
(ii) Students have limited information about what to expect.
(iii) Instructor makes general assumption about what is helpful.

### During Class

(i) Students try to follow along.
(ii) Instructor tries to get through all the material.

### After Class

(i) Students attempt the homework, usually with delayed feedback.
(ii) Instructor grades past work.

### Office Hours

(i) Students want confirmation about what to study.
(ii) Instructor often repeats what was in lecture.

## What are the key elements of the flipped classroom?

### 1. Provide an opportunity for students to gain first exposure prior to class.

The mechanism used for first exposure can vary, from simple textbook readings to lecture videos to podcasts or screen casts. These videos can be created by the instructor or found online from YouTube, or other similar sources.

### 2. Provide an incentive for students to prepare for class.

The assignment can vary; that ranged from online quizzes to worksheets to short writing assignments, but in each case the task provided an incentive for students to come to class prepared by speaking the common language of undergraduates: points. In many cases, grading for completion rather than effort can be sufficient, particularly if class activities will provide students with the kind of feedback that grading for accuracy usually provides.

**3. Provide a mechanism to assess student understanding.**

The pre-class assignments that students complete as evidence of their preparation can also help both the instructor and the student assess understanding. Pre-class worksheets can also help focus student attention on areas with which they're struggling, while pre-class writing assignments help students clarify their thinking about a subject, thereby producing richer in-class discussions. Importantly, much of the feedback students need is provided in class, reducing the need for instructors to provide extensive commentary outside of class (Walvoord and Anderson, 1998). In addition, many of the activities used during class time (e.g., clicker questions or debates) can serve as informal checks of student understanding

**4. Provide in-class activities that focus on higher level cognitive activities.**

If the students gained basic knowledge outside of class, then they need to spend class time to promote deeper learning. Again, the activity will depend on the learning goals of the class and the culture of the discipline. Students may spend time in class engaged in debates, data analysis, or synthesis activities. The key is that students are using class time to deepen their understanding and increase their skills at using their new knowledge.

## Why is it significant?

In a traditional lecture, students often try to capture what is being said at the instant the speaker says it. They cannot stop to reflect upon what is being said, and they may miss significant points because they are trying to transcribe the instructor's words. By contrast, the use of video and other prerecorded media puts lectures under the control of the students: they can watch, rewind, and fast-forward as needed. This ability may be of particular value to students with accessibility concerns, especially where captions are provided for those with hearing impairments. Lectures that can be viewed more than once may also help those for whom English is not their first language. Devoting class time to application of concepts might give instructors a better opportunity to detect errors in thinking, particularly those that are widespread in a class. At the same time, collaborative projects can encourage social interaction among students, making it easier for them to learn from one another and for those of varying skill levels to support their peers.

## Conclusion

With the teacher at the front and seats in rows, the classroom has barely changed in the last century. But we now know that there's no "one size fits all" approach to learning – and the flipped classroom model brings together advances in education and technology to provide a personalized, engaging learning experience for every student – whatever their learning style, pace, or ability.

# 34

# Blended Learning

## Introduction

Blended learning is a formal education program in which a student learns at least in part through online delivery of content and instruction with some element of student control over time, place, path or pace. While still attending a "brick-and-mortar" school structure, face-to-face classroom methods are combined with activities. Defining Hybrid or Blended Education is a trickery task than one might think options vary wildly on the matter. The sloab consortium defined hybrid courses as those that "Integrated online witch traditional face to face class activities in a planned pedagogically valuable manner"

## History of the term

The concept of blended learning has been around for a long time, but its terminology was not firmly established until around the beginning of the 21st century. The meaning of blended learning widely diverged to encompass a wide variety of synthesis in learning methods until 2006, when the first *Handbook of Blended Learning* by Bonk and Graham was published. In this publication Graham challenged the breadth and ambiguity of the term's definition, and defined 'blended learning systems' as learning systems that "combine face-to-face instruction with computer mediated instruction." Currently, use of the term *blended learning* mostly involves "combining Internet and digital media with established classroom forms that require the physical co-presence of teacher and students."

### Advantages

Proponents of blended learning argue that by incorporating the "asynchronous Internet communication technology" into courses serves to "facilitate a simultaneous independent and collaborative learning experience", and this incorporation is a major contributor to student satisfaction and success in such courses. The use of information and communication technologies has been found to improve access to as well as student attitudes towards learning. By incorporating information technology into class projects, communication between lecturers and part-time students was improved, and students were able to better evaluate their understanding of course material via the use of "computer-based qualitative and quantitative assessment modules".

### Disadvantages

Blended learning has a strong dependence on the technical resources with which the blended learning experience is delivered these tools need to be reliable, easy to use, and up to date in order for the use of the Internet to have a meaningful impact on the learning experience. Additionally, IT literacy can serve as a significant barrier for students attempting to get access to the course materials, making the availability of high quality technical support paramount.

It has been observed that the use of lecture recording technologies can result in students falling behind on the material in a study performed across four different universities, it was found that only half of the students watched the lecture videos on a regular basis, and nearly 40% of students watched several weeks worth of videos in one sitting.

### Community

The Blackboard learning management system helped develop a better feel for an online community where discussions can be held to better aid students. This Virtual Learning Environment helps connect professors with students without physically being present, thus making this a 'Virtual Cafe'. Many schools use this online tool for online classes, class work, question & answer forums, and other school related work. Blended learning yielded positive results from the online community.

## Learning Materials About Blended Learning

1. Hybrid Course
2. M-learning
3. E-learning
4. Flip teaching
5. Media psychology
6. Networked learning
7. Virtual education
8. Virtual University

## M-learning

M-Learning or mobile learning offers modern ways to support learning process through mobile devices, such as handheld and tablet computers MP3players, smart phones and mobile phones.

It presence unique attributes compared to conventional e-learning personal portable, collaborative, interactive, contextual and situated. It emphasizes "just -in-time-learning" as instruction can be delivered anywhere and at anytime through it. Moreover, it is an aid to formal and informal learning and thus holds enormous potential to transform the delivery or education and training.

## E-learning

E-learning (or eLearning) is the use of electronic media and information and communication technologies (ICT) in education. E-learning is broadly inclusive of all forms of educational technology in learning and teaching. E-learning is inclusive of, and is broadly synonymous with multimedia learning, technology-enhanced learning (TEL), computer-based instruction (CBI), computer managed instruction,[1] computer-based training (CBT), computer-assisted instruction or computer-aided instruction (CAI), internet-based training (IBT), web-based training (WBT), online education, virtual education, virtual learning environments (VLE) (which are also called learning platforms), m-learning, and digital educational collaboration. These alternative names emphasize a particular aspect, component or delivery method.

E-learning includes numerous types of media that deliver text, audio, images, animation, and streaming video, and includes technology applications and processes such as audio or video tape, satellite TV, CD-ROM, and computer-based learning, as well as local intranet/extranet and web-based learning. Information and communication systems, whether free-standing or based on either local networks or the Internet in networked learning, underly many e-learning processes.

E-learning can occur in or out of the classroom. It can be self-paced, asynchronous learning or may be instructor-led, synchronous learning. E-learning is suited to distance learning and flexible learning, but it can also be used in conjunction with face-to-face teaching, in which case the term blended learning is commonly used.

## Flip Teaching

Flip teaching or a flipped classroom is a form of blended learning in which students learn new content online by watching video lectures, usually at home, and what used to be homework (assigned problems) is now done in class with teachers offering more personalized guidance and interaction with students, instead of lecturing. This is also known as backwards classroom, flipped classroom, reverse teaching, and the Thayer Method." Flipped classrooms free class time for hands-on work. Students learn by doing and asking questions. Students can also help each other, a process that benefits both the advanced and less advanced learners.

## Networked Learning

Networked learning is a process of developing and maintaining connections with people and information, and communicating in such a way so as to support one another's learning. The central term in this definition is connections. It takes a relational stance in which learning takes place both in relation to others and in relation to learning resources.

It has been suggested that networked learning offers educational institutions more functional efficiency, in that the curriculum can be more tightly managed centrally, or in the case of vocational learning, it can reduce costs to employers and tax payers. However, it is also argued that networked learning is too often considered within the presumption of institutionalized or educationalised learning, thereby omitting awareness of the benefits that networked learning has to informal or situated learning.

## Virtual Education

Virtual education refers to a variety of teaching formats that don't involve students and instructors collaborating in person, at least not in the same room. While some of these forms of education do involve real-time meetings, the teacher and student usually are in different locations and connected via computer to each other. Moreover, not all forms of virtual education feature real time connections. Sometimes material is prepared in advance and any discussion occurs with time delays, such as discussion over email. These varied forms of virtual learning continue to increase in popularity and provide alternatives to the face-to-face learning environment of the traditional classroom.

## Conclusion

Whatever one choose to call it, Blended method of learning which combines classroom and online education is going places and making headlines along the way while education experts continue to debate the efficacy of hybrid learning. Its very existence has challenged them to re-evaluate not just the technologies place in and out of the classroom, but also how to reach and teach students more effectively.

# 35

# Flipped Classroom

## Introduction

Learning is one of the most valuable of all human activities while time is the fundamental key to all learning activities. Increasing the amount of time available for learning and making it more productive are keys to improved learning. Both learning and time is central to the teacher's responsibility to manage. Yet, American students have less learning time allocated to them than do students in other industrial countries. The idea of time and learning describes scheduled time as the umbrella component from which the allotted instructional time and learning time are achieved. Scheduled time, therefore, must be maximized so that, ultimately, high amounts of instructional and learning time can be obtained. "flipping the classroom" means that students gain first exposure to new material outside of class, usually via reading or lecture videos, and then use class time to do the harder work of assimilating that knowledge, perhaps through problem-solving, discussion, or debates. The flipped classroom approach has been used for years in some disciplines, notably within the humanities.

*The Flipped* Classroom *Info graphic* a new method of teaching is turning the traditional classroom on its head. Share your thoughts in the comments below and subscribe to our monthly newsletter to find out when we release our next info graphic. The flipped classroom is a pedagogical model in which the typical lecture and homework elements of a course are reversed. Short video lectures are viewed by students at home before the class session, while in-class time is devoted to exercises, projects, or discussions. The video lecture is often seen as the key ingredient in the flipped approach, such lectures being either created by the instructor and posted online or selected from an online repository. While a prerecorded lecture could certainly be a podcast or other audio format, the ease with which video can be accessed and viewed today has made it so ubiquitous that the flipped model has come to be identified with it. The notion of a flipped classroom draws on such concepts as active learning, student engagement, hybrid course design, and course podcasting

## Defining Flipped Learning

In the Flipped Learning model, teachers shift direct learning out of the large group learning space and move it into the individual learning space, with the help of one of several technologies. Teachers record and narrate screen casts of work they do on their computer desktops, create videos of themselves teaching, or curate video lessons from internet sites.

Many educators start flipping their classroom by using these readily available materials. The videos or screen casts are available for students to access whenever and wherever it is convenient—at home, during study hall, on the bus, even in the hospital—as many times as they like, enabling them to come to class better prepared (Musallam, 2011). Teachers also can use class time to check on each student's understanding and, if necessary, help them develop procedural fluency. Teachers can provide individualized support as students work through the activities designed to help them master the material, meeting them at their readiness level.

## Traditional Class Room

A teacher stands at the front of the classroom, delivering a lecture on the Civil War and writing on a white board. Students are hunched over desks arranged in rows, quietly taking notes. At the end of the hour, they copy down the night's homework assignment, which consists of reading pages from a thick textbook and answering the questions at the end of the chapter. This dramatic, defining period in our nation's history, which left questions unanswered that are as relevant today as they were then, has been reduced to a dry, if familiar, exercise. The teacher is acutely aware that many students do not understand the day's lesson but does not have the time to meet with them individually during the 50-minute class period.

The next day, the teacher will collect and briefly review the homework assignment. If students have additional questions there won't be much time to linger. The class cannot fall behind schedule. There is a lot of material to cover before the test at the end of the unit.

## The Important Key Elements of the Flipped Classroom

1. Provide an opportunity for students to gain first exposure prior to class.
2. Provide an incentive for students to prepare for class.
3. Provide a mechanism to assess student understanding.
4. Provide in-class activities that focus on higher level cognitive activities.

The flipped classroom—the term is widely used to describe almost any class structure that provides prerecorded lectures followed by in-class exercises... Instructors might lead in-class discussions or turn the classroom into a studio where students create, collaborate, and put into practice what they learned from the lectures they view outside class. As on-site experts, instructors suggest various approaches, clarify content, and monitor progress. They might organize students into an ad hoc workgroup to solve a problem that several are struggling to understand. Because this approach represents a comprehensive change in the class dynamic, some instructors have chosen to implement only a few elements of the flipped model or to flip only a few selected class sessions during a term.

## The Flipped Classroom Concept

The flipped classroom concept upon first inspection seems to be another in a series of clever ploys for teachers who don't want to (or can't) really work hard to shift much of the task of educating onto their students. For what many teachers get paid, especially in the public sector, they could work quite a bit harder for the level of salaries they are earning.

## Traditional vs. flipped teaching

The traditional pattern of teaching has been to assign students to read textbooks and work on problem sets outside school, while listening to lectures and taking tests in class. "My teacher explaining what motivated her to adopt flipped teaching. In flip teaching, the students first study the topic by themselves, typically using video lessons prepared by the teacher or third parties. In class students apply the knowledge by solving problems and doing practical work. The teacher tutors the students when they become stuck, rather than imparting the initial lesson in person. Complementary techniques include] differentiate instruction project based learning. Flipped classrooms free class time for hands-on work. Students learn by doing and asking questions. Students can also help each other, a process that benefits both the advanced and less advanced learners.

Flipping also changes the allocation of teacher time. Traditionally, the teacher engages with the students who ask questions — but those who don't ask tend to need the most attention. "We refer to 'silent failures,' " said one teacher, claiming that flipping allows her to target those who need the most help rather than the most confident. Flipping changes teachers from "sage on the stage" to "guide on the side", allowing them to work with individuals or groups of students throughout the session. This is also known as backwards classroom, flipped classroom, reverse teaching, and the Thayer Method.

Teachers found that shorter videos (3–6 minutes) were the most effective. The school uses audio files, readings and videos from the Khan Academy, and other sources. Students favored the changes. Students unable to watch the videos at home watch the videos in school.

1. In-class programs
2. Local field trips
3. grant opportunities
4. Professional development workshops
5. Local science exhibits

## Flipped Mastery

Traditionally, each topic in class receives a fixed amount of time for all students. Students who do not master the material get no extra time. Mastery learning was briefly popular in the 1920s, and was revived by Benjamin Bloom in 1968. Students who initially turn in shoddy work must correct it before moving on. Before flipping, mastery learning was impractical in most schools worn each exercise or project when they have mastered the precursors. Advocates claim that its efficiency allows most students to do a year's work in much less time. Advanced students work on independent projects while slower learners get more personalized instruction. Some students might not get through the year's material, but demonstrated competence on the parts they did complete.

## Flipped Learning Requires Flexible Environments

Flipped classrooms allow for a variety of learning modes; educators often physically rearrange their learning space to accommodate the lesson or unit, which might involve group work, independent study, research, performance, and evaluation. Flipped educators accept that the in-class time will be somewhat chaotic and noisy, as compared with the quiet typical of a well-behaved class during a lecture. Furthermore, educators who flip their classes are flexible in their expectations of student timelines for learning and how students are assessed. Educators build appropriate assessments systems that objectively measure understanding in a way that is meaningful for students and the teacher.

## Four Pillars of Flipped Learning

The four Pillars of F-L-I-P are:

1. Flexible Environment
2. Learning Culture,
3. Intentional Content, a
4. Professional Educator

Just as no two traditional classrooms are identical, such is the case with flipped classrooms. Because Flipped Learning focuses on meeting individual student learning needs as opposed to a set methodology with a clear set of rules, a cadre of experienced educators from the Flipped Learning Network, along with Pearson's School Achievement Services identified the key features, or pillars, of flipped classrooms that allow Flipped Learning to occur.

## Flipped Learning Requires Flexible Environments

Flipped classrooms allow for a variety of learning modes; educators often physically rearrange their learning space to accommodate the lesson or unit, which might involve group work, independent study, research, performance, and evaluation. Furthermore, educators who flip their classes are flexible in their expectations of student timelines for learning and how students are assessed. Educators build appropriate assessments systems that objectively measure understanding in a way that is meaningful for students and the teacher.

## Learning Culture

In the traditional teacher-centered model, the teacher is the main source of information; the teacher is the "sage on the stage" i.e. the sole content expert who provides information to students, generally via direct instruction lecture. Flipped educators help students explore topics in greater depth using student-centered pedagogies aimed at their readiness level or zone of proximal development, where they are challenged but not so much so that key are demoralized .

## Seven Tools for the Flipped Classroom

"Flipping the classroom" has become something of a buzzword in the last several years, driven in part by high profile publications in The New York Times, The Chronicle of Higher Education and Science.

## Bloom's Taxonomy (Revised)

In terms of Bloom's revised taxonomy (2001), this means that students are doing the lower levels of cognitive work (gaining knowledge and comprehension) outside of class, and focusing on the higher forms of cognitive work (application, analysis, synthesis, and/or evaluation) in class, where they have the support of their peers and instructor. This model contrasts from the traditional model in which "first exposure" occurs via lecture in class, with students assimilating knowledge through homework; thus the term "flipped classroom."

"The Flipped Classroom: Pro and Con" — one of the most concise and balanced views I've read on the buzz-wordy concept of flipping the classroom. Advocates say that "flipped classrooms" help overburdened teachers differentiate their instruction to reach more learners, provide an avenue into more hands-on and student-driven learning during class time, and shift the teacher's role from "sage on the stage" to learning coach and facilitator

A flipped class is one that inverts the typical cycle of content acquisition and application so that

1. Students gain necessary knowledge before class, and
2. Instructors guide students to actively and interactively clarify and apply that
3. Knowledge during class.

There are many benefits of screen recording on computer teaching and training from Wonder Share they are listed as follows:

## 1. Fully reflect the subjectivity of students, and drive the entire class to complete the task and explore more

With the video tutorials recorded from screen, it

### 2. Breaks restriction of time and space in learning

Usually, students listen to the teacher in the class, and then go to practice. If they don't focus their minds, some operations or main points may be unable to grasp. And it is not practical for teachers do repeat the course.

### 3. All levels of students are taken in consideration

There are some differences of learning progress among Students. It is more conducive for different levels of students if there are detailed video tutorials. Students who master fast and do some deep exploring while students who master slowly can spend more time and opportunity to consolidate their learning.

### 4. A big help for teachers

There will be more time for teachers to manage and guide students in computer course learning. And there will be more time for Students to collaborate with peers, and more opportunities for exchanges opinions with their teachers.

### 5. Screen recording documents can be done by both extra-curricular and in class

The screen recording documents need to be prepared before such computer courses. If necessary, teachers can install the screen recording software to help students deal with some unexpected problems in class. On-site recording and distributing is a necessary complement for pre-class preparation improvement.

### Inverted Classroom

To help ensure student preparation for class, students were expected to complete worksheets that were periodically but randomly collected and graded. Class time was then spent on activities that encouraged students to process and apply economics principles, ranging from mini-lectures in response to student questions to economic experiments to small group discussions of application problems. Both student and instructor response to the approach was positive, with instructors noting that students appeared more motivated than when the course was taught in a traditional format.

### Peer Instruction

The Peer Instruction (PI) model requires that students gain first exposure prior to class, and uses assignments to help ensure that students come to class prepared. Class time is structured around alternating mini-lectures and conceptual questions. Importantly, the conceptual questions are not posed informally and answered by student volunteers as in traditional lectures; instead, all students must answer the conceptual question, often via "clickers", or handheld personal response systems, that allow students to answer anonymously and that allow the instructor to see (and display) the class data immediately.

## Personal Learning Environments in the Flipped Classroom

The flipped classroom has its roots in creating personal learning environments for students. In these classrooms technology tools and points of information referencing become a viable foundation in supporting student learning. The PLE (Personal Learning Environment) distinguishes the role of the individual as a self motivated learner who is capable in organizing his or her own learning through facilitation and instructional guidance. The creation of a PLE is based on the idea that learning can and will take place in co-collaborative learning environments and will not be provided by a single "one shoe fits all" learning provider.

## How to Flip a Classroom

"Flipping" a classroom refers a new approach to teaching in which the students are allowed to participate in a mobile learning environment. To create a flipped classroom the teacher will need to create a plethora of videos, podcasts or podcasts that substitute for classroom lectures. These mobile learning media rich lessons are posted to a blog, or wiki, allowing students to have on demand access to learning and the review of learning at all times. These resources of podcast, podcast, or video streams from the internet are the skill sets represented within the standards.

## How to Construct Screen Captures

Usually this is a digital image taken by the host operating system or software running on the computer device, but it can also be a capture made by a camera or a device intercepting the video output of the computer. Screenshots, screen dumps, or screen captures can be used to demonstrate a program, a particular problem a user might be having or generally when computer output needs to be shown to others or archived, or to simply show off what you do on your computer to others."

The video tutorials can be made readily available and accessed on demand by learners who require additional support with using a Web 2.0

technology. Screen cast tutorials may include simple tasks such as Find an Unknown in a Proportion, to more complex task of using CPI Index in economics problem. Instructional recorded tutorials that demonstrate how to use an application can be created by the teacher in about the same time it takes to teach the skill.

## Conclusion

Flip teaching or a flipped classroom is a form of blended learning in which students learn new content online by watching video lectures, usually at home, and what used to be homework is now done in class with teachers offering more personalized guidance and interaction with students, instead of lecturing. This is also known as backwards classroom; Educators have been working to break this lecture-centered instructional model by shifting the focus from the curriculum pacing guide to student learning needs as the driver of instruction. They are, increasingly, turning to an alternative model of instruction called Flipped Learning in which digital technologies are used to Shift direct instruction outside of the group learning space to the individual learning space, usually via videos. Time becomes available for students to collaborate with peers on projects, engage more deeply with content, practice skills, and receive feedback on their progress. Teachers can devote more time to coaching their students, helping them develop procedural fluency if needed, and inspiring and assisting them with challenging projects that give them greater control over their own learning.

## References

1. Hallberg, Sara (2010). "An Alternate Approach in the Application of the Thayer Concept of Teaching ".
2. Tina Barseghian (February 5, 2011), Three Trends That Define the Future of Teaching and Learning, KQED.
3. The flip: Turning a classroom upside down, Washington Post, 4. June, 2012.

# 36

# Learning Through Mobile in Future

## Introduction

There is a global technology revolution where there is a shift from desktop to the use of mobile technology in society. Mobile technology is changing the way people work, learn, conduct business, interact with each other, and access information. With mobile web usage expected to double within five years and overtaking the PC access to the Web, we are in the mobile generation. This trend is supported by recent statistics. At the end of 2010, there were an estimated 5.3 billion mobile cellular subscriptions worldwide (ITU, 2010). According to the 2011 Horizon report, by 2015, 80 percent of people will be accessing the Internet using mobile devices. The use of mobile learning has been increasing over the last few years with a rapid increase in developing countries which have the fastest growth rate in the acquisition of mobile technology. At the same time, there are also many international initiatives on mobile learning.

The International Association of Mobile was formed recently to bring together mobile learning experts from around the world to share expertise and work collaboratively on mobile learning projects. Mobile technologies have been used broadly across sectors to provide goods and services to consumers. For example, libraries are being digitized and information formatted for access by mobile technology – "a library in everyone's pocket"

(Ally & Needham, 2010). In the financial sector, customers now have the access to bank services using mobile technology - "in the pocket banking" (The Economist, 2007). The travel industry is using mobile technology to make travel convenient for customers and governments are moving to mobile government (Ally, 2006). The healthcare system is also making significant use of mobile technology to provide services to patients (Kenny et al., 2009; Taylor et al., 2010). Individuals are using mobile technology for entertainment – "entertainment in the pocket" and to shop – "in the pocket shopping".

## Learning

Learning is the act of acquiring new, or modifying and reinforcing, existing knowledge, behaviors, skills, values, or preferences and may involve synthesizing different types of information. The ability to learn is possessed by humans, animals and some machines. Progress over time tends to follow learning curves. Learning is not compulsory; it is contextual. It does not happen all at once, but builds upon and is shaped by what we already know. To that end, learning may be viewed as a process, rather than a collection of factual and procedural knowledge. Learning produces changes in the organism and the changes produced are relatively permanent.

## Defining the Term Mobile Learning

The ADL Mobile Learning Team believes that a fixed definition of "mobile learning" could limit our strategy and objectives. Many of the existing definitions of mobile learning are usually too learner-focused or too device-focused. A universally accepted definition seems improbable. Therefore, ADL believes that both the learner and the device should be considered to provide a more flexible view of mobile learning for the next generation learner and next generation learning environment. ADL describes mobile learning as:

This description is intentionally generalized to allow for a growing number of mobile learning scenarios as well as future capabilities of new technology and device types. Mobile learning should be viewed as a way to augment the learner through the use of ubiquitous technology that provides access to learning content and information, anytime and anywhere. Unlike other learning technologies, mobile learning is unique in that it can accommodate both formal and informal learning in collaborative or individual learning modes.

## The Reason For Mobile Learning

The interest in mobile learning has come from a number of places:

A. Advances in technology and high levels of mobile phone penetration have made mobile devices the ideal targets for mobile learning applications

B. As well as these advances in technology reshaping learning, the characteristics and behaviours of Generation Yi, and the environment they have grown up in mean that Generation Y are driving changes in learning design for all generations

C. It is as important to have behavioural change as well as technological change: social norms are rapidly evolving and for most people the benefits of the mobile phone now outweigh its disadvantages – educators need to tap into the new behaviours and technologies rather than trying to change or resist them

D. Mobile learning offers many benefits for learning

1. 'Just enough' learning
2. Highly applied, easily digestible learning for increasingly busy executives
3. 'Just-in-time' learning
4. Convenient, ûexible and relevant learning at the exact moment learning is required
5. 'Just-for-me' learning
6. Learner-driven learning in a suitable format
7. Technology
8. Mobile learning can be cost effective and using a learner's own mobile device eliminates
9. Technological barriers to accessing learning.

### *Why is Mobile Learning Important for Executive Education?*

"Whether we like it or not, whether we are ready for it or not, mobile learning represents the next step in a long tradition of technology-mediated learning. It will feature new strategies, practices, tools, applications, and resources to realize the promise of ubiquitous, pervasive, personal, and connected learning. It responds to the on-demand learning interests of connected citizens in an information-centric world. It also connects formal educational experience....with informal, situated learning experience".

Although executive education has evolved considerably over the last 50 years, the industry is now faced with a series of signiûcant trends that offer the potential to create dramatic new opportunities for effective learning. The powerful mobile technologies are now a normal part of everyday life and while executive education providers do not use them as tools for learning their potential cannot be exploited. In addition to the beneûts described previously, there are also a number of further reasons for embracing mobile learning in executive education.

### *Mobile technologies are already in the classroom*

Participants coming to business schools have their own mobile devices and will increasingly expect to use mobile devices as part of their studies. The mobile learner wants to undertake learning activities that could not be done before, as well as wanting to be able to access materials and connect with others in more convenient ways that are in tune with evolving practices at work and in their lives more generally. There is a need to provide more ûexible opportunities for study that build in some choice in how participants will use technology.

### *Participants have increased use and expectations*

As described, ownership of personal technologies is now pervasive and mobile technologies are becoming more embedded, ubiquitous and networked. Learners are increasingly depending on technology to help them fit learning into their complex, demanding lives. This is driven both by Generation Y as well as developments in technology that provide shortcuts in people's lives.

### *Employers and organizations are already making use of mobile learning*

Mobile learning can be an excellent way to support work based learning and professional updating. An increasing number of employers and organizations recognise this and now make use of mobile communications and mobile delivery for continuous development and training.

### *The importance of mobility*

Mobile learning can be suitable for all ages and stages of education although the mobility issue is more important for those in executive education (not bound by the classroom as much as school students and university learners). Mobile technologies have provided the means and the methods for demonstrating that learning no longer needs to be classroom bounded and so learning is moving more into the learners' environment.

### *Increasing participation and engagement*

Communication by sending brief messages, web links or photos is an effective way of increasing participation and engagement in situations where they might otherwise be reluctant to contribute. Mobile devices also offer a way of keeping in touch with participants, or for participants to maintain contact, interact or collaborate with one another.

### *Supporting pre- and post-programme learning*

Mobile devices can support pre- and post-programme learning; for example, pre-programme podcasts can be used to support classroom delivery and maximize face-to-face teaching time. Pre-programme assessments can be conducted quickly and simply prior to face to face sessions to enable educators to determine learners' level of knowledge and plan their sessions accordingly. In terms of post-programme learning, mobile devices can offer educators and organizations further opportunities to maintain contact, and conduct any follow-up actions. Participants can also use mobile devices to record reûections and observations of learning once they are back in the workplace.

### *Extending opportunities to learn*

People use their mobile phone in situations during 'dead time'. These periods of time might be given over to random surfing or entertainment, but they could also be opportunities for some alternative, learning related ways that keep up their interest in their studies (e.g. 'light- touch' prompted reûection or planning).

Increasing constraints on the time of a busy executive at present are not necessarily matched to demands for increased reûection and learning. Quite the opposite; many executives are time starved, over worked yet under increasing pressure to make the best decisions in both an increasingly competitive and litigious environment. These behaviours may well drive learning away from short term priorities and yet mobile learning offers a powerful opportunity to introduce learning 'on demand'. It allows the individual to connect to executive education at a time that suits them and in a way that can support current business challenges. The learner is no longer dependent on the classroom – mobile devices allow the learner to connect in those times of reûection – a long train journey, a daily commute – where the mind is alert and open to new insights.

## Advantages of M-learning

1. One can access lessons, video clips and audio libraries from anywhere, including public places and moving buses and trains.
2. Interaction with fellow students and instructors will be a great help. It is an accepted fact that learning is made easier when information is shared and questions answered through a sort of combined study. This helps several students to work together on assignments even while remaining at far-flung locations.
3. Portability is a very big plus, as a PDA is compact and very lightweight, and enables a student to take notes or enter all types of data directly into the device.
4. There is a psychological factor; owning handheld devices increases student motivation and deepens the commitment to using and learning with them. Further, the present generation of students has a fascination with handhelds like PDAs, mobile phones and similar carry-around devices. The learning material is mostly colorful and inviting which may prompt students to go back and forth and practice more.
5. It is a fact that most handheld devices are more affordably priced than larger systems, and already a major percentage of the population owns them.
6. Flexible hours of learning are indeed a great boon as students can access the system anytime 24-7 and from any location. What is more, teacher support can now be expected even outside classrooms and other learning environments.
7. Each student can learn at his or her own pace - some student may be slower learners. The students who pick up things fast need not waste time going repeatedly through basic lessons.
8. Yet another blessing is a huge saving in the cost of learning materials and also commuting expenses.

## Disadvantages of M-learning

1. There is the definite inconvenience of size, as the student has to learn while hunched over the small screen of a mobile phone and PDA.
2. There is no denying that the storage capacities of PDAs are limited.
3. Anyone who has a mobile gadget knows that the short battery life and frequent changes of batteries is a great nuisance.
4. Add to this the absence of a common hardware platform; this makes it extremely difficult to develop content for use by all.

5. Devices may become outdated quickly and students have to keep combating obsolescence.
6. There is limited wireless bandwidth and chances are that it may further decrease with the number of users ever on the increase.
7. In the M-Learning venue, students are incapable of printing, simply because it requires a network connection. This is obviously not feasible in a number of real-life situations.

As a society, we have come to rely on technology to help in everyday life. M-learning is growing powerful, not just for education, but for business and personal use as well. As technology grows and gets better, we'll discover more ways in which we can use it.

## Conclusion

The utilization of this Mobile Learning technology by the learners would be able to provide problem-solving, guided institution with analytical thinking, active participation and self-pacing in flexible learning environment. Hence, it is essential factors for the teachers and students to adopt this technology to face the challenges in the emerging knowledge based society. Therefore teachers and students must work together to enhance the level of utilization of Mobile Learning technology in the teaching-learning process.

## Reference

1. Ally, M., & Tsinakos, A. (Eds.) (2014). Increasing access through mobile learning. Vancouver, BC: Commonwealth of Learning Press.
2. Brown, J. S. (2005). New Learning Environments for the 21st Century. Retrieved from www.johnseelybrown.
3. Hassan, M., Hamdan, Z., & Al-Sadi, J. (2012). A new mobile learning content design process. International Journal of Academic Research, 4(1), 23-28.
4. Muir, D. J. (2013). An international perspective on mobile learning. In Z. L. Berge & L. Y. Muilenburg (Eds.), Handbook of mobile learning. New York, NY: Routledge.
5. Stoerger, S. (2013). Becoming a digital nomad: Transforming learning through mobile devices. In Z. L. Berge & L. Y. Muilenburg (Eds.), Handbook of mobile learning. New York, NY: Routledge.
6. Sutch, D. (2010). Education futures, teachers and technology. Future lab Report. http://www2.
7. Futurelab.org.uk/resources/documents/other_research_reports/ Education_futures.pdf.

8. Traxler, J. (2013). Mobile learning across developing and developed worlds: Tackling distance, digital divides, disadvantage, disenfranchisement. In Z. L. Berge & L. Y. Muilenburg (Eds.), Handbook of mobile learning. New York, NY: Routledge.
9. Traxler, J. (2009). Learning in a Mobile Age. International Journal of Mobile and Blended learning, 1(1), 1-12.
10. Tsinakos, A., & Ally, M. (2013). Global mobile learning implementation and trends. Beijing, Wang, M., Shen, R., Novak, D., & Pan, X. (2009). The impact of mobile learning on students' learning behaviours and performance: Report from a large blended classroom. British Journal of Educational Technology, 40(4), 673-695.

# 37

# Learning Without Limits: Every Child is Special

## Introduction

Learning is basic to human behaviour. The psychological study of learning embraces much more than the learning of skills or academic subjects; it also bears upon the fundamental problems of emotional development, motivation, social behaviour, and personality (Hilgard et. al. 1975). In the words of Montessori, children are to be respected as different from adults and individuals who are different from each other. Children create themselves through purposeful activities. Schools have existed historically to teach children to observe, to think, to judge. Montessori introduces children to the joy of learning at an early age and provides a framework in which intellectual and social discipline go hand-in-hand (Arulsamy, 2013).

Education becomes an act of depositing, in which the students are depositories and teacher is a depositor. Instead of communicating, the teacher issues communiqués and makes deposits in which students patiently receive, memorise and repeat. This is the banking concept of education, in which the scope action allowed to the students extends only as far as receiving, filling and storing the deposits (Freire, 1971). Paulo

Freire's writings vehemently criticize this banking system which seems to be the conventional system used around the world. The banking model of education has been generating greater and greater failure (Tiphange, 2013). Treating students as depositories make them feel that they are capable only to receive information and no actions to be attempted other than responding whatever they received from the teacher. The expectation of all the stakeholders is invariably achievement irrespective of the interests and abilities of the students. This puts all the limits to the learning. India's leading education advocacy group, Pratham, released the findings of Annual State Education Report (ASER). ASER can be credited with beginning the conversation about the quality of education at a time when, buoyed by the big push of the Sarva Shiksha Abhiyaan, everyone was talking about quanitative targets only. What ASER did was to remind us that kids were learning astoundingly little in school.

The first-ever survey of higher education in the country shows that Scheduled Castes and Sheduled Tribes have not been able to reap the benefits. The survey reveals that though Gross Enrollment Ratio (GER) has gone up to about 20%, private unaided colleges have the lowest number of students. It is expected that when the final results of survey appear by year-end, enrollment would be go up across the spectrum. But the provisional data for SCs/STs is a cause for worry. Enrollment of SC students is only 10.2%; male (10.3%) and female (4.3%), in case of STs, the situation is alarming at 4.4%; male students (4.3%) and female students (4.6%). With such a poor GER for SCs/STs is natural that they have a poor presence as college and university teachers. Only 7.4% of teachers belong to SCs and 2.9% are STs (The Times of India, 2012).

## Learning and Creativity

In the information age we live in, it is a creative challenge to filter excessive information. Rolf Doblli in his book called, The Art of Thinking Clearly details how we can suffer from an information bias. Creativity is the ability to use space, with limited resources, to create beauty or to sustain a functional need. For instance, in a village in Rajasthan, illiterate adult women learnt the alphabet by increasing the script on pots so that they could learn it while they walked in a line to the water well. Perhaps creativity could then be viewed as how we process the facts to add up to our own experiential wisdom (Shyam, 2014). But, the main problem with our education system, everywhere there is terrible destruction of imagination. If you see some of the board exam papers, they are an insult to our childtren's potential. The system stops citizens from thinking about why the world is as it is. It almost feels like a conspiracy by the ruling elite to keep those who are down from ever rising (McLaughlin, 2014)

## Learning without Limits and the Teachers

It is the supreme art of the teacher to awaken the joy in creative expression and knowledge. – Albert Einstein. Grouping by abilities holds children back argues head teacher Alison Peacock, whose school went from failing to outstanding when the whole staff worked to ban limiting beliefs about fixed abilities and fixed futures and became a listening school. The study of our primary school has shown what is possible when teachers trust in every child's learning capacity, and focuses their energy on planning high quality learning experiences. Colleagues have increasingly felt free to inspire children and to engage them actively in discovering "what works" for each teacher and class instead of trying to perform to a standard model of classroom practice (Peacock, 2014)

It is not helpful to children, or to teachers, to categorise children as being 'more able', 'less able' or 'average', and plan for their education on that basis. These are not fixed attributes that can be reliably predicted from an early age. There are many complex ways in which ideas of fixed ability, and the practices based on them, can place limits on learning, as decades of research have shown .The Fixed Ability Paradigm must be contested if we are to realise the unlimited potential of the working class, a basic premise of Marxism, it is lacking in two respects: first its inherent social democratic politics, and second, its lack of concern within the curriculum (Mike, 2008). So, the teachers should understand the learners with their real potential and the thirst for learning and creativity, and the role of leadership in creating of professional learning right across the school, and to understand the importance of providing an environment where colleagues and children experience emotional stability. It is the duty of the teachers to find ways to encourage the growth of inventiveness and openness to new ideas. Teachers who share commitments to teaching and learning should reflect the core idea of 'transformability': the idea that things can change, even dramatically, through the choices that teachers and young people make.

## Conclusion

In producing learning without limits environment and in order to exploit to the full their power to make future learning, teachers make principled choices designed to increase young people's active engagement in, and control over, their learning; encourage learning as a collective experience, making choices that are in the interest of every member of the community; trust in child's capacity to learn and to become a better learner given enabling conditions; make learning experiences as open as possible. Recognising that all young people are unique, complex individuals, who are constantly growing and changing in unpredictable ways. The big idea of transformability and the four practical, pedagogical principles outlined above would help us inform and inspire to create learning without limits environment for all the children including children with special needs.

## Reference


1. Alphonse, Xavier. (2012). New Thinking, New Possibilities – Road Map of Higher Education in India – 2020. *New Frontiers in Education,* vol.45:3.
2. Arulsamy, S. (2013). Philisophical and Socialogical Perspectives on Education. Neelkamal Publications, New Delhi. p 149-152.
3. Freire, Paulo. (1971). The Banking Concept of Education. Retrieved from http://learning.writing101.net/wp-content/readings/freire the banking concept of education.pdf.
4. McLaughlin, Peter. (2014). The Discovery of Doon. *Fortune India,* April 2014 p 104-106.
5. Mike,Cole. (2008). Learning Without Limits: a Marxist Assessment, *Policy Futures in Education,* 6(4), 453-463. http://dx.doi.org/10.2304/pfie.2008.6.4.453.
6. Peacock, Alison. (2014). Learning Without Limits. Retrieved from http://learningwithoutlimits.educ,cam.ac.uk on April 28, 2014.
7. Shyam, Anuradha. (2014). A Universe of Creativity. *The Hindu, Education Plus.* April 21, 2014, p. 3.
8. The Hindu. (2014). In The Classroom, Enrollment Levels in Schools, 2013. January 24, 2014.
9. The Times of India. (2012). Poor SC/ST Enrollment in Higher Education: Survey. September 2, 2012.
10. Vaidhyasubramaniam, S. (2012). Labyrinth of Higher Education. *The New India Express,* August 18, 2012.
11. http://learningwithoutlimits.educ,cam.ac.uk.
12. http://www.goolereads.com/quotes/75838. Retrieved on April 28, 2014.
13. http://www.ncert.nic.in/publication/journals/pdf_files/jie/jie_may_2010.pdf Retrieved on April 28, 2014.

# 38

# Life Long Learning: A Way to the Best Society

## Introduction

The quality of any nation depends on the quality of its members. If the people have abilities, attitudes, social service, knowledge, aptitudes, hardworking nature, broadminded ness, socialisation and skills that nation develops a lot. Might be great or small, but every individual contributes for the nation. That means, the quality of the members depends on the quality of education they receive. So, Providing education for all, is the main aim of governing bodies, but getting education in a regular mode properly by everybody may not be possible, because of the persons may be destitute, physically challenged, working people, economically weaker section and discontinued education for various reasons. But they may have thrust and need of learning. Even the educated also cannot be quite without learning new things, and sharing his knowledge with others. A quick glance over the past 30 years so, shows how rapidly education patterns have changed. It seems that the natural curiosity will and should be transformed via Life Long Learning framework into a learning revolution. The different requirements in education mirror the different requirements in the society.

## Learning

Learning means knowing the unknown things. It is a lifelong process. According to D.W.Johnson and R.T.Johnson(1997) there are three different ways to carry out the learning process, Individualistic learning, competitive learning and cooperative learning. If the members of the society learn something about everything of the society and everything about some important aspects. Learning can occur through practice and experiences. It may be through formal or informal or non formal. Formally one can learn through schools, colleges and universities, informally, no formally by mingling with the public, socialisation, through mass media, through experiences one may learn many things. Even apart from Formal education system, there are many types of educational systems through which one can get education, viz., Distance education, Inclusive education, Integrated education, Open system, Alternative system etc. Integrated, inclusive education normalizes the life and education of children with disabilities along with non- disabled children to promote child-to-child learning.

## Learning Without Limitation

This new concept develops teaching and learning approaches free from limitations ideas about ability. It is a synonymous to the lifelong learning. We can categorise this at two levels.

## At school Level

In the formal way, Teachers trust in everybody's capacity to learn and to become a better learner make learning experience as open as possible recognizing that all young people are unique. When teachers trust in every child's capacity and focus their energy on planning high quality learning experiences.

In this way the sense of competitive ness comes from a desire to compete the oneself in order to achieve, not from a desire to outperform others in the class.

Open education and Alternative education are the different approaches to extend education to the learners through in and non-formally. The basic advantage of open education system in terms of time, pace, place, age, occupation certainly gives a new hope to the learners who were not able to continue the traditional formal system of education. The strength of National Institute of open Schooling curriculum is its wider range of options for course selection and facility to learn at the pace of the Learner. Alternative schooling includes a number of approaches to teaching and learning other than mainstream of traditional education. The possibility of alternative schooling such as night schools, evening schools, package programmes etc may also be explored for proving need-based services and develop skills like social, academic and pre vocational skills among children.

New courses which are needed to the present society can be introduced, students can learn on their interest.

## At Higher Level

The post graduates of today are the academic teachers and learners of tomorrow. Lifelong learning provides the environment that is inclusive, human enabling for everybody a place free from the damaging effects of fixed ability thinking and practices. It highlighting and sharing new trends and practices, giving unlimited chance for professionalization by educating everybody. Learning as a collective experience, making choices that are in the interests of members of the community.

Through the Hybride Course model, where the course will be scheduled as a mix of on-line and face-to-face periods. The ICT-tools and the web material that make up the frame of the activities during the on-line period continue to play their role during the face-to-face periods.

## Features of Learning without Limits

It gives importance to 7dispositions to learners as well as teachers. Openness, questioning, inventiveness, persistence, emotional stability, generosity, empathy.

It is not addressed issues of ethnicity, class, gender and disability explicitly, but these issues taken into account in an empowering way.

Now-a-days, Many universities offering MOOC Massive Open Online Courses, for the learners to get more degrees and most knowledge through internet which can lead to learning without limits. The Internet is well suited to Open and Distance Learning (ODL)for reasons such being ubiquitous, flexible, timeless and interactive ( Kenney, 1996).

Virtual lectures (multi media based teaching),virtual seminars (electronic discussion boards), virtual tutorials (live text chats) and virtual exams(computer based assignments) came to existence, which provides broad and distance learning opportunities to the people. Such environment foster "anytime/ anyplace" learning models that are not only a different way of delivering knowledge, but also a powerful means of creating knowledge ( Wilson, 1996).

The existence of enabling technologies as educational tools facilitate and promote the learning process while the support traditional Models and techniques of teaching which in fact are still within the infrastructure of new and hybrid teaching methods such as Computer Assisted Learning, Open and Distance Learning and Intelligent Tutoring Systems.

Learning without limit is useful to the exceptional students also. Disabled or gifted, they can learn what ever courses they want on their own pace. Career development or professionalization can acquire. Women, socially weaker section, economically weaker section can also enrich themselves by getting financial freedom, recognition through education.

### Learning without limits is beneficial for 2reasons

1. Vertical mobility: any person can upgrade in his profession through updating his proficiency by learning without limit.(qualitative)

2. Horizontal mobility: any one can get thorough knowledge of different aspects /courses/ degrees which can provide him to select better opportunity.(quantitative)

With the above two types of betterment lead a person to have intrinsic motivation as well as extrinsic motivation. With his intention to learn more make him to be self satisfied again lead to intrinsic motivation. It also brings praises and admiration from the others as an extrinsic motivation. If everybody learns without limit that nation does not have the problems of unemployment, poverty, illiteracy.

Learning means knowing the unknown things, if the members of the society learn something about everything and everything about something without limits that will become better society

### Role of Mass-media in Learning without Limits

Through news papers, periodicals, television channels and through computers, anybody can learn knowingly and unknowingly about political, medical, educational, financial, sociological, cultural, amusement, health aspects, psychological aspects, moral values, current events, disasters, prevention measures.... What not? Anything and everything from regional to universe, from past to future through present one may learn without limits.

## Benefits of Life Long Learning

1. Traditional school age or adult learners are becoming more informed consumers with faster and regional boundaries. The demand for education is fulfilling by using open and distance education, online education or technology-enhanced education.
2. Leads to innovative and qualitative learning.
3. Educate and civilize individual and societies and increase employability.
4. Provides Vocational Excellency.
5. Creates a better society.
6. Make lives richer and more prosperous.
7. Offer prospects for progression and enhance earning power.
8. Promote respect of the individual within society.
9. Acquire competitive skills and therefore competitive advantages.
10. Bridge the gap between haves and have outs.

## Conclusion

Learning is a process of " Woomb to Tomb" Anybody can learn Anything from Anywhere at Any time. If all the members in the society were educated by learn something about everything and everything about something, that society will flourished in all aspects. A burning lamp can only lighten the other lamps, a learned person only make the others to learn for betterment of life, betterment of the society.

## References

1. Ogborn, J. (1990), A Future for Modelling in Science Education, Journal of Computer Assisted Learning, 6103-12.
2. Bates, A.(1991), Third Generation Distance Education: The challenge of New Technology, Research in Distance Education, 3(2) 10-15.
3. Maria Jose O.L.Goncalves (2001) Distance Continuing Education for Enterprises in European Universities.
4. Wilson,G.(1996), Constructivist Learning Environments: Case studies in Instructional Design. Englewood Cliffs, UJ, Educational Technology Publication.
5. Kenny,J(1996) Integrated Internet Services for in-service Training. In technology and communications: Catalyst for education change. Vol.2.INTE New orlean, 96: proceedings of the 13th International Conference on Technology on Education, New Orleans, 17-20 March Vol.2 pp 452-454.

6. Rosenberg, M.J (2001), E learning strategies for delivering knowledge in th Digital age McGrqw-Hill, Newyork.
7. Learning without Limits: Developing the Next Generation of Education, Proceedings of the EDEN 10th Anniversary Conference, held in Stockholm, Sweden, 10-13 June, 2001.

# 39

# Blended Learning

After nearly 2 years of research in blended learning, and detailed interviews with more than 30 companies, we find that blended learning is replacing "e-learning" as the next big thing. Our research finds that blended learning programs are perhaps the highest impact, lowest cost way to drive major corporate initiatives. Companies have discovered unique and powerful methodologies for selecting the "right media" to solve a given business problem. The biggest challenges companies face include technology and the change management and business processes required to roll out major programs. Results: Blended Learning solves the problem of speed, scale, and impact-and leverages e-learning where it's most appropriate, without forcing e-learning into places it does not fit. Go to article. The first generation of e-learning or Web-based learning programs focused on presenting physical classroom-based instructional content over the Internet. The experience gained from the first generation of e-learning often riddled with long sequences of "page-turner" content and point-and-click quizzes, is giving rise to the realization that a single mode of instructional delivery may not provide sufficient choices, engagement, social contact, relevance, and context needed to facilitate successful learning and performance.

## Introduction

One of the problems with e-learning in the early days was that learners worked on their own without any interaction with an instructor or other learners. It soon became clear that social interaction was an important ingredient in many learning situations, and that it might need to be built into some e-learning solutions. This was essentially the beginning of the concept of "blended learning". This term refers to a learning solution that incorporates a mix of online and face-to-face elements. It has been further refined to mean a learning solution that contains a mix of formats, media and experiences, comfortable with the new world of online learning. Mix and match, duck and dive: This 12th Think Tank in our series examines key questions that face learning and development professionals in every organization, In these days, various types of scientific exchange and expert reports are often held in universities to demonstrate and improve their teaching and academic level. While for the limitation of space and time, how to present all the valuable lectures to more students is the main problem. it not only can live streaming the overall audio, video media and computer desktop information but also can make recording of brilliant performance for future VOD service anywhere anytime.

## Defining Blended Learning

Blended learning uses the tools of the provincial learning management system (LMS) to teach and support learning in a face-to-face class. Through blended learning, K-12 students can access high-quality course materials, course calendars, and assignments during and outside school hours. Students can also take part in face-to-face lessons and communicate with their teacher and classmates using a suite of secure online tools inside the password-protected LMS. These tools help students learn or review key concepts, stay organized, show what they have learned, submit assignments, track their achievement, and communicate with others. This suite of online secure tools includes:

## Introducing Blended Learning

An experience of uncertainty for students in the United Arab Emirates The cultural dimension of Uncertainty Avoidance is analyzed in this study of an introduction to blended learning for international students. Content analysis was conducted on the survey narratives collected from three cohorts of management undergraduates in the United Arab Emirates. Interpretation of certainty with blended learning was found in: student skills with technology; student acknowledgement of course organization; and student appreciation of online feedback. Uncertainty with the introduction of blended learning was found: when membership was assigned for group work, higher quality research methods were introduced; where course structure lacked detail, increased time was required for new and different online activities. The implications of these findings are discussed, and strategies suggested for introducing blended learning to international students. The limitations of the study are considered, and a direction for future research is suggested. This is the first study on undergraduates in the Middle East for the effects of a cultural dimension when introducing blended learning. The findings increase the body of knowledge that relates to learning technology in the international business classroom.

We study the effect of one dimension, from within a culture framework, on the introduction to blended learning for business undergraduates at a university in the United Arab Emirates People are not generally aware of the tremendous impact that national culture has on their vision and interpretation of the world. Because culture colors nearly every aspect of human behavior, a working knowledge of culture and its influences can be useful to executives operating in a multicultural business environment.

## Implications for K-12 Education

### Restructuring the Class:

One of the most difficult challenges of transforming a traditional K-12 class into a blended learning classroom requires a shift in an educator's teaching paradigm. Instead of preparing the necessary materials for the off-line setting of a traditional classroom, the blended learning K-12 teacher now must also organize and maintain the on-line, virtual classroom. The time, planning, and organization needed to restructure a K-12 blended classroom requires the educator to, in essence, plan and organize a class in two settings, which complement each other in terms of scheduling, content, lesson flow, and organization.

A blended learning classroom requires the K-12 instructor to develop teaching materials prior to the start of class. Other K-12 classroom models have also used other characteristics of blended learning for instructing students through the Web and other electronic tools. Web-enhanced campus courses, Web-centric courses, Web-courses using distance learning and campus settings, and traditional distance courses have implemented web use to certain degrees. Each category of web integration requires a varied percentage of packaged developed material, ranging from fifty to one hundred percent. (Boettcher and Conrad 1999) However, the percent-age of prepared material web material in blended K-12 course ultimately depends on teacher preference, student/school technological capabilities, and other lesson dependent factors.

Like the other models of Web integration in the K-12 classroom, blended learning courses need to successfully address and incorporate four of the following components:

1. **Administration** – organization of the syllabus, increase teacher productivity/efficiency, distributing/collecting material, and scheduling duties
2. **Assessment** – providing feedback, tracking student progress, and testing opportunities
3. **Content Delivery** – communicating content through different learning styles, using multimedia, incorporating learning activities, using the Internet for the acquisition of knowledge
4. **Community** – building the classroom community through synchronous/threaded chats, providing office/help hours to communicate online

## Benefits of Blended Learning

One of the more potentially impacting benefits of blended learning is in the area of student accessibility. According to Jeffrey, the ability to use the Web for the classroom has the potential to serve any student, at any time, in any place. (Jeffrey 2003) Likewise, the characteristics of blended learning also allow its K-12 students the same advantages in terms of accessibility. A blended learning's online course components could possibly minimize the accessibility concerns for the following K-12 students who cannot meet in the traditional classroom:

1. Students in rural or small school districts where the proximity of the classroom is the main challenge to content/material accessibility
2. Home-schooled students with instruction in subjects their parents feel unable to teach
3. Handicapped or hospitalized students who cannot travel to the traditional classroom
4. Expelled students who are required not to attend the traditional classroom as a consequence but still can have access to material to prevent falling behind academically

We contend that educators may not be aware of the impact of culture, and that it is useful for an educator to recognize the influence of culture on their students. For culture will impact both the perception of the learning environment and learner's behavior. Of course this is equally true of the educator's vision and interpretation, but that is for a separate study. In the culture model, the UAE is classified within the Middle East cluster of nations, and we investigate Uncertainty Avoidance (UA) because of the high score in that region for this cultural dimension .UA is defined as "the extent to which the members of a culture feel threatened by ambiguous or unknown situations" A confidential survey to evaluate the introduction of blended learning was administered to three cohorts of students. Content analysis of collected narrative data revealed student certainty and uncertainty for the introduction of a blended learning environment. Three indicators of certainty with a blended learning environment were found:

1. Student skills in the use of technology;
2. Student acknowledgement of course organization; and
3. Student appreciation of online feedback. Uncertainty with the blended environment was also indicated:

Awareness about the cultural dimension of UA increased this educator's ability to diagnose potential challenges that may affect the introduction of blended learning. Some lessons learned, and changes in pedagogy are suggested as a consequence of the study. The findings add to the body of knowledge, as this is the first study to be conducted on the effect of a cultural dimension for the introduction of blended learning to There was appreciation for the organization of assignment deadlines available to students in the LMS However, data about assignments revealed increased time on task due to searching for quality sources in the virtual library Comments about time on task were found in the context of "deadlines", appearing at twice the rate in the uncertainty than the certainty classification. Keywords "research" and "sources" were associated with the less positive classification because of time and difference to the norm of searching online. Learners commented on interaction as "different" in a blended classroom to the previous experience of a more traditional class. However, the key word "difference" also revealed uncertainty with change associated with new tasks, especially where change related to traditions in exam format. An "open laptop" exam format with individual questions introduced the potential risk of failure for students. Unless students considered they had received a lot of practice, e.g. in online exam preparation or in searching for sources.

There were misconceptions also about unfamiliar activities, and a desire for more information expressed with in this study of learners from a high UA culture, there was evidence of reliance on Professor Feedback the professor was also expected to be flexible in expectations for the use of technology. Quotation 14 relates to student use of competence with technology, but needing flexibility in its use. A learner revealed how knowledge was attained through online group work The interpretation was that interaction is beneficial Students appreciated group work, although there was a sense of uncertainty with unfamiliar classmates To follow is a discussion about the themes that arose as implications for teaching and learning when a blended environment is introduced to students with high UA.

## Discussion

The emergent themes revealed implications for changes in pedagogy to avoid uncertainty when introducing students to blended learning. These implications are contained in the final column of and are considered further in this discussion. Our study findings did not reveal student certainty or uncertainty about the shift to a more technologically supported classroom, concurring with findings related to this generation's familiarity with technology. However, as Bennett, Matron, and Kevin argue, familiarity with technological tools is not the whole debate, surrounding the introduction of learning technology for the "Next Generation", of so called "digital natives" Our research firmly places culture into the debate about learning technology/blended learning. The cultural dimension of high UA requires the international educator to consider culture and adapt blended learning to avoid potential resistance by those who are risk averse to a new learning environment.

As there is a tendency for less structure in blended learning, those from cultures who prefer more structure may perceive the environment rather vague Uncertainty manifested itself through survey narrative in students' requests for more structured learning, e.g. explicit verbal and written direction was wanted ambiguity for students, there is an opportunity to post asynchronous "diagnostic feedback", on why answers are wrong, and "prescriptive feedback", on how the answers could be improved for next time Although an educator risks student uncertainty, because of less structured pedagogy, employment preparation is of concern as more structure is considered to stifle innovation in the workplaces.

Lectures as a mode of structured instructional delivery were complemented, in this blended environment, with instructor facilitation of online group activities when the professor changes her or his role from the more traditional delivery of knowledge to become a student guide towards online material and facilitator in online group discussion and projects, it can increase uncertainty for students. The professor assigned team membership to introduce cultural diversity into online groups Hwang and Francesco 2010; Hwang, Kessler, and Francesco 2004). However, students expressed their uncertainty on this practice through less than positive survey comments. A preference was for certainty in the attitudes of familiar others, known performance, or regular decision making. However, for online discussions that carried less weight in the final grading criteria, the professor continued to assign student group members. This practice was aligned with skills needed for a global workplace, as team orientation is vital for the ability to work across boundaries, to influence people without formal authority and to lead teams composed of different cultures.

Assignments were formulated to increase knowledge about local issues. Students in this region require exposure to management in the Arab world because many will be employed in the Middle East Students were familiar with searching online through the Internet for sources to complete assignments. However, a pedagogical approach to improve research quality, through use of the virtual library, created and therefore, "seamless linking of e-learning and e-library" becomes crucial further links to library sources were embedded in the LMS, and a research workshop was later introduced in an attempt to ameliorate UA when searching for quality regional and global sources.

A change in the exam norm caused students to exhibit uncertainty, as revealed in narrative relating to perceived unfairness and increased time on activity. Education for those with high UA must "encourage gradual acquisition of knowledge and skills practiced in a supportive environment, where mistakes are never fatal" Progressive change is suggested to reduce UA, e.g. a change to exam format, from written to electronic, followed later with other changes to exam procedure. The results agree with findings that learners from high UA cultures spend more time completing online tasks and attribute results to circumstances rather than acknowledging self-control for learning the introduction of blended learning makes necessary a longer view of time for knowledge acquisition that is more fitting with learners from high UA cultures

## Limitations and future research direction

A limitation of article length only allowed analysis of one dimension, (UA), in a culture framework to be applied to this introduction of blended learning. A further limitation is that data collected were from learners who were also taught by the survey creator. There was potential bias in data interpretation by the teacher/creator/collector. To ameliorate bias, a research colleague reviewed the results, and a future survey is planned to collect data from learners taught by others. Survey data collected in other courses, and interpreted through other cultural dimensions, will extend the value of a culture framework for blended learning.

## Conclusion

The mid semester LCLC survey addressed the research question, i.e. what evidence is there of learner uncertainty or certainty on the introduction of blended learning? To investigate the introduction of blended learning, an analysis of the cultural dimension of UA was conducted. Interpretation of certainty with blended learning was found in: student skills with technology; student acknowledgement of course organization; and student appreciation of online feedback. Uncertainty with the introduction of blended learning was found: when membership was assigned for group work, higher quality research methods were introduced; where course structure lacked detail, increased time was required for new and different activities. Findings increased the international researcher's ability to interpret collected data on learner experiences within a cultural dimension. A culture framework also offers valuable insights for the educator to effectively introduce blended learning to international students.

## References

1. Abdurrahman, H. & Storti, G. (2011) 'Organizational training across cultures: variations in practices and attitudes', Journal of European Industrial Training, vol. 35, no. 1, pp. 45–70. Publisher Full Text
2. Adeoye, B. & Went ling, R. M. (2007) 'The relationship between national culture and the usability of an E-learning system', International Journal on E-learning, vol. 6, no. 1, pp. 119–146.
3. Alebaikan, R. & Troudi, S. (2011) 'Blended learning in Saudi universities: challenges and perspectives', Research in Learning Technology, [online] Available at: http://www. researchinlearning technology.net/index.php/rlt/article/view/10750/12370
4. Alodiedat, A. & Eyadat, Y. (2008) 'The effect of intranet use on students' achievement and self-confidence', International Management Review, vol. 4, no. 1, pp. 72–87, 109.

# 40

# Recent Emerging Technology in Classroom: Blended Learning

## Introduction

Blended learning is a term increasingly used to describe the way e-learning is being combined with traditional classroom methods and independent study to create a new, hybrid teaching methodology. It represents a much greater change in basic technique than simply adding computers to classrooms; it represents, in many cases, a fundamental change in the way teachers and students approach the learning experience. It has already produced an offshoot the flipped classroom that has quickly become a distinct approach of its own. No single, reliable definition of blended learning exists, or evens a universal agreement on the term itself. Many use terms like hybrid, mixed, or integrative to describe the same trend. But the trend is significant. In 2000 an estimated 45,000 K-12 students took an online course, but almost a decade later more than 3million took courses that way, many of them using computers in the schools themselves.

## A Learning Model in Three Parts

There is a general consensus among education innovators that blended learning has three primary components:

1. In person classroom activities facilitated by a trained educator.
2. Online learning materials, often including prerecorded lectures given by that same instructor.
3. Structured independent study time guided by the material in the lectures and skills developed during the classroom experience.

## Forms of Blended Learning

1. Face-to-face Driver
2. Rotation
3. Flex
4. Online Lab
5. Self-Blend
6. Online Driver

## Face-to-face Driver

Face-to-face driver is a blended learning model in which teachers deliver most of the curriculum. Teachers lead the class in a lecture following an established protocol taking precedence and technology being a secondary thought. However, they also produce online resources to supplement or revise course material which students can study at home, in the classroom or in a technology lab.

## Rotation

In the Rotation model of blended learning: within a given course, a student rotates on a fixed schedule between learning online in a one-to-one, self-paced environment and sitting in a classroom with a traditional face-to-face teacher.

## Flex

Flex model of blended learning features an online platform that delivers most of the curricula. It's the model where most of the learning is done online and the face-to-face model exists to provide on-site support for a flexible and adaptive, as required basis through in person tutoring sessions and small group sessions.

## Online Lab

Online lab is a model of blended learning that characterizes programs that rely on an online platform to deliver the entire course but in a brick and mortar lab environment. The entire course and teaching are done online. Teachers interact with students through prerecorded videos, audio and video conferences or discussion forums and email.

### Self-Blend

The Self - Blend model is a fully individualized approach that allows students to choose to take one or more courses online to supplement their traditional school's catalog. Maximum part of the learning is done online, but the student will still attend face-to-face classes.

### Role of Teacher in Blended Learning

In the blended learning approach, a student's day typically includes a combination of online learning and small group instruction time with teachers. This learning model shifts the classroom teacher's focus away from more traditional curricular and administrative tasks in the direction of working with data and providing more individualized support to students. Because the focus in this model has shifted from planning lessons and delivering content to being a facilitator of student learning, the classroom teacher's role can expand in challenging and stimulating ways

Rather than follow the traditional roles of sharing content and grading papers, classroom teachers in the blended learning model must:

### Be willing to learn

In a blended learning program, the teacher should be prepared to:

1. Access, analyze and aggregate data
2. Use data as an integral part of the planning process for each individual student, groups of students and the whole class
3. Use benchmark tests and other assessments to direct instruction at different levels (individual, group, class)
4. To help teachers learn their new roles and to understand online learning, many blended learning programs require that the teachers take an online class themselves as part of the required professional development.
5. Having an experienced blended learning mentor as a guide and participating in training on the data management system also is important.
6. With proper professional development, a "traditional" teacher can develop the data-analysis skills needed to get the most out of the blended learning model.

## Be open to new teaching strategies

The blended learning teacher should:

1. have a wide breadth of content knowledge in order to teach multiple subjects
2. differentiate instruction based upon student needs (as determined by the data)
3. focus on academic intervention and enrichment
4. While blended learning instructors still need to be able to maximize learning time and manage a classroom effectively, they have more individual time with students and can give them the attention and support they need.

## Be leaders

To help guide students in a blended learning environment, teachers should:

1. Model learning and show students how to find information and answers
2. Be able to manage project based learning activities
3. Have strategies in place to keep students on task, engaged and motivated
4. The blended learning instructor helps students move beyond simply "regurgitating" rote responses to learning to apply content to new situations. Just as the teacher must interpret and analyze information, students need to learn to reason, integrate information and demonstrate knowledge through application.

## Facilitators Focus on Four Key Areas

1. Development of online and offline course content.
2. Facilitation of communication with and among students, including the pedagogy of communicating content online without the contextual clues students would get in person.
3. Guiding the learning experience of individual students, and customizing material wherever possible to strengthen the learning experience.
4. Assessment and grading, not unlike the expectations for teachers within the traditional framework.

## Blended Learning: Personalizing Education for Students

Blended learning is a new educational model with great potential to increase student outcomes and create exciting new roles for teachers. In this course you will learn about the different types of blended learning and the best practices from real schools using these models. In addition, you will develop the tools you need to build your own blended learning program.

### Advantages

Proponents of blended learning argue that by incorporating the "asynchronous Internet communication technology" into courses serves to "facilitate a simultaneous independent and collaborative learning experience", and this incorporation is a major contributor to student satisfaction and success in such courses. The use of information and communication technologies has been found to improve access to as well as student attitudes towards learning. By incorporating information technology into class projects, communication between lecturers and part-time students was improved, and students were able to better evaluate their understanding of course material via the use of "computer-based qualitative and quantitative assessment modules.

### Disadvantages

Blended learning has a strong dependence on the technical resources with which the blended learning experience is delivered these tools need to be reliable, easy to use, and up to date in order for the use of the Internet to have a meaningful impact on the learning experience. Additionally, IT literacy can serve as a significant barrier for students attempting to get access to the course materials, making the availability of high quality technical support paramount.

It has been observed that the use of lecture recording technologies can result in students falling behind on the material in a study performed across four different universities; it was found that only half of the students watched the lecture videos on a regular basis, and nearly 40% of students watched several weeks' worth of videos in one sitting.

### Conclusion

In some situations, the move to blended learning has inspired educators to redefine traditional roles. The word "facilitator" has emerged as an alternative to "teacher," bringing with it a slightly different focus. The facilitator places an emphasis on empowering students with the skills and knowledge required to make the most of the online material and independent study time, guiding students toward the most meaningful experience possible. So, what might blended learning mean to teachers? Continued growth as they modify their existing strategies to lead students to become independent learners themselves? Technology can also give teachers crucial information to understand individual needs of students to support and strengthen their learning. When teachers use good technology effectively, it provides them the power to become even greater experts in the content areas they teach.

## References

1. Bow Valley College. (2007). Annual report. Retrieved October 21, 2007.
2. Chickering, A., &Ehrmann, S. (1996), implementing the seven principles: Technology as lever. Retrieved February 15, 2009.
3. Dziuban, C. D., Hartman, J. L., &Moskal, P. D. (2004, March 30). Blended learning. (Research Bulletin, Issue 7). Boulder, CO: EDUCAUSE Center for Applied Research. Retrieved March 2, Hijazi, S., Crowley, M., Smith, M. L., Shaffer, C. (2006). Maximizing learning by teaching blended courses. Retrieved March 4, 2009,

# 41

# The Use of Cloud Computing in innovative Learning

## Introduction

Cloud computing in general can be portrayed as a synonym for computing over a network, with the ability to run a program or application on many connected computers at the same time. It specifically refers to a computing hardware machine or group of computing hardware machines commonly referred as a server connected through a communication network such as the Internet, an intranet, a local area network (LAN) or wide area network (WAN) and individual users or user who have permission to access the server can use the server's processing power for their individual computing needs like to run an application, store data or any other computing need. Therefore, instead of using a personal computer every-time to run the application, the individual can now run the application from anywhere in the world, as the server provides the processing power to the application and the server is also connected to a network via internet or other connection platforms to be accessed from anywhere.

## Advantages

The cloud focuses on maximizing the effectiveness of the shared resources. Cloud resources are usually not only shared by multiple users but are also dynamically reallocated per demand. This can work for allocating resources to users. For example, a cloud computer facility that serves European users during European business hours with a specific application (e.g., email) may reallocate the same resources to serve North American users during North America's business hours with a different application (e.g., a web server). This approach should maximize the use of computing power thus reducing environmental damage as well since less power, air conditioning, rackspace, etc. are required for a variety of functions. With cloud computing, multiple users can access a single server to retrieve and update their data without purchasing licenses for different applications.

### Hosted (Host) services

The term "cloud computing" is mostly used to sell hosted services in the sense of application service provisioning that run client server software at a remote location. Such services are given popular acronyms like 'SaaS' (Software as a Service), 'PaaS' (Platform as a Service), 'IaaS' (Infrastructure as a Service), 'HaaS' (Hardware as a Service) and finally 'EaaS' (Everything as a Service). End users access cloud-based applications through a web browser, thin client or mobile app while the business software and user's data are stored on servers at a remote location. Examples include Amazon Web Services and Google App engine, which allocate space for a user to deploy and manage software "in the cloud".

In early 2008, Eucalyptus became the first open-source, AWS API-compatible platform for deploying private clouds. In early 2008, Open Nebula, enhanced in the RESERVOIR European Commission-funded project, became the first open-source software for deploying private and hybrid clouds, and for the federation of clouds. In the same year, efforts were focused on providing quality of service guarantees (as required by real-time interactive applications) to cloud-based infrastructures, in the framework of the IRMOS European Commission-funded project, resulting in a real-time cloud environment. By mid-2008, Gartner saw an opportunity for cloud computing "to shape the relationship among consumers of IT services, those who use IT services and those who sell them" and observed that "organizations are switching from company-owned hardware and software assets to per-use service-based models" so that the "projected shift to computing ... will result in dramatic growth in IT products in some areas and significant reductions in other areas."

## Growth and popularity

The development of the Internet from being document centric via semantic data towards more and more services was described as "dynamic web". This contribution focused in particular in the need for better metadata able to describe not only implementation details but also conceptual details of model-based applications.

The present availability of high-capacity networks, low-cost computers and storage devices as well as the widespread adoption of hardware virtualization, service-oriented architecture, and autonomic and utility computing have led to a growth in cloud computing.

## Origin of the term

The origin of the term *cloud computing* is unclear, although it is often attributed to the Internet Systems Division of Compaq Computer (George Favaloro, Philip Reagan, Jeff Whatcott, Ken Evans, Ricardo Cidale, and others). The expression *cloud* is commonly used in science to describe a large agglomeration of objects that visually appear from a distance as a cloud and describes any set of things whose details are not inspected further in a given context.

1. **Meteorology:** a weather cloud is an agglomeration.
2. **Mathematics:** a large number of points in a coordinate system in mathematics is seen as a point cloud;
3. **Astronomy:** a cloud of gas and particulate matter in space is known as a nebula (Latin for mist or cloud),
4. **Physics:** The indeterminate position of electrons around an atomic kernel appears like a cloud to a distant observer

The term became popular after Amazon.com introduced the Elastic Compute Cloud in 2006.

## Similar systems and Concepts

Cloud Computing is the result of evolution and adoption of existing technologies and paradigms. The goal of cloud computing is to allow users to take beneût from all of these technologies, without the need for deep knowledge about or expertise with each one of them. The cloud aims to cut costs, and help the users focus on their core business instead of being impeded by IT obstacles.

The main enabling technology for cloud computing is virtualization. Virtualization generalizes the physical infrastructure, which is the most rigid component, and makes it available as a soft component that is easy to use and manage. By doing so, virtualization provides the agility required to speed up IT operations, and reduces cost by increasing infrastructure utilization. On the other hand, autonomic computing automates the process through which the user can provision resources on-demand. By minimizing user involvement, automation speeds up the process and reduces the possibility of human errors.

### Cloud computing shares characteristics with:

1. **Client–server model** — *Client–server computing* refers broadly to any distributed application that distinguishes between service providers (servers) and service requestors (clients).
2. **Grid computing** — "A form of distributed and parallel computing, whereby a 'super and virtual computer' is composed of a cluster of networked, loosely coupled computers acting in concert to perform very large tasks."
3. **Mainframe computer** — Powerful computers used mainly by large organizations for critical applications, typically bulk data processing such as: census; industry and consumer statistics; police and secret intelligence services; enterprise resource planning; and financial transaction processing.
4. **Utility computing** — The "packaging of computing resources, such as computation and storage, as a metered service similar to a traditional public utility, such as electricity."
5. **Peer-to-peer** — A distributed architecture without the need for central coordination. Participants are both suppliers and consumers of resources (in contrast to the traditional client–server model).
6. **Cloud gaming** — Also known as on-demand gaming, is a way of delivering games to computers. Gaming data is stored in the provider's server, so that gaming is independent of client computers used to play the game. One such current example, would be a service by OnLive which allows users a certain space to save game data, and load games within the OnLive server.

### Cloud clients

Users access cloud computing using networked client devices, such as desktop computers, laptops, tablets and smart phones. Some of these devices – *cloud clients* – rely on cloud computing for all or a majority of their applications so as to be essentially useless without it. Examples are thin clients and the browser-based Chromebook. Many cloud applications do not require specific software on the client and instead use a web browser to interact with the cloud application. With Ajax and HTML5 these Web user interfaces can achieve a similar, or even better, look and feel to native applications. Some cloud applications, however, support specific client software dedicated to these applications (e.g., virtual desktop clients and most email clients). Some legacy applications (line of business applications that until now have been prevalent in thin client computing) are delivered via a screen-sharing technology.

## Deployment models

### Controlled cloud

Controlled cloud services are not publicly available; users are specifically authorized by services vendors. Access to the controlled cloud may be through the Internet; however, connections would be encrypted. The cloud vendor employs various techniques and technologies to prevent unauthorized access Use of services is governed by contracts, and which specify the responsibilities of the vendor and the responsibilities of the customer with regard to data stewardship.

The services vendor discloses to customers its processes for managing customer data. Any subprocessors used in processing customer data are identified to customers. Data protection schemes, such as administrative controls, encryption methods, and other appropriate technical and organizational measures (TOMs) to protect data are described and demonstrated to customers.

### Private cloud

Private cloud is cloud infrastructure operated solely for a single organization, whether managed internally or by a third-party and hosted internally or externally. Undertaking a private cloud project requires a significant level and degree of engagement to virtualize the business environment, and requires the organization to reevaluate decisions about existing resources. When done right, it can improve business, but every step in the project raises security issues that must be addressed to prevent serious vulnerabilities. Self-run data centers are generally capital intensive. They have a significant physical footprint, requiring allocations of space, hardware, and environmental controls. These assets have to be refreshed periodically, resulting in additional capital expenditures. They have attracted criticism because users “still have to buy, build, and manage them” and thus do not benefit from less hands-on management, essentially "[lacking] the economic model that makes cloud computing such an intriguing concept".

### Public cloud

A cloud is called a "public cloud" when the services are rendered over a network that is open for public use. Technically there may be little or no difference between public and private cloud architecture, however, security consideration may be substantially different for services (applications, storage, and other resources) that are made available by a service provider for a public audience and when communication is effected over a non-trusted network. Generally, public cloud service providers like Amazon AWS, Microsoft and Google own and operate the infrastructure and offer access only via Internet (direct connectivity is not offered).

### Community cloud

Community cloud shares infrastructure between several organizations from a specific community with common concerns (security, compliance, jurisdiction, etc.), whether managed internally or by a third-party and hosted internally or externally. The costs are spread over fewer users than a public cloud (but more than a private cloud), so only some of the cost savings potential of cloud computing are realized.

### Hybrid cloud

Hybrid cloud is a composition of two or more clouds (private, community or public) that remain distinct entities but are bound together, offering the benefits of multiple deployment models. Hybrid cloud can also mean the ability to connect collocation, managed and/or dedicated services with cloud resources.

Gartner, Inc. defines a hybrid cloud service as a cloud computing service that is composed of some combination of private, public and community cloud services, from different service providers. A hybrid cloud service crosses isolation and provider boundaries so that it can't be simply put in one category of private, public, or community cloud service. It allows one to extend either the capacity or the capability of a cloud service, by aggregation, integration or customization with another cloud service.

### Distributed cloud

Cloud computing can also be provided by a distributed set of machines that are running at different locations, while still connected to a single network or hub service. Examples of this include distributed computing platforms such as BOINC and Folding@Home.

## Conclusion

According to Gartner's Hype cycle, Cloud computing has reached a maturity that leads it into a productive phase. This means that most of the main issues with Cloud computing have been addressed to a degree that Clouds have become interesting for full commercial exploitation. This however does not mean that all the problems listed above have actually been solved, only that the according risks can be tolerated to a certain degree. Cloud computing is therefore still as much a research topic, as it is a market offering.

## Works sited

1. University of Michigan http://it.umich.edu/initiatives/cloud/content/what-cloud. Retrieved 15 January 2014. Missing or empty |title= (help)
2. National Institute of Standards and Technology. Retrieved 24 July 2011.
3. "What is Cloud Computing?". *Amazon Web Services*. 2013-03-19. Retrieved 2013-03-20.
4. It.tmcnet.com. 2011-08-24. Retrieved 2011-12-02.

# 42

# Futuristic 21st Century Skills For Preparing Students Beyond Digital age

## Introduction

At present 21st century is considered as Digital Age – a time of unprecedented growth in technology and its subsequent information explosion. The tools for information access and management system made such a vast impact on the way we live, work, shop and play. New technologies and tools multiply daily in a vast manner and the new technologies of today are outdated almost as soon as they reach the market. Everywhere we are occupied with new innovation based technology gadgets available today that guides the students and teachers with new emerging digital skills in the field of learning and teaching process in education. The concept of emerging digital skills will outdated the some of the basic skills which are essential for sustaining human life. Numerous studies and reports have emerged over the past decade that seek to identify the life, career, and learning skills that define the skills needed for success in the 21st century world apart from the digital skills.

Over the last decade, there were tremendous advances in the science of learning, made possible by the convergence of research in the cognitive sciences, neuroscience, human development, and technology. As a result, we know more today about how people think and learn. For starters, the research clearly shows that students learn more when they are engaged in meaningful, relevant, and intellectually stimulating work (Newmann, 2001). While all learning is deeply personal, the frequency and relevance of such moments increase when technology enables us to tap outside experts; visualize and analyze data; link to real-world contexts; and take advantage of opportunities for feedback, reflection, and analysis. Technology influences learning in three significant ways. A synthesis of recent research and national skill sets shows that technology can be a driver of change, a bridge to academic excellence, and a platform for informed decision making and accountability:

1. A Driver for Change: The 21st Century Skills
2. A Bridge to High Academic Achievement Technology
3. A Platform for Informed Decision Making and Accountability

**A Driver for Change: The 21st Century Skills** Technology has catapulted us into knowledge based, global society. It is clear that success in this society will require significantly different skills than in the past. However, policymakers and educators have not yet clearly defined what ıt means to be "educated" in a Digital Age. The irony of a call for 21st century skills in this era of high stakes testing based on conventional metrics is not lost on teachers. To fully realize the educational opportunities that 21st century skills can bring to students, education leaders must formally incorporate them into the mainstream of school curriculum, instruction, and assessment.

**A Bridge to High Academic Achievement Technology** serves as a bridge to more engaged, relevant, meaningful, and personalized learning—all of which can lead to higher academic achievement. Research indicates that when technology is used appropriately, children learn more, even as measured by conventional tests (Newmann et al., 2001). It is important to demonstrate this research link to teachers, thereby encouraging them to incorporate technology into the mainstream of student learning.

**A Platform for Informed Decision Making and Accountability** Technology provides a platform for more informed decision making using timely, meaningful data to shape learning opportunities. This situation translates into more personalized learning based on continuous feedback available to students, teachers, and parents. The challenge lies in building such accountability systems on the foundation of the right indicators—indicators that lead to high academic standards and 21st century skills. Only this foundation will enable true Digital Age readiness. While there are some differences in how the skills are categorized or interpreted, there are some common skills that essential for human life is given below.

1. **Creativity and Innovation** Using knowledge and understanding to create new ways of thinking in order to find solutions to new problems and to create new products and services.
2. **Critical Thinking and Problem Solving** Applying higher order thinking to new problems and issues, using appropriate reasoning as they effectively analyze the problem and make decisions about the most effective ways to solve the problem.
3. **Communication** Communicating effectively in a wide variety of forms and contexts for a wide range of purposes and using multiple media and technologies.
4. **Collaboration** Working with others respectfully and effectively to create, use and share knowledge, solutions and innovations.
5. **Information Management** Accessing, analyzing, synthesizing, creating and sharing information from multiple sources.
6. **Effective Use of Technology** Creating the capacity to identify and use technology efficiently, effectively and ethically as a tool to access, organize, evaluate and share information
7. **Career and Life Skills** Developing skills for becoming self-directed, independent learners and workers who can adapt to change, manage projects, take responsibility for their work, lead others and produce results.
8. **Cultural Awareness** Developing cultural competence in working with others by recognizing and respecting cultural differences and work with others from a wide range of cultural and social backgrounds.

## Integrating 21st Century Skills with Digital Age and Content

These skills are about the thinking processes and behaviours students will use as they learn subject area content and work with others to deepen their understanding of the content. All of the frameworks emphasize the need to ground 21st century skills in core content, and especially in an interdisciplinary fashion. Organizing instruction around important concepts and "big ideas" helps students create conceptual structures for storing, retrieving and using information in new and unanticipated ways. As the 21st century skills are integrated into content, some key design principles include

1. Connecting the content knowledge to real-world applications and problem situations that enable students to see how what they are

learning connects with their lives and the world around them. The work that is asked of students must be authentic work that is relevant and that mirrors real life.

2. Emphasizing deep understanding of the learning by focusing on projects and problems that require students to use the content knowledge in new ways and to extend their understanding through collaboration with others.
3. Using technology to help students access, analyze, organize and share what they are learning and allow students to independently locate appropriate tools for the task.
4. Providing opportunities for students to become "creators as well as consumers of published information" (Apple, 2008) by providing opportunities for creating and verifying their own entries in collaborative sites and evaluating contributions of others.
5. Engaging students in solving complex problems that require higher order thinking and application of content and that result in new perspectives and solutions to problems.
6. Providing opportunities for students to work collaborative as they gather information, solve problems, share ideas, and generate new ideas.
7. Developing life and career skills by creating opportunities for students to become self-directed learners who take responsibility for their own learning and who learn how to work effectively with others.
8. Helping students make connections between subjects, concepts and ideas and with others, including those outside of the classroom.

## Preparation of Students for Success in the 21st Century

The 21st century skills are not really different. We have always wanted students to be creative thinkers and problem solvers who have the skills necessary to function effectively in society and in the workplace. However, the way in which these skills are incorporated in the classroom and how technology is integrated will greatly change instruction. Indeed, with technology, today's classroom transcends physical walls and reaches around the globe. In addition, we need to plan instruction with an understanding of the "digital natives" (Prensky, 2001) who have grown up in the Digital Age and who expect learning to be interactive, engaging and up-to-date. Instruction that meets the needs of today's students will incorporate.

1. A variety of learning opportunities and activities

2. The use of appropriate technology tools to accomplish learning goals
3. Project- and problem-based learning
4. Cross-curricular connections
5. A focus on inquiry and the student-led investigations
6. Collaborative learning environments, both within and beyond the classroom
7. High levels of visualization and the use of visuals to increase understanding
8. Frequent, formative assessments including the use of self-assessment.

## Role of Teachers in fostering skills

The role of teachers in a 21st century classroom shifts from that of the "expert" to that of the" facilitator." The focus for instruction shifts from "knowing" to being able to use and apply information in relevant ways. Students who are being prepared for the 21st century will be involved in "continuous cycles of learning" (Lemke, et al, 2003) that lead to deeper understanding of the subject area content and that develop the critical skills for meeting the challenges of the future.

## Emerging challenges

To prepare students for their future lives and careers, they need to wrestle with real-life problems that are engaging and relevant. Their involvement in the problem-solving process builds a culture of inquiry, in which asking and answering their own questions becomes the centerpiece of the learning process. As problem solvers, students use high levels of thinking as they apply content knowledge in innovative ways. The curriculum must incorporate the "four important C's" of 21st century skills: creativity, critical thinking, collaboration and communication. Students work together to create innovative solutions to real-world problems and communicate their solutions with others. As they carry out their investigations and projects, they must access, analyze, and use the information they need to complete the learning tasks.

While working through the task, students build important life and career skills by learning to manage their time, to become self-directed workers and to collaborate effectively with others. Using appropriate technology tools to complete their task, students discover the most effective and efficient ways to access and manage the world of digital information that is available to them. "Digital natives" find a. classroom an inviting and challenging environment that incorporates their need to be interactive participants in their learning.

## Conclusion

Integrating 21st century skills like creativity, critical thinking, collaboration and communication can be achieved into the classroom are application, connections and participation. Many research findings revealed that retention is very low when there context for the learning and when the learning is not reinforced with practice. Most humans tend to forget 50% of newly learned knowledge in a matter of days or weeks. Meaningful material takes only about one tenth the efforts to learn and the forgetting is relatively gradual." Infusing 21st century skills with subject area content, and especially cross-curricular content, provides students with strong learning capacity and helps them retain the learning for ongoing use. This will create students to tackle any problems with acquired skills that provide everlasting peaceful sustainable life.

## Reference

1. American Association of School Librarians & Association for Educational Communications and Technology. (1998). Information *literacy standards for student learning* Chicago: American Library Association.
2. National Science Board. (2002). *Science and engineering indicators.* Arlington, VA: National Science Foundation. Retrieved April 12, 2003, from http://www.nsf.gov/sbe/srs/seind02/start.htm
3. Newmann, F. (1996). *Authentic achievement: Restructuring schools for intellectual quality.* San Francisco: Jossey-Bass.
4. Weisberg, R. W. (1999). Creativity and knowledge: A challenge to theories. In R. Sternberg (Ed.), *Handbook of creativity* (pp. 226-250). Cambridge, MA: Cambridge University Press.
5. *Quality Science Education and 21st Century Skills.* Publication. National Science Teachers Association, (2011). Web. <http://science. nsta.org/ nstaexpress/ Position Statement Draft_21st Century Skills. pdf.

# 43

# Cloud Computing –A Subscription Based Service Provider

## Introduction

Cloud computing is the delivery of computing services over the Internet. Cloud services allow individuals and business peoples to use software and hardware that are managed by third parties at remote locations. Cloud services include online file storage, social networking sites, webmail, and online business applications (Lewis, Grace, 2010). The cloud computing model allows access to information and computer. Now- a-days cloud computing is receiving a great deal of attention, both in publications, researches and among users, from individuals to professionals not only in the field of business sector but also it plays a vital application in the field of education.

Cloud computing is a subscription-based service provider that can provide information from networked storage space and computer resources. The best example for cloud computing is to consider our experience with e-mail. E-mail service providers like Yahoo, Gmail, Hotmail, and so on, takes care of housing all of the hardware and software necessary to support our personal email account. Instead of keeping data on our own hard drive or updating applications for our needs, we use a service over the

Internet, at another location, to store our information or use its applications (Lewis, Grace, 2010). The short representation of cloud computing can be given in the pictorial format.

## Requirements of cloud computing

The basic requirement for implementing cloud computing is one that need to have an internet connection in order to access the cloud. In order to look at or access at a specific document have housed in the cloud, we must first establish an internet connection either through a wireless or wired internet or a mobile broadband connection. The benefit is helps one can to access that same document from wherever with any device that can access the internet. These devices could be a desktop, laptop, tablet, or phone. This can also helps business to function more smoothly because anyone can connect to the internet and your cloud can work on documents, access software, and store data. Imagine picking up smart phone and downloading a pdf document to review instead of having to stop by the office to print it or upload it to our laptop. This is the freedom that the cloud can provide for organization. There are different types of cloud providers which serves the different purposes upon the choosing a cloud provider.

## Choosing a cloud provider

Each provider serves a specific function, giving users more or less control over their cloud depending on the type. For choose a provider, compare our needs to the cloud services available. Our cloud needs will vary depending on how we intend to use the space and resources associated with the cloud. If it will be for personal home use, we will need a different cloud type and provider than if we will be using the cloud for business. Keep in mind that cloud provider will be pay-as-we-go, meaning that if our technological needs change at any point can purchase more storage space (or less for that matter) from cloud provider. There are three types of cloud providers that can subscribe to: Software as a Service (SaaS), Platform as a Service (PaaS), and Infrastructure as a Service (IaaS). These three types differ in the amount of control that have over our information, and conversely, how much can expect our provider to do for us.

1. **Software as a Service** - A SaaS provider gives subscribers access to both resources and applications. SaaS makes it unnecessary to have a physical copy of software to install on our devices. SaaS also makes it easier to have the same software on all of our devices at

once by accessing it on the cloud. In a SAAS agreement, we have the least control over the cloud.

2. **Platform as a Service** - A PaaS system goes a level above the Software as a Service setup. A PaaS provider gives subscribers access to the components that they require to develop and operate applications over the internet.
3. **Infrastructure as a Service** - An IaaS agreement, as the name states, deals primarily with computational infrastructure. In an IaaS agreement, the subscriber completely outsources the storage and resources, such as hardware and software that they need.

We can choose our level of control over our information and types of services that want from a cloud provider. For starting up our own small business. We cannot afford to purchase and store all of the hardware and software necessary to stay on the cutting edge of our market. By subscribing to an Infrastructure as a Service cloud, we would be able to maintain our business with just as much computational capability as a larger, more established company, while only paying for the storage space and bandwidth that we use (Strowd, Harrison & Lewis, Grace, 2010). However, this system may mean we have to spend more of our resources on the development and operation of applications.

## Types of clouds

There are different types of clouds that you can subscribe to depending on your needs. As a home user or small business owner, you will most likely use public cloud services.

1. Public Cloud - A public cloud can be accessed by any subscriber with an internet connection and access to the cloud space.

2. Private Cloud - A private cloud is established for a specific group or organization and limits access to just that group.

3. Community Cloud - A community cloud is shared among two or more organizations that have similar cloud requirements.

4. Hybrid Cloud - A hybrid cloud is essentially a combination of at least two clouds, where the clouds included are a mixture of public, private, or community.

## Security

The information housed on the cloud is often seen as valuable to individuals with malicious intent. There is a lot of personal information and potentially secure data that people store on their computers, and this information is now being transferred to the cloud. This makes it critical to understand the security measures that our cloud provider has in place, and it is equally important to take personal precautions to secure our data. No matter how careful we are with our personal data, by subscribing to the cloud you will be giving up some control to an external source. This distance between from us and the physical location of our data creates a barrier. It may also create more space for a third party to access your information. However, to take advantage of the benefits of the cloud, you will have to knowingly give up direct control of your data. On the converse, keep in mind that most cloud providers will have a great deal of knowledge on how to keep your data safe (Jansen, Wayne and Grace, Timothy, 2011)). A provider likely has more resources and expertise than the average user to secure their computers and networks.

## Applications

1. The cloud makes it possible to access information from anywhere at any time.

2. The cloud removes the need to be in the same physical location as the hardware that stores data.

3. Cloud provider can both own and house the hardware and software necessary to run home or business applications.

4. This is especially helpful for businesses that cannot afford the same amount of hardware and storage space as a bigger company.

5. Small companies can store their information in the cloud, removing the cost of purchasing and storing memory devices.

6. We can purchase more space or reduce their subscription as their business grows or as they find they need less storage space.

### Conclusion

Today the cloud provides many options for the everyday computer user as well as large and small businesses. Most of the people often feel that cloud computing is especially useful and applicable in the field of business sector. It opens up the world of computing to a broader range of uses and increases the ease of use by giving access through any internet connection. But it is well known that most of the service providing types of cloud computing is well applied in the field of education. Policy level designers and curriculum makers must considers the importance and implement the concept of cloud computing as a better resource accessing in the field of education especially to teaching and learning process.

## Reference


1. Lewis, Grace. (2009). *Cloud Computing: Finding the Silver Lining, Not the Silver Bullet* http://www.sei.cmu.edu/newsitems/cloudcomputing.cfm.
2. Lewis, Grace. (2010). *Basics about Cloud Computing.* http://www.sei.cmu.edu/library/abstracts/whitepapers/cloudcomputingbasics.cfm.
3. Jansen, Wayne and Grace, Timothy. (2011). *Guidelines on Security and Privacy in Public Cloud Computing.* National Institute of Standards and Technology.
4. Strowd, Harrison & Lewis, Grace.(2010). *T-Check in System-of-Systems Technologies: Cloud Computing (CMU/SEI-2010-TN-009).* Software Engineering Institute, Carnegie Mellon University. http://www.sei.cmu.edu/library/abstracts/reports/10tn009.cfm.

# 44

# Blended Learning – A Realistic Step Towards Learning Process

## Introduction

A blended learning approach combines face to face classroom methods with computer-mediated activities to form an integrated instructional approach. Kerres(2002) called it 'hybrid learning', mixed learning or multi-method learning'. Classroom time can be used to engage students in advanced interactive experiences while the online portion can address individual student needs. In this components of blended learning is divided in to two major views i.e., online and offline. Criterias are the principles and policies, which shape the choice of components in a blended solution. In this context we introduced drivers of blended learning. Since blended learning is mostly understood as a way of blending face-to-face and technology-based teaching and it is further described as one approach to be used. The program should include opportunities for faculty to learn how to redesign their courses, teach well online, and effective use of technology.

The meaning of blended learning widely diverged to encompass a wide variety of synthesis in learning methods until 2006, when the first *Handbook of Blended Learning* by Bonk and Graham was published.

Blended learning often refers specifically to the provision or use of resources which combine e-learning with other educational resources. Kerres(2002) called it 'hybrid learning', mixed learning or multi-method learning'. Blended learning is a formal education program in which a student learns at least in part through online delivery of content and instruction with some element of student control over time, place, path or pace. A blended learning approach combines face to face classroom methods with computer-mediated activities to form an integrated instructional approach. Learning activities that otherwise would have taken place during classroom time can be moved online. According to Elliot Masie, it is the use of two or more distinct methods of training. This may include combinations such as: blending classroom instruction with online instruction, blending online instruction with access to a coach or faculty member, blending stimulations with structured courses, blending on the job training with brown bag informal sessions, blending managerial coaching with e-learning activities.

## Goal

The goal of blended approach is to join the best aspects of both face to face and online instruction. Classroom time can be used to engage students in advanced interactive experiences while the online portion can address individual student needs.

Six major waves of technological innovation in learning:

1. Writing
2. Printing
3. Broadcast media
4. Consumer storage media
5. PC and CD-ROM
6. Internet technology

Writing can be considered as the first technological innovation, with phonetic alphabets, papyrus and paper. Printing was the second, with moveable type. The third was broadcast media such as film, radio and television. The fourth was a range of mass media storage devices including audio cassette, videotape with CD-ROM. The sixth is the current networked, web-based e-learning revolution.

## Components of Blended Learning

### Six online component groups

1. Online learning content

2. e-tutoring, e-coaching or e-mentoring
3. Online collaborative learning
4. Online knowledge management
5. The web
6. Mobile learning

**Six offline component groups**

1. Workplace learning
2. Face-to-face tutoring, coaching or mentoring
3. Classroom
4. Distributable print media
5. Distributable electronic media
6. Broadcast media

**Online components**

**1. Online learning content**

E-learning content can include: simple learning resources, interactive generic content, interactive customized content, performance support and simulations.

**2. e-tutoring, e-coaching or e-mentoring**

One-to-one, electronic support can include: e-tutoring, e-coaching, e-mentoring and 360 degree feedback.

**3. Online collaborative learning**

Collaborative learning can include:

i. Asynchronous collaboration: e-mail and bulletin boards

ii. Synchronous collaboration: Text chat, application sharing, audio conferencing, video conferencing and virtual classrooms.

**4. Online knowledge management**

Knowledge systems include: Searching knowledge bases, Data mining, Document and file retrieval and Ask an expert

**5. The Web**

This is the future itself. As the internet becomes bigger, better faster, quicker and cheaper, it becomes an indispensable tool. The main features of internet access include: Search engines, Websites, User groups and e-commerce sites.

### 6. Mobile learning

Mobile devices include: Laptops, PDAs and mobile phones

## Offline components

### 1. Workplace learning

There are many ways in which workplace learning can be formalized: Learning on the job, Projects, Apprenticeships, Placements, Site visits

### 2. Face-to-face tutoring, coaching or mentoring

One-to-one, face-to-face support can include, Tutoring, Coaching, Mentoring, 360 degree feedback

### 3. Classroom

Classroom learning covers a huge range of activities including: Lectures/presentations, Tutorials, Workshops, Seminars, Role play, Simulations, Conferences.

### 4. Distributable print media

Print still a primary learning resource: Books, Magazines, Newspapers, Workbooks, Keeping a journal and Review/learning logs.

### 5. Distributable electronic media

Distributable electronic media include: Audio cassettes, Audio CD, Videotape, CD-ROM, DVD, Pen drive

### 6. Broadcast media

It includes TV, RADIO, Interactive TV, Satellites(Especially for education)

## Criterias of Blended learning

Components are the elements that can be pieced together and integrated into a blended solution. Criteria are the principles and policies, which shape the choice of components in a blended solution. Six criterias:

1. Learning

2. Learners
3. Maintenance
4. Scalability
5. Resources
6. Sustainability

## 1. Learning

A considerable amount of work has been produced by cognitive psychologists over the last 50 years. These include Bloom, Gagne, Mager, Belbin, Bruner, Biggs and Collins, Pedler, Merriam and Caffarella. In practice the schemas produced by these authors are very similar, resulting in the following general categories:

Knowledge, Procedural skills, Mental skills, Interpersonal skills, Psychomotor skills, Attitudes and Aspirational learning.

*Procedural skills* involve following processes or routines from memory, manuals or computers. Knowledge of a range of procedures is required and learners appreciate the significance of the parts in relation to the whole. It may be expected to apply demonstrate, calculate, complete, solve, modify, relate, classify or find.

*Mental skills* involve the application of methods and theories in new situations; solve problems using required skills or knowledge. Problem solving is demonstrated by coming up with effective solutions.

*Interpersonal skills* have been increasingly recognized as a distinct skill set in themselves, along with emotional intelligence. These are skills in listening, questioning, presenting, interviewing, counseling, appraising and so on. Writing skills, telephone skills and electronic communication skills using email etc are also included.

*Psychomotor skills* involve the acquisition of skilled movements and perceptual abilities. These may be in sports, dance, music, driving, crafts, keyboard skills or flying an aircraft. *Attitudinal change* requires the learner to be made aware of existing attitudes and, if there's a gap between those and the new attitudes or values, to be able to understand and apply those new attitudes.

## 2. Learners

To understand blended learning we must focus on learners. Learners blend anyway. They'll learn through lots of different learning encounters. In learning a language the learner is likely to take some classes, use online resources, CD-ROMs, audio cassettes, audio CDs, videos, watch TV, listen to radio programmes in that language, use books, access dictionaries, get a pen-pal, speak to native speakers, even go to that country for practice. Blended learning was always the norm-for learners.

The learner population has to be profiled, including

1. Number of learners
2. Geographic dispersion of learners
3. Available time by learners
4. Learner's motivation to learn
5. Novices versus experts
6. Academic versus non-academic

### 3. Maintenance

Different types of content need different levels of maintenance. Non-volatile factual content such as basic science may need little or no updating. Middle ground content such as management skills may need a modest amount updates. However, induction, product knowledge, legislative issues and many other topics will need major updates.

### 4. Scalability

Scalability is the ability of a delivery mechanism to cope with large numbers, on-demand at little incremental cost. Scalability is usually achieved through technology. A hand written letter can be scaled through word-processing, photocopying, printing and ultimately, the most scalable of all, email, where huge numbers can be delivered instantly, on demand and at a tiny incremental cost. The classroom is only scalable in the sense of having more people in the room at any one time. A good example would be a conference with thousands of people seeing a keynote speech by experts.

### 5. Sustainability

The sustainability of your blend will make the difference between short and long-term success. Cultural resistance is usually the major obstacle to change and if you exist in a culture where change difficult, newer components may be difficult to implement. At one level sustainability will depend on cultural issues and change management may be needed. On another level, sustainability will depend on the ability of your blend to support an ongoing learning culture within the organization.

## 6. Resources

Whatever may be the intentions in blended learning, if you don't have the human, organizational, technical and fiscal resources, you're bound to fail. The type of blend you want may be different from the blend you can deliver.

Resources consider include:

1. Human resources
2. Physical infrastructure
3. Technical resources
4. Budget

## Drivers of Blended Learning

1. Improve ability to personalize learning.
2. Potential for individual progress.
3. Improve student engagement and motivation.
4. Shift to online state tests starting in 2015
5. Need to extend time and stretch resources.
6. Potential to extend the reach of effective teachers.
7. Ability to improve working conditions.
8. Decrease device costs.
9. Student and parent adoption of learning apps.
10. Interest in narrowing the digital divide.

## Approaches

Since blended learning is mostly understood as a way of blending face-to-face and technology-based teaching and it is further described as one approach to be used within other pedagogical approaches it would be interesting to look at different kinds of approaches to blend face-to-face and technology-based teaching. Bersin(2008) offers two concrete approaches and finds that the goal of blended learning is to synthesize the face-to-face and technology-based teaching into an integrated mix. In this way one can tailor the teaching basing on actual needs. First of all-the technology can compliment traditional instructor-led program and second it can compliment technology-based training where the socialization process is lacking and where the students lack motivation and excitement from an instructor. From this thought Bersin finds two general approaches to blended learning.

1. The 'Program flow' model: a step-by-step curriculum that integrates

several media into a chronological program or syllabus. The cheapters are building on each other. It ends in an exercise or assessment to measure total learning. This model is comparable to a college or high-school course.

2. The 'core-and-spoke'model: One fundamental training approach with other materials, interactivities, resources and assessments as 'supporting materials, optional or mandatory materials that surround and complement the primary approach.

## Conclusion

In designing, developing and delivering different types of blends – we must be sure that we have thought about the learning outcomes, learners, culture, learning resources, electronic infrastructure, scalability and maintainability of the proposed solution. Increasing choice is not an end in itself. They are carefully crafted blends of complementary tastes, where the sum is greater than the parts. The concept of Blended learning has been with us for some time and really builds on the good practice of blending teaching and learning styles for the benefit of the learner. Teachers', who adopt a variety of teaching styles are more likely to offer their learners a more rewarding and successful educational experience. Therefore, it is essential to introduce and expand a new culture of knowledge, based on active users who are able to create, search, analyze, communicate and share information and knowledge. In this respect, blended learning constitutes a strategic environment which facilitates the adoption of the new educational paradigm based on active learning. A policy frame work should be developed, which explicity states how blended learning supports the vision, values, and principles of the institution. Faculty development program should be central to success of an institutions blended learning initiative. The program should include opportunities for faculty to learn how to redesign their courses, teach well online, and effective use of technology.

## References

1. Bersin, J.(2008). The blended learning book: best practices, proven methodologies, and lesions learned, San Francisco: Pfeiffer.
2. Throne, K.(2012). Blended learning: How to integrate online and traditional learning, Kogan page Limted, Londan.
3. 10.Kerres, M., & De Witt C.(2002). A didactical framework for the design of blended learning arrangements. Journal of Educational Media, 28, pp 2-3.

4. Richard, J, A., Muthaiah, N. & Bond, H.(2012). Can Blended Learning Enhance Teaching Skills/University News, vol. 50, No. 11, pp 1-6.

# 45

## Learning Without Limit

### Introduction

Grouping by ability holds children back argues head teacher Alison Peacock, whose school went from failing to outstanding when the whole staff worked to ban limiting beliefs about fixed abilities and fixed futures and became a listening school. Learning without Limits College Preparatory Elementary School helps students to become leaders who are passionate, curious and equipped with the skills and knowledge needed for high achievement. We build on the knowledge students bring with them to school and monitor their progress closely to ensure success's convincing. "The style and language used by the authors make the book readable and therefore a book that practicing teachers can actively use as a guide to improve their practice ...it is amply demonstrated that teaching can and should be an activity whose primary focus is to enhance students' learning capacity and not limit it." The authors analyze these case studies and identify the key concept of transformability as a distinguishing feature of these teachers' approach. They construct a model of pedagogy based on transformability: the mind-set that children's futures as learners are not pre-determined, and that teachers can help to strengthen and ultimately transform young people's capacity to learn through the choices they make.

Literature and research spanning many decades have drawn attention to the damaging effects of ability labeling on young people's learning and life chances. Yet determinist beliefs about ability continue to have currency in schools. Indeed, the idea that child are born with a given amount of intellectual power, has gained renewed strength and legitimacy in recent years. Government-sponsored initiatives to raise standards and improve practice in schools have placed particular emphasis upon the need to differentiate by 'ability'. Teachers are expected to make explicit in their schemes of work how this differentiation is to be achieved.

"Creating Learning without Limits' takes on one of the most important issues in education today. In the last decade schools in England have taken a path towards putting all children into boxes, attaching are capable of achieving. This book shows the possibility of a different educational path, one in which all students are encouraged to achieve the greatest they can. Importantly the book also documents ways in which courageous teachers can do this - promoting fair and engaging learning environments for all students. This is a must-read for educators, policy makers and parents alike".

"College is a place where a professor's Lecture notes go straight to the student's lecture notes, without passing through the brains of either "- Edwin Emory Slosson.

Learning without Limits College Preparatory Elementary School is the right fit for you and your child if you are looking for a school that treats you like a partner. At LWL, we are dedicated to seeing all children make dramatic progress. Students who attend LWL agree to make one another feel loved and cared about. When students feel a sense of belonging at school, they are able to give their full attention to their work and when they do that, they learn without limits! The Learning without Limits project is dedicated to developing approaches to teaching and learning that do not rely on determinist beliefs about ability. The purpose of the project is to support the development of approaches to education that allow every child's learning to flourish, free from such externally imposed limits.

## 'Special Educational Needs'

Learning without Limits website The big idea of 'transformability' and the four practical, pedagogical principles outlined above have been used to inform and inspire whole-school development; to support teachers in initial training and courses of further professional development; they have helped to inform a foundation degree course in Higher Education and a local authority support service dedicated to fostering the inclusion of children deemed to have 'special educational needs'.

## Small Group Section

1. Support small, closed study groups within a larger course:
2. On-campus class announcements
3. Closed forums
4. Notes and note-taking tools
5. Instructor access to grades for the students in the section
6. Facilitate closer interactions between instructors, TAs and students
7. While benefiting from the richness of interaction in a larger community.

## Flexibility in Course Structure

1. High-quality online content
2. Produced locally or adopted from another institution
3. High-touch interaction with local instructor
4. Active learning, problem solving, personal attention to students
5. Self-selected level of guidance – Multi-campus or multi-section enrollment
6. Attention from instructor.

## Digital Learning

Park Manor has developed an Accelerated Learning Framework to help us effectively integrate digital learning into our curriculum in ways that accelerates the learning of all of our students. The Accelerated Learning Framework was just published in Michael Fullan's latest book "Stratosphere 'students as seekers, users and creators of their own knowledge'.

## Perception and Recall

Perception requires that the learner selectively focus on and make sense of stimulation in the environment, including the learner's own internal states and responses (thoughts, feelings, and physiological states). Recall involves the ability to remember and make use of relevant prior learning, as well as of the learning acquired in a given situation.

1. **Organization affects perception;** that is, events, ideas, words, concepts, and other stimuli that are not organized in some meaningful way are more difficult to understand and remember than those that are.
2. **Perception and recall can be aided by comparison and contrast;** similarity and grouping also assist recall.

3. **Presentations that focus on differences are distinguished better by learners** and their contents may be easier to recall.
4. **Modeling and demonstrations** can result in learning. While learners eventually must become active in the process of acquiring skills and knowledge, students can also learn while watching.
5. **Repetition and review** increase learning up to a point. (Depth of understanding, breadth of proficiency).

## Concept Formation and Higher-order Thinking

The learning of concepts or principles is often intended to be part of a process leading to engagement with other, related concepts. In formulations such as Gagne's (1970), below, the learning sequence is hierarchical, and as the learner moves up the sequence, more complex orders of reasoning are required:

1. **Signal learning**; involuntary responses; for example, the startle response, or removing a hand from heat.

2. **stimulus-response learning**; involuntary, selective responses; for example, signaling in response to a specific cue, or imitating an action.

3. **motor-chain learning**; performing a sequence of actions in a certain order; for example, dancing, parallel parking, or replacing a light bulb.

4. **verbal association or verbal chaining**; reciting correct responses to cues; for example, singing the lyrics of a song, reciting the alphabet, or translating a word from one language to another.

5 .**Multiple discrimination**; responding differently to similar stimuli; for example, distinguishing individual

6. **concept learning**; responding to new stimuli according to properties they share with previously encountered stimuli, or comparing properties of phenomena.

7. **Principle learning**; putting two or more concepts together in a relationship (without necessarily being able to explain the underlying rule governing the relationship)

8. **Problem-solving**; recalling previously learned principles and using them in combination to achieve a goal.

## Media, Modes, and Learning

Technologies, as channels through which modes (symbols acting as stimuli) pass, differ in the responses they evoke in users. For example, text is a mode of presentation. Print-on-paper is one possible medium (channel) for text, but there are others: a computer monitor, an overhead projection, a television screen, film (moving or still), etc. In this way, media may help to reduce "transactional distance" in learning the communication gap or psychological distance between participants which may open in a teaching-learning situation.

## Media Characteristics and Impacts on Learning

Five types of media, from print to multimedia defined as "the integration of video, audio, graphics, and data within a single computer workstation"; The argument here is that, as technologies continue to evolve, it will be increasingly possible, technically, to use ever more complex media, including multimedia as defined above, to deliver instruction.

## Print and Text

There is no medium more ubiquitous than print, and no mode more familiar than text in its many forms. Print was part of the first teaching machine—the book—and books was the first mass-produced commodity. Print has been the dominant medium to date in distance education, and distance students have traditionally spent most of their time studying alone, often using print materials only. The chief strengths of print and text have traditionally included:

- **Cost**—reports that print is one of the lowest cost one-way technologies.
- **Flexibility and robustness**—print scores highest on these features.
- **Portability** and ease of production—with desktop publishing hardware and software, printing has become enormously simpler and its quality much higher. In addition, costs can be reduced with local production.
- In **stability** organization and sequencing are positively affected, since text-only printed and online materials can be reorganized and resequenced with relative ease by cut-and-paste operations, using word-processors and HTML editors.
- **Convenience,** familiarity, and economy—instruction and feedback are facilitated by the medium's familiarity, as, for adept learners and the highly literate, are higher-order thinking and concept formation.

## Video and Animation

According to Roberts (1998), video adds a sense of direct involvement and physical presence among geographically dispersed learners.

- Provides quality learning opportunities
- Gives distant sites live, interactive learning opportunities.
- Enables the delivery of global expertise to remote learners.
- Eliminates or reduces travel time and time away from jobs and family.

The advantages in actual practice of various forms of video continue to be debated. In some studies, animation has been shown to result in a reduction in study time, "suggesting that animation results in more efficient learning" with learning effects persisting over time, when compared with "highly imaginative examples and illustrations," the advantages of animated simulations were less obvious in concluded from his analysis that "any widespread belief in the superiority of animation over non-animated instruction within the context of computer-based instruction is at odds with the research" According to Roberts (1998), critical issues in the delivery of video-based training include those listed below.

1. Proper training of instructors.
2. User self-consciousness.
3. Integration of other media into video presentations.
4. Optimum length of sessions and size of groups.
5. Session variety.
6. Technical design and support.
7. Professional quality visual elements.

Obviously, video delivery is complex, potentially costly, and of uncertain benefit for some teaching tasks over simpler, more economical media. A clear pedagogic and business case is obviously needed for its use. Despite these potential limitations and weaknesses, multimedia also has potential strengths when used appropriately. Advantages of multimedia for instruction:

- Multiple, active learning modalities.
- Accommodation of different learning styles and preferences, including disabilities.
- Effective instruction across learning domains, including affective and psychomotor (with simulations, case studies, and other representational and interactive uses), promoting development of higher-order thinking skills, and concept formation.
- Realism, especially when coupled with graphics and video.
- Potential interactivity.
- Consistent experiences, compared with group-based face-to-face instruction.
- Potential for high levels of learner control.

## The Internet

As noted at the outset of this chapter, "online learning" almost always denotes learning "on the Internet." The Internet offers both advantages and challenges to educators and trainers. The advantages arise from the Internet's enormous capacity to link participants with information and with each other. But problems with navigation, structure, interactivity, complexity, security, and sheer consumption of time must be addressed.

The Internet is potentially a powerful linking and communication vehicle. Two related Internet-based media show particular instructional promise for those with the skill and discipline to use them well, especially in relation to organization and sequencing challenges presented by the Internet: hypermedia and hypertext. Hypermedia is the linking of multimedia documents, while hypertext is the linking of words or phrases to other words or phrases in the same or another document. Internet delivery may be hyperlinked or linear.

## Conclusion

Online learning is still in its early infancy. There are many outstanding, and, in some cases, vexing issues: costs are declining, but still limit widespread access; many users (teachers, trainers and learners) feel they do not have all the skills they need to make mature use of online learning's potential; administrators and policy-makers often overstate the likely impacts of going online and the relation of learning outcomes to technology use, for specific populations and in particular circumstances, has not been clearly identified, and is not well understood. Although these realities prove that there must be evolution before online learning can be seen as mature, at the same time there are promising signs. Finally, in-service training is increasingly available to potential users. Whether online learning follows this path or not, it has a good chance to grow because online access to information—wired or wireless, structured or user-driven—and interaction using various computer-based technologies are established social and economic realities.

## References

1. Bates, A. W. (1988). Technology for distance education: A 10-year prospective. Open Learning, 3(3), 3-12.
2. Bates, A. W. (1995). Technology, open learning and distance education. New York: Rutledge.

3. Bates, A. W., Harri ngton, R., Gilmore, D., & van Sorest, C. (1992). Compressed video and video-conferencing in open and distance learning: A guide to current developments. Unpublished manuscript, The Open Learning Agency, Burnaby, BC.
4. Bloom, B. S. (1976). Human characteristics and school learning. Toronto: McGraw-Hill.
5. Bloom, B. S. (1984, June-July). The 2-sigma problem: The search for methods of group instruction as effective as one-to-one tutoring. Educational Researcher, 4-16.

# 46

# Flipped Classroom

## Introduction

A flipped classroom is where students receive the key instructional elements at home. Then in the classroom, they apply the knowledge. Instruction can be provided through videos, podcasts, websites, DVDs, CDs, or any other form that provides a clear instructional message. In the classroom, students work together under the guidance of the teacher in applying the instruction to complex problems. In a Flipped Classroom students receive their direct-instruction through video which can be watched in or out of class. No longer is the teacher using the majority of classroom time to lecture; instead students are engaging in various learning activities with increased face-to-face classroom time. The general focus of the Flipped Classroom in this study was to make the learning environment more students centered by moving the learning from a passive format to an active one.

Flip teaching or a flipped classroom is a form of blended learning in which students learn new content online by watching video lectures, usually at home, and what used to be homework (assigned problems) is now done in class with teachers offering more personalized guidance and interaction with students, instead of lecturing. This is also known as backwards classroom, flipped classroom, reverse teaching, and the Thayer Method.

Teachers are blending the advantages of flipped learning with traditional in-class lecturing through tools like edu canon that keep students accountable to video lessons at home through time-embedded formative assessments. Flipping also changes the allocation of teacher time. Flipping changes teachers from "sage on the stage" to "guide on the side", allowing them to work with individuals or groups of students throughout the session.

## Flipped Classroom

There is no single model for the flipped classroom the term is widely used to describe almost any class structure that provides prerecorded lectures followed by in-class exercises. In one common model, students might view multiple lectures of five to seven minutes each. Online quizzes or activities can be interspersed to test what students have learned. Immediate quiz feedback and the ability to rerun lecture segments may help clarify points of confusion. Instructors might lead in-class discussions or turn the classroom into a studio where students create, collaborate, and put into practice what they learned from the lectures they view outside class. As on-site experts, instructors suggest various approaches, clarify content, and monitor progress. They might organize students into an ad hoc workgroup to solve a problem that several are struggling to understand. Because this approach represents a comprehensive change in the class dynamic, some instructors have chosen to implement only a few elements of the flipped model or to flip only a few selected class sessions during a term.

## Defining the Flipped Classroom

The flipped classroom is a pedagogical model in which the typical lecture and homework elements of a course are reversed. Short video lectures are viewed by students at home before the class session, while in-class time is devoted to exercises, projects, or discussions.

## Significant of flipped classroom

In a traditional lecture, students they are trying to transcribe the instructor's words, but in flipped classroom it is contrast, the use of video and other prerecorded media puts lectures under the control of the students, At the same time, collaborative projects can encourage social interaction among students, making it easier for them to learn from one another and for those of varying skill levels to support their peers.

An effective flip requires careful preparation. Recording lectures should carefully integrate the, out-of-class and in-side-class elements for students to understand the model and be motivated to prepare for class. As a result, instructor may require new skills. Those who see themselves as attending class to hear lectures may feel it is safe to skip a class that focuses on activities and might miss the real value of the flip. Finally, even where students embrace the model, their equipment and access might not always support rapid delivery of video.

## Educational Effectiveness and the Flipped Classroom

Flipped classroom represents a unique combination of both student-centered and conventional lecture-based teaching methods; the flipped classroom may perform better than purely problem-based approaches on knowledge outcomes, while still working toward broad learning goals that conventional teaching methods usually ignore. This statement represents the central motivating hypothesis of the present work. Successful evaluation of this theory will allow educators and future researchers to make more informed decisions that will hopefully lead to higher overall educational effectiveness.

## Reviews and related literature

Strayer (2007) surveyed university students on learning environment and learning activity. The study included a class that received traditional instruction and a class that was given flipped instruction. The results of the study showed that students in the Flipped Classroom "preferred and experienced a higher level of innovation and cooperation in their classroom". Strayer noted that, although students enjoyed the innovation and cooperation aspects the Flipped Classroom offered,

Day and Foley (2006) conducted a study similar to Strayer (2009). Two introductory human-computer interaction upper-level undergraduate classes were studied. One received traditional in-class lecture, and the other class received web based out of class lecture. Day and Foley sought to determine what effect the Flipped Classroom had on student achievement and student enjoyment. There results confirmed their hypothesis that the Flipped Classroom increased student achievement. Those students in the experimental Flipped Classroom scored higher grades on every assignment and every exam and, as a result, scored higher in the course.

## Conclusion

Flipped classrooms are shifting the way teachers provide instruction by inverting traditional teaching methods to engage students in the learning process. Using technology, lectures are moved out of the classroom and delivered online as a means to free up class time for interaction and collaboration. In order to effectively implement a flipped classroom, teachers must possess a set of requisite technical skills, conceptual knowledge and pedagogical expertise. Through this study, teachers are interested to making web-based instructional modules to implementing in flipped classroom for quality learning.

## Reference


1. Day,J.A.,&Foley,J.D.(2006).Evaluating a web lecture intervention in a human–computer interaction course. IEEE Transactions on Education, 49 (4), 420–431.
2. Green, G. (2012, January 18). My View: Flipped classrooms give every student achance to succeed. *CNN.* Retrieved from http://schoolsofthought.blogs.cnn.com/2012/01/18/my-view-flipped-classrooms-give-every-student-a-chance-tosucceed/
3. Guskey, T. R (2007). Closing Achievement Gaps: Revisiting Benjamin S. Bloom's"Learning for Mastery". *Journal of Advanced Academics, 19*(1), 8-31.
4. Knight, J. K., & Wood, W. B. (2005). Teaching More by Lecturing Less. Cell Biology
5. Education, 4(4), 298-310.
6. Toppo, G. (2011, October 7). 'Flipped' classrooms take advantage of technology. USA
7. Today. Retrieved from http://usatoday30.usatoday.com/news/education/story/
8. 2011-10-06/flipped-classrooms-virtual-teaching/50681482/1
9. Toto, R., & Nguyen, H. (2009, October) "Flipping the Work Design in an Industrial.
10. Engineering Course," Proceedings, 39th ASEE/IEEE Frontiers in Education Conference, San Antonio, Texas, USA.

# 47

# Achievement and Stress among students and Teachers in Modern Scenario

## Introduction

The aim of the study is to determine the stress in teaching, learning towards by promoting technology in teaching and learning for the achievement among students and teachers. Recent progresses in the technology have provided a new direction to instructional method in the classroom. One among those which has become prominent is called the flipped classroom, where the idea is to flip the instructional approach. The traditional classroom usually spent 90% of class time on delivery and review of content and only 10% is spent on application and evaluation. Hence, there is no enough time for differentiation. In flipped classroom, the primary delivery of the concept or content is online which makes a flipped classroom different from the traditional classroom. It promotes a unique combination of learning theories which is derived from constructivist ideology and direct instruction methods based on behaviorist theories (Bishop & Verleger, 2013). The study focused on promoting flipped class room teaching and learning pattern to overcome hurdles in its achievement (Stalker & Horn, 2012).

This paper studies what we know and don't know about flipped class room. Detailed reviews of the theory, research on flipped class room, and the extensive literature on how flipped class rooms should be utilized in teaching. Earlier reviews provide the foundation for proposing specific learning outcomes and generic techniques to integrate the traditional class rooms into flip model across the educational curriculum.

Stress is a common feature in our lives, especially as the pace of development increases. Work is a common term which is applied for all sorts of occupation. An occupational stress is any force that pushes a psychological or physical factor behind its range of stability, producing a strain within the individuals. As occupational stress begins to take toll on the body and mind, a variety of symptoms can result ("job stress" 1992). Working in organizations' not only provides individuals with life sustaining income but also exerts its own pressures on them. On several occasions, different students commented they wished other classes would operate in the same manner because they enjoyed the reduction in stress and work level that came along with being able to interact with the teacher during the assignment rather than waiting until the assignment was due to discover it was incorrect.

Flipped Classroom model is an innovative classroom model which synthesis the idea that blended or unified learning happens where students have some control over time, place, path and pace. This facilitates the students to choose the setting where the learners receive the content of learning. The model utilizes educational technology and various activities in such a way that it has a positive impact on the learning atmosphere. The role of the instructor or teacher has changed as a facilitator, coach and a guide who empowers then to actively engage them in the learning process. The goal of the class room time or a period is to master the concepts and to encourage collaborative work. "Research shows that a discipline problem of a classroom was drastically reduced due to practice of flipped model. This also leads to self -directed learning and taking ownership of one's own learning."(O'Neil et al, 2012). The article is divided into four sections: (a) why use flipped class rooms? (b) Modern teaching technology in the classroom, (c) selecting appropriate flips, (d) conclusions.

## Objective of the Study

### *(a) Why use flipped class rooms?*

In a Flipped Learning setting, teachers make lessons available to students to be accessed whenever and wherever it is convenient for the student. Teachers can deliver this instruction by recording and narrating screen casts of work they do on their computers, and students can watch the videos or screen casts as many times as they need to, enabling them to be more productive learners in the classroom.

### *(b) Modern teaching technology in the Classroom*

Among all of the tools currently available, which ones do students use and which ones have potential for classroom use? The answers to those questions are examined in the following two sections: (a) tools of the trade for students, Today's *Net Generation* of students is so sophisticated with technology that they have been branded as *digital natives* (Prensky, 2001, 2006) and (b) tools for the classroom.

### *(c) Selecting appropriate flips*

Requirements towards Flipped class rooms are:

(i) Flexible environments, (ii) A shift in learning culture, (iii) Intentional content, and (iv). Professional educators

**(i) Flexible environments:** Flipped classrooms allow for a variety of learning modes; educators often physically rearrange their learning space to accommodate the lesson or unit, which might involve group work, independent study, research, performance, and evaluation. Students choose when and where they learn. Furthermore, educators who flip their classes are flexible in their expectations of student timelines for learning and how students are assessed.

**(ii) A shift in learning culture:** A student-centered approach, where in-class time is meant for exploring topics in greater depth and creating richer learning opportunities. Students move from being the product of teaching to the center of learning. A student-centered pedagogy aimed at their readiness level or zone of proximal development, where they are challenged but not so much so that they are demoralized (Vygotsky, 1978).

**(iii) Intentional content:** Flipped educators evaluate what content they need to teach directly, since lectures are an effective tool for teaching particular skills and concepts, and what materials students should be allowed to first explore on their own outside of the group learning space.

**(iv) Professional Educators:** Professional Educators are reflective in their practice and are more important than ever. Educators continually observe their students, provide them with feedback relevant in the moment, and continuously assess their work.

## Research on Flipped Learning

Quantitative and rigorous qualitative research on Flipped Learning is limited, but great deal of research supports the key elements of the model with respect to instructional strategies for engaging students in their learning. A significant body of research on active learning strategies supports the effectiveness of these approaches in increasing student learning and achievement (e.g.; Prince, 2004). Active learning provides students with opportunities to interact with content through reading, writing, listening, talking, and reflecting (University of Minnesota Center of Learning and Education, 2008). Evidence indicates that active learning also improves student academic performance (Hake, 1998; Knight & Wood, 2005; Michael, 2006; Freeman et al., 2007; Chaplin, 2009); increases student engagement and critical thinking; and improves student attitudes (O'Dowd & Aguilar-Roca, 2009).

Eric Mazur at Harvard University is a leading researcher on "peer instruction" (1996), which emphasizes the kind of in-class interactional elements made more practical in a flipped classroom. In Mazur's model, students are engaged by having them confront the logical progression of their thinking and their misconceptions (Berrett, 2012). Bloom (1984) observed that the constant feedback and correction students receive significantly improves learning and achievement.

Little formal data exist to show the effect of Flipped Learning on special populations, such as English language learners. Marshall and DeCapua (2013) note that, in traditional classrooms, English language learners "put most of their effort into the lower levels" of Bloom's Taxonomy (understanding and remembering) as they attempt to follow the teacher's instruction. In the flipped classroom, the teacher and students can focus on the upper levels of the taxonomy (applying, analyzing, evaluating, and creating).

## Concerns about Flipped Learning

Skeptics of Flipped Learning say that there is little that is new in it. They say that good teachers always try to meet the needs of individual students and use the tools that will help them do that. And, as noted previously, the potential of Flipped Learning lies not in the videos but in how delivering direct instruction in a different environment opens up time and space inside the classroom to engage in higher leverage instructional practices and individualize learning. Even critics acknowledge that the changeover to the Flipped Learning model encourages teachers to re-evaluate their teaching (e.g.; Stumpenhorst, 2012).

Another concern is it undervalues the power of good, engaging, face-to-face Socratic teaching. Teachers cannot to that kind of teaching because class time is devoted to students collaborating, student-generated and -led activities, and other interactive exercises. However, Marshall (2013) points out that teacher are more important than ever in Flipped Learning and their role is to “lead from behind.” In other words, the teacher has the tasks of “observation, feedback, and assessment” and guiding the learners’ thinking, in the best spirit of the Socratic Method.

Gary Stager, a critic of Flipped Learning voiced three major concerns, that the model emphasizes traditional homework and lectures, although their position is flipped. Second, it requires that students study ahead of time. Finally, this model is a means of standardizing learning and in the future that the direct instruction delivered via video will be outsourced to mediocre, low-cost teachers to replace more highly paid veteran teachers.

In regard to Stager’s concern about mass-produced, cheaply made videos becoming the mainstay of flipped classrooms, Sams and Bergmann think that the model works best when teachers make their own videos for their own classes. However, the use of videotaped lessons does make it possible for the teacher to find great instruction produced by others, such as those found on Khan Academy or TED-Ed.

Another concern that is raised is that not all students have access to the high-speed Internet or computers. Bergmann and Sams (2012) noted that for lower elementary grades, Flipped Learning might be appropriate for certain lessons or units, but not entire classes.

## Analysis

A positive feedback from learners is quite encouraging as it suggests that it has really helped some of them grasp the key concepts better. It has seen students get a great deal of support from me as a guide, because I am not presenting as much information in class it allows me to spend my time clarifying concepts, working with students individually or in groups. The main advantage is as a facilitator I am able to present students with a range of rich stimulating tasks to complete in class. This permits them to combine the key concepts and problem skills required. More than 75% of the students suggest that it really supports their learning and it helps them to grasp the key concepts quicker. 90% express that they watch the videos more than once in order understand the key concepts. This technology allows them to pause & rewind when it is needed and often the criticism of presenting information in the classroom is that many of the students feel left behind. This pedagogy and technology is supportive of teaching any subject to any year level and should be used considered as only one strategy to be utilised. The most important part is still what happens in the classroom and this requires the teacher to prepare innovative challenging materials to support what is presented on the videos. Teachers can also record any presentation that is done throughout the lesson and post this for students to review at a later stage.

Instead of going through this numerous times with students, because they had forgotten what I had said I am now able to get them to watch the video again which allows me to work with students in extending and improving their investigations. The learning group prefer video lectures and collaborative classroom to lectures.

### *(d) Conclusion*

The present study has provided comprehensive information about stress among the students and teachers. Students reported lower stress levels in this type of classroom environment compared to other classes. While semester grades showed improvement, exam grades did not show significant improvement. Overall, students displayed positive feelings towards the treatment and enjoyed the associated benefits of being able to choose their own assignments and explore concepts they found interesting more in-depth.

This will also enhance the engagement of High Achievers as they are challenged to think and low or struggling students to receive enough effective remediation. This is so 90% of class time spent on application of content and 10% of time spent on delivery of content.

The improvement will be to make the videos more interactive and fun for students. The formal process that students need to complete at home (watch video, take notes and apply concepts) needs to be further developed and modified to make students more accountable and have time to think about the key concepts. The development of classroom materials will need to continue to provide students with open ended, higher order challenging questions that extends students problem solving and reasoning skills.

## References

1. Bergmann, J. & Sams, A. (2012). *Flip Your Classroom: Reach Every*

*Student in Every Class Every Day.* International Society for Technology in Education.

2. Berrett, D. (2012, February 19). How 'flipping' the classroom can improve the traditional lecture. *The Chronicle of Higher Education.* Retrieved from http://chronicle.com/article/How-Flipping-the-Classroom/130857/
3. Bloom, B. S. (1984). The 2 sigma problem: The search for methods of group instruction as effective as one-to-one tutoring. *Educational Researcher, 13(6),* 4-16.
4. Chaplin S. (2009). Assessment of the impact of case studies on student learning gains in an introductory biology course. *J. College Science Teaching, 39,* 72–79.
5. Classifying K-12 blended learning by Heather Staker and Michael B. Horn, may 2012, http://files.eric.ed.gov/fulltext/ED535180.pdf ERIC differently? *On the Horizon, 9*(6).
6. Freeman S., O'Connor E., Parks J. W., Cunningham M., Hurley D., Haak D., Dirks C., Wenderoth M. P. (2007). Prescribed active learning increases performance in introductory biology. *CBE Life Science Education, 6,* 132–139.
7. Hake, R. (1998). Interactive-engagement versus traditional methods: a six-thousand-student survey of mechanics test data for introductory physics courses. *American Journal of Physics, 16,* 64–74.
8. House. http://stumpteacher.blogspot.com/2012/12/not-flipping-for-flipped.html http://www.marcprensky.com/writing/).
9. http://www.slideshare.net/lainemarsh/3-reasons-to-flip-tesol-2013-32113.
10. Kathrine O'Neil, Teresa Kelly, Sheryl Bone, Kaplan University, United States World Conference on Educational Multimedia, Hypermedia and Telecommunications, Jun 26, 2012 in Denver, Colorado, USA ISBN 978-1-880094-95-2Publisher: Association for the Advancement of Computing in Education (AACE), Chesapeake, VA.
11. Knight J. K., & Wood W. B. (2005). Teaching more by lecturing less. *Cell Biology Education, 4,* 298–310.
12. Marshall, H. W. & DeCapua, A. (in press). *Making the transition: Culturally responsive teaching for struggling language learners.* University of Michigan Press: Ann Arbor, MI.
13. Marshall, H. W. (2013, March 21). *Three reasons to flip your classroom.* Retrieved from.
14. Mazur, E. (1996). *Peer Instruction: A User's Manual.* Addison Wesley: Boston, MA.

15. Michael, J. (2006). Where's the evidence that active learning works? *Advances Physiology Education, 30,* 159–167.
16. O'Dowd, D. K., & Aguilar-Roca, N. (2009). Garage demos: using physical models to illustrate dynamic aspects of microscopic biological processes. *CBE Life Science Education, 8,* 118–122.
17. Prensky, M. (2001). Digital natives, digital immigrants, part II: Do they really think
18. Prensky, M. (2006). *"Don't bother me mom I'm learning."* St. Paul, MN: Paragon
19. Stumpenhorst, J. (December 3, 2012). *Not Flipping for Flipped.* Retrieved from
20. The Flipped Classroom: A Survey of the Research, Jacob Lowell Bishop, Utah State University Dr. Matthew A Verleger, Embry-Riddle Aeronautical Univ., Daytona Beach, Paper ID #6219, 120th ASEE, Annual Conference and Exposition, June 23-26, 2013
21. Vygotsky, L. S. (1978) *Mind in society: The development of higher psychological processes.* Harvard University Press: Cambridge, MA.

# 48

# Implementation of Cloud Computing in Education

## Introduction

Innovation is necessary to ride the inevitable tide of change and one such hot recent area of research in Information Technology (IT) is cloud computing. Cloud computing is a distributed computing technology offering required software and hardware through Internet. It also provides storage, computational platform and infrastructure which are demanded by the user according to their requirement. Due to the growing need of infrastructure educational institutes, organizations have to spend a large amount on their infrastructure to fulfill the needs and demands of the users. Cloud computing is a next generation platform that allows institutions and organizations with a dynamic pools of resource and to reduce cost through improved utilization.

In the present scenario, many education institutions are facing the problems with the growing need of IT and infrastructure. Cloud computing which is an emerging technology and which relies on existing technology such as Internet, virtualization, grid computing etc. can be a solution to such problems by providing required infrastructure, software and storage. In this paper a basic research has been carried out to show how cloud computing can be introduced in the education to improve teaching, agility and have a cost-effective infrastructure which can bring a revolution in the field of education. It also tries to bring out its benefits and limitations.

In other words cloud computing provides shared resources, software and information through Internet as a PAYGO (Pay-as-you-go) basis. In the recent years, where educational institutes, universities, industries are giving their full contribution in transforming the society and entire world economy. Various researches are carried out to update the present IT infrastructure especially in the area of education.

Cloud computing can be a welcomed optioned in the universities and educational institutes for higher studies. It gives a better choice and flexibility to the IT departments by building multipurpose computational infrastructure once and then Manuscript received. Amazon, Google have already started providing their facilities for large business group. With the help of cloud computing the platform and application the user uses can be on-campus or off-campus or combination of both depending on the institutions need. Due to the evolution of cloud computing number of services have migrated from the traditional system to the online form. At present, as many universities are trying to update their IT infrastructure and data, but they are facing few challenges.

## Defining the cloud

Broadly, the cloud can be described as on-demand computing, for anyone with a network connection. Access to applications and data anywhere, anytime, from any device is the potential outcome. The consumer-level cloud is a good starting point for this – sites like Flickr and Face book act as digital repositories for data and we can access this data from any internet-enabled device, from our iPhones to our desktop computers. In the case of Flickr and the like, storage of our digital images is, from the consumer point of view, somewhere in the cloud. We don't need to know where specifically, we just need our Flickr login credentials and a web connection. We can see this model as evident in web-based email too.

The starting point (the bottom layer) is the physical hardware – the servers in data centers, whether owned by a firm or university for internal use or by the likes of Amazon or Google for public access. The next layer is virtualization. Virtualization allows a single physical server to run many independent virtual servers and is a necessary part of gaining the efficiencies (built on economies of scale) that cloud computing can offer those running the data centers. Automating the allocation of computing resources amongst the virtual servers and tracking user (customer) resource use requires a management layer. As Naone (2009a) highlights, this allows "true pay-as-you-go" billing which is part of the appeal of the cloud for users.

The cloud, however, doesn't stop here. The provision of software (services) to end-users mediated by the web is what has come to be known as Software as a Service (resulting in the rather clumsy acronym SaaS). This builds a further layer – the software running in the cloud and being accessed by users through their browser or other web-compliant tool. Firms like Salesforce.com have successfully built their business model entirely around providing web-based software, with the users' data storage and the processing of that data taking place in the cloud, rather than on the clients' own servers or their local machines.

**Which can be solved by cloud computing. The challenges are**;

**Cost:** choose the subscription or PAYGO plan.

**Flexibility:** cloud computing allows to dynamically scale the investment in infrastructures as demand fluctuate.

**Accessibility:** making the data and services available publicly without losing the sensitive information

## Services of Cloud

With an aim of reducing the expenditure of the universities for IT infrastructure and the complexity faced by universities and institutions, the traditional installed software on the campus computers are now replaced by cloud computing. With the power of cloud, today higher education can gain significant flexibility and agility and can migrate the sensitive data into remote and world wide data center ' the cloud' itself. To use the cloud services the universities and the institutions has to first define their requirements and has to take a special attention for the privacy and critical issues.

## There are several cloud services as follows;

1. Software as a Service (SaaS): the application service provider is hosting the application which runs and interacts through web browser, hosted desktop or remote client. It eliminates the need to install and run the application on customer own computer and simplifying maintenance and support.

2. Infrastructure as a Service (IaaS): can be used to satisfy the infrastructure needs of the students, faculties or researcher globally or locally with some specific hardware configuration for a specific task.
3. Platform as a Service (PaaS): certain providers are opening up application platforms to permit customer's to build their own application without the cost and complexity of buying and managing the underlying hardware and software layers.
4. Computing as a Service (CaaS): providers offer access Implementation of Cloud Computing in Education – A Revolution.

## Cloud Architecture for Education

Due to the higher accessibility, availability and efficiency of cloud services many universities, businesses are trying to make use of these services. Today's cloud computing providers are offering higher education, the opportunity to substitute their data and information in the 'cloud' for universities with existing data centers, servers and application replacing these traditional campus machines. Developing a cloud architecture for education can be distinct according to the purpose and infrastructure of the institution and can be challenging. The universities has to follow all the rules and regulation of the state and country for developing a cloud for education as many countries are very strict in cross broader transfer of information. Once the university establishes where their data will reside and gives the measure of data security an agreement called SLA (Service Level Agreement) can be made with the cloud service provider.

The SLA is a document which can ensure educational cloud users regarding the services provided by the cloud. It tries to identify the users need and simplifies complex issues and creates a relationship between the user and the service provider. It helps to specify the privacy, consistency and integrity. Privacy is one of the important factors which have to be taken care for cloud computing, as the service provider may require some personal information which is related to the data on what the user is trying to store in the cloud. So the universities should be very careful before disclosing the data and it should not lose the integrity of educational data.

There are many solutions that can ensure the security and protection of sensitive data in the cloud. These are;

1. Mask or de-identify of the data
2. Firewalls

3. Encryption and decryption
4. Authorization identity management.

Institutes can develop their own cloud called as 'private cloud' by making use of their existing Resources or multiple universities can come together and can develop a hybrid cloud called as 'educational cloud', in which they can share all the resources from the various universities. Private cloud makes use of the local network whereas the educational cloud makes use of public network to access the services provided by the cloud. Both private and educational cloud which is developed for education has to specify the services provided by them. Following table shows the differences between private and educational cloud.

## Benefits and Limitations of Cloud Computing

Due to the recent development in IT technologies, infrastructure and continuous upgrades in software and hardware has put a great deal of pressure on the budgets and expenses of universities and educational institutes. Cloud computing development provides many universities with an opportunity to take advantage of new IT technologies at an affordable cost. Allows the lecturer to get their work done in their web browsers rather storing and carrying it on the hard drive.

## Its gives the TEN benefits

### 1. Flexibility

The second a company needs more bandwidth than usual, a cloud-based service can instantly meet the demand because of the vast capacity of the service's remote servers. In fact, this flexibility is so crucial that 65% of respondents to an InformationWeek survey said "the ability to quickly meet business demands" was an important reason to move to cloud computing.

### 2. Disaster recovery

When companies start relying on cloud-based services, they no longer need complex disaster recovery plans. Cloud computing providers take care of most issues, and they do it faster. Aberdeen that businesses which used the cloud were able to resolve issues in an average of 2.1 hours, nearly four times faster than businesses that didn't use the cloud (8 hours). The same study found that mid-sized businesses had the best recovery times of all, taking almost half the time of larger companies to recover.

### 3. Automatic software updates

In 2010, UK companies spent 18 working days per month managing on-site security alone. But cloud computing suppliers do the server maintenance – Including security updates –themselves, Freeing up their customers' time and resources for other tasks.

### 4. Cap-Ex Free

Cloud computing services are typically pay as you go, so there's no need for capital expenditure at all. And because cloud computing is much faster to deploy, businesses have minimal project start-up costs and predictable ongoing operating expenses.

### 5. Increased collaboration

Cloud computing increases collaboration by allowing all employees – wherever they are – to sync up and work on documents and shared apps simultaneously, and follow colleagues and records to receive critical updates in real time. A survey by Frost & Sullivan found that companies which invested in collaboration technology had a 400% return on investment.

### 6. Work from anywhere

As long as employees have internet access, they can work from anywhere. This flexibility positively affects knowledge workers' work-life balance and productivity. One study found that 42% of working adults would give up some of their salary if they could telecommute, and on average they would take a 6% pay cut.

### 7. Document control

According to one study, "73% of knowledge workers collaborate with people in different time zones and regions at least monthly". Cloud computing keeps all the files in one central location, and everyone works off of one central copy. Employees can even chat to each other whilst making changes together. This whole process makes collaboration stronger, which increases efficiency and improves a company's bottom line.

### 8. Security

Some 800,000 laptops are lost each year in airports alone. This can have some serious monetary implications, but when everything is stored in the cloud, data can still be accessed no matter what happens to a machine.

### 9. Competitiveness

The cloud grants SMEs access to enterprise-class technology. It also allows smaller businesses to act faster than big, established competitors. A study on disaster recovery eventually concluded that companies that didn't use the cloud had to rely on tape backup methods and complicated procedures to recover – slow, laborious things which cloud users simply don't use, allowing David to once again out-manoeuvre Goliath.

### 10. Environmentally Friendly

Businesses using cloud computing only use the server space they need, which decreases their carbon footprint. Using the cloud results in at least 30% less energy consumption and carbon emissions than using on-site servers. And again, SMEs get the most benefit: for small companies, the cut in energy use and carbon emissions is likely to be 90%.

## Limitations

Cloud computing has the potential for improving the efficiency, cost and convenience for the universities and educational sectors, but it has few limitations such as;

1. Not all application run on cloud
2. Risk related to data protection and security and its integrity
3. Organizational support
4. Dissemination politics, intellectual property
5. Security and protection of sensitive data
6. Maturity of solutions
7. Lack of confidence
8. Standard adherence & Speed and lack of Internet can affect work methods

## Conclusion

Cloud computing is an emerging computing paradigm and next generation platform that can provide tremendous value of information of any size. The shift towards cloud computing would enable the universities and educational institutions to save money and take benefit of the developing technology. Both private and educational cloud can provide the necessary computational facility on demand of the user without any expense and can create a common platform for sharing the various resources from the various institutions. In spite, of limitations of cloud computing and keeping in mind the present scenario of economic crisis many universities, educational intuitions, organizations etc are trying to adopt cloud computing as a solution to the developing technologies and try to reduce their expenses. The main objective of the paper was to identify the essentials of cloud computing which can be considered as a new dawn to the higher education and has the full potential to make a 'revolution' in the field of education.

## Reference


1. J. L. Nicholson. Cloud Computing: Top Issues for Higher Education.
2. A. S. Dutta, Use of Cloud Computing in Education.
3. B. R. Kandukuri, V. R. Paturi, and A. Rakshit, "Cloud Security," in proceedings of the 2009 IEEE International Conference on Services. Computing, Washington, DC, USA, 2009, IEEE Computer Society, pp. 517-520.
4. R. N. Katz, The Tower and the Cloud: Higher Education in the age of cloud computing, 2008.
5. T. Ercan, "Effective Use of Cloud Computing in Educational Institutions," Procedia Social and Behavioral Science, vol. 2, pp 938-942, 2010.

# 49

# Blended Learning

## Introduction

Blended Learning, the combination of traditional face –to face teaching methods with authentic online learning activities, has the potential to transform student learning experiences and outcomes the technologies are not enough on their own to make a difference, but that teachers bring a particular understanding of language and the needs of their learners to the creation of suitable activities. It will show that the use of technologies is also changing our understanding of the profession of language education and that socio-cultural theory can help us understand why this is occurring. Blended learning as a type of classroom activity will be explored showing how different methods may be interpreted in the classroom context.

This paper will explore what language educators need to know in order to make effective use of learning technologies, the current stage of educational technology development that blended learning is the most appropriate solution for many teachers working in traditional classrooms who want to make use of digital technologies as an aspect of their practice. the advent of Web 2.0 we have seen a massive increase in the availability of tools that can potentially be used in a variety of different ways to blend regular classroom practice. Blended learning is a term increasingly used to describe the way e-learning is being combined with traditional classroom methods and independent study to create a new, hybrid teaching methodology. It represents a much greater change in basic technique than simply adding computers to classrooms. Traditional education (especially at the college level) tends to place an emphasis on delivering material by way of a lecture, while in a blended learning model lectures can be videotaped ahead of time so the student can watch on their own time. The classroom time is more likely to be for structured exercises that emphasize the application of the curriculum to solve problems or work through tasks.

## What is Blended Learning?

1. Blended learning combines online with face-to-face learning. The goal of blended learning is to provide the most efficient and effective instruction experience by combining delivery modalities.

2. "The term blended learning is used to describe a solution that combines several different delivery methods, such as collaboration software, Web-based courses, EPSS, and knowledge management practices

## Why Use Blended Learning?

1. "Students not only learned more when online sessions were added to traditional courses, but student interaction and satisfaction improved as well."
2. "Providing several linked options for learners, in addition to classroom training, increased what they learned."
3. Speedier performance was detected on real world tasks by those who learned through blended strategies as opposed to those that learned via e-learning along.
4. "Adults don't just "learn" in one way. Likewise, associations should not make the mistake of providing just one way for adult learners to receive their educational content."

## Concepts of Blended Learning

It consists of four different concepts of blended learning

1. To combine or mix modes of web-based technology (e.g., live virtual classroom, self-paced instruction, collaborative learning, streaming video, audio, and text) to accomplish an educational goal.
2. To combine various pedagogical approaches (e.g., constructivism, behaviorism, cognitive) to produce an optimal learning outcome with or without instructional technology.
3. To combine any form of instructional technology (e.g., videotape, CD-ROM, web-based training, film) with face-to-face instructor-led training.

4. To mix or combine instructional technology with actual job tasks in order to create a harmonious effect of learning and working

## What Medium can be used in Blended Learning?

The medium is not limited to technology and can include:

1. Stand-alone, Asynchronous, Or Synchronous Online Learning / Training
2. Performance Support Tools (Knowledge Management Tools)
3. Traditional Classroom, Labs, Or Other "Hands-on" Experiences
4. Reading Assignments, Cd-rom Or Other Self-paced Learning
5. Teletraining / Telelearning, or Other media

## Blended Learning Strategies

Blended learning is a powerful strategy for many reasons. If well designed, it addresses more Learning style requirements, a wider audience and increased performance or learning results.

Making the best selection of method (media) will greatly enhance these results. Learning professionals now have a plethora of choices which include e-learning, classroom (live or virtual), workshops, websites, job aids, simulations, books (hard copy or virtual) and many, many other choices.

## Synchronous Instructional Methods

Methods in this domain consist of traditional classrooms, virtual classrooms, live product practice (labs), interactive chats and mentoring (coaching).

## Asynchronous Instructional Methods

Methods in this domain consist of documents and web pages, web-based training (WBT), Computer-based training (CBT), CD-ROM, assessments, tests, surveys, simulations and labs and Recorded live events.

## Developing A Schoolwide Approach To Blended Learning

1. Blended learning means that some learning must occur outside of the classroom. This is a big psychological hurdle for some teachers to overcome, as they have grown accustomed to thinking of the learning environment only within the four walls of the classroom.
2. Blended learning requires that students have the skills to be self-regulated.

3. Blended learning requires a progression. Eighth graders should not be doing the same thing as sixth graders. There comes a time when a scope and sequence of blended learning experiences is needed.
4. Blended learning requires a school wide approach. There will always be individual teachers who are wondrously innovative and adventurous—thank goodness we all have them on our faculty. But without a mechanism for school wide discussions, planning, and curriculum development, these innovators exist in silos.

## Advantages of Blended Learning

Classroom: is good for workshops, coaching, exercises, feedback on activities and paper-based tests.

Self-paced e-learning: is good for simulations, online case studies, interactive learning modules, e-mail, bulletin boards interactions, online assessments, and other forms of CBT (computer based training).

Live e-Learning: is good for application exercises, online coaching, and interaction between students, online feedback, assessment, chats and instant messaging

## Implications

1. Development of online and offline course content.
2. Facilitation of communication with and among students, including the pedagogy of communicating content online without the contextual clues students would get in person.
3. Guiding the learning experience of individual students, and customizing material wherever possible to strengthen the learning experience.
4. Assessment and grading, not unlike the expectations for teachers within the traditional framework.

## Conclusions

The blended learning program is to improve both student outcomes and levels of satisfaction. It is clear that this environment can help teaching and learning engage students more effectively and allow greater participation than traditional models. Since technology is constrained by neither time nor space, it can improve the quality of subject learning by the students who are geographically dispersed. The only requirement is that the technology resources should be available for the use of technology in teaching, technology awareness should be intensified. Change of mindset to learn is needed by all the role players in the teaching-learning process. teachers need to be trained as online facilitators, and that the teachers also need to be subject-matter experts and reflective learners o f their teaching practices other teacher needs include communicating with online colleagues to provide support and possible solutions to teaching issues and challenges such as group size in the online learning environment. .The nature of the learning environments that most people inhabit – four physical walls with the possibility of one of these walls being expanded by connections to the Internet – and the enormous possibilities that Web 2.0 tools offer to both teachers and learners, make it inevitable that learning blends will be a feature of the language learning and more general educational landscape in the coming years.

## Referrences

(1) Blended Learning Book: Best Practices, Proven Methodologies, and Lessons Learned by JoshBersin. Jossey-Bass, 2004. (352 pages).

(2) "Blended Learning Strategies for Best Results," E-learning! Magazine. Winter 2006.

(3) Blended Learning: Let's Get Beyond the Hype by Dr. Margaret

(4) Bonk C.Olson,T., Wisher R.& Orvis, (2002). Learning from focus groups: An examination of Blended Learning. Journal of distance education, 17(3).

(5) Voos,R.(2003), Blended Learning: what is it & where might it take us? Slon–C view 2(1),2-5.

(6) Blended Learning Definition from Wikipedia http://en. wikipedia. org/wiki/Blended learning.

# 50

# Ict in Education: the Indian Perspective

## Introduction

Education is the most effective instrument which can instill people with the knowledge, skill and capability to observe and analyze the sense of purpose and confidence for building a dynamic energetic, just and unified nation able to take care of its entire people. Education does not have accumulation of information as its terminus. It should engender wisdom, which comprises tolerance, understanding, compassion and large-heartedness in outlook. Perhaps, this is what Plato meant when he said that the purpose of education is "not to fill an empty vessel but to turn the eye of the soul towards light".

## Information & Communication Technology

ICTs stand for information and communication technologies and are defined as a "diverse set of technological tools and resources used to communicate, create, disseminate, store, and manage information." These technologies include computers, the Internet, broadcasting technologies (radio and television), and telephony. Information technology defines an industry that uses computers, networking, software programming, and other equipment and processes to store, process, retrieve, transmit, and protect information.

## Growth of Higher Education in India

India's higher education system is the third largest in the world after China and the United States. Since independence the higher education in India has increased manifold in its institutional capacity as can be observed from the given table:

**Table 1. Institutional Capacity expansion in Higher Education**

| Institutional capacity indicator | 1950 | 2008 |
|---|---|---|
| Number of University Level Institutions (including 11 Private University) | 25 | 431 |
| Number of Colleges | 700 | 20,677 |
| Number of Teachers | 15,000 | 5,05,000 |
| Number of Students Enrolled | 1,00,000 | 1,16,12,000 |

Source: UGC – Hogher Education in India – issues related to expansion, Inclusiveness,

Quality & Finance, November 2008.

## The Aim of Involvement of Ict in Education

For developing countries like India, ICTs have the potential for increasing access to and improving the relevance and quality of education. It thus represents a potentially equalizing strategy for developing countries. ICTs greatly facilitate the acquisition and absorption of knowledge, offering developing countries unprecedented opportunities to enhance educational systems, improve policy formulation and execution, and widen the range of opportunities for business and the poor.

One of the greatest hardships endured by the poor, and by many others, who live in the poorest countries, is their sense of isolation. The new communications technologies promise to reduce that sense of isolation, and to open access to knowledge in ways unimaginable not long ago. However, the reality of the Digital Divide—the gap between those who have access to and control of technology and those who do not—means that the introduction and integration of ICTs at different levels and in various types of education will be a most challenging undertaking. Failure to meet the challenge would mean a further widening of the knowledge gap and the deepening of existing economic and social inequalities. The multifaceted aim of involvement of ICTs in education may be given as follows:

## ICTs for expanding access to education

ICTs are a potentially powerful tool for extending educational opportunities, both formal and non-formal, to previously underserved constituencies—scattered and rural populations, groups traditionally excluded from education due to cultural or social reasons such as ethnic minorities, girls and women, persons with disabilities, and the elderly, as well as all others who for reasons of cost or because of time constraints are unable to enroll on campus.

### (a) Anytime, anywhere

One defining feature of ICTs is their ability to transcend time and space. ICTs make possible asynchronous learning, or learning characterized by a time lag between the delivery of instruction and its reception by learners. Online course materials, for example, may be accessed 24 hours a day, 7 days a week. ICT-based educational delivery (e.g., educational programming broadcast over radio or television) also dispenses with the need for all learners and the instructor to be in one physical location. Additionally, certain types of ICTs, such as teleconferencing technologies, enable instruction to be received simultaneously by multiple, geographically dispersed learners.

### (b) Access to remote learning resources.

Teachers and learners no longer have to rely solely on printed books and other materials in physical media housed in libraries (and available in limited quantities) for their educational needs. With the Internet and the World Wide Web, a wealth of learning materials in almost every subject and in a variety of media can now be accessed from anywhere at any time of the day and by an unlimited number of people. This is particularly significant for many schools in developing countries, and even some in developed countries, that have limited and outdated library resources. ICTs also facilitate access to resource persons— mentors, experts, researchers, professionals, business leaders, and peers—all over the world.

### (c) ICTs for better Grooming of Students for the modern workplace

One of the most commonly cited reasons for using ICTs in the classroom has been to better prepare the current generation of students for a workplace where ICTs, particularly computers, the Internet and related technologies, are becoming more and more ubiquitous. Technological literacy, or the ability to use ICTs effectively and efficiently, is thus seen as representing a competitive edge in an increasingly globalizing job market. Technological literacy, however, are not the only skill well-paying jobs in the new global economy will require.

### (d) ICTs to improve the quality of education

Improving the quality of education and training is a critical issue, particularly at a time of educational expansion. ICTs can enhance the quality of education in several ways as follows:

1. **Motivating to learn**: ICTs such as videos, television and multimedia computer software that combine text, sound, and colorful, moving images can be used to provide challenging and authentic content that will engage the student in the learning process. Computers with Internet connectivity can increase learner motivation as it combines the media richness and interactivity of other ICTs with the opportunity to connect with real people and to participate in real world events.
2. **Facilitating the acquisition of basic skills**. The transmission of basic skills and concepts that are the foundation of higher order thinking skills and creativity can be facilitated by ICTs through drill and practice. Most of the early uses of computers were for computer-based learning (also called computer-assisted instruction) that focused on mastery of skills and content through repetition and reinforcement.
3. **Enhancing teacher training** ICTs have also been used to improve access to and the quality of teacher training. Institutions are taking advantage of the Internet to provide better teacher professional development opportunities to in-service teachers. At Indira Gandhi National Open University, satellite-based one-way video- and two-way audio-conferencing was held in 1996, supplemented by print-materials and recorded video, to train 910 primary school teachers and facilitators from 20 district training institutes in Karnataka State. The teachers interacted with remote lecturers by telephone and fax. In China, large-scale radio and television-based teacher education has for many years been conducted by the China Central Radio and TV University.
4. **ICTs to transform the learning environment into one that is learner-centered**. Research has shown that the appropriate use of ICTs can catalyze the paradigmatic shift at the heart of education reform in the 21st century. If designed and implemented properly, ICT-supported education can promote the acquisition of the knowledge and skills that will empower students for lifelong learning. When used appropriately, ICTs—especially computers and Internet technologies— enable new ways of teaching and learning rather than simply allow teachers and students to do what they have done

before in a better way. These new ways of teaching and learning are underpinned by constructivist theories of learning and constitute a shift from a teacher-centered pedagogy—in its worst form characterized by memorization and rote learning—to one that is learner-centered.

## Forms of Icts in Education

### Radio and TV Broadcasting

Radio and television have been used widely as educational tools since the 1920s and the 1950s, respectively. There are three general approaches to the use of radio and TV broadcasting in education:

(a) Direct Class Teaching: Where broadcast programming substitutes for teachers on a temporary basis.
(b) School Broadcasting: Where broadcast programming provides complementary teaching and learning resources not otherwise available.
(c) General Educational Programming Over Community: National and international stations which provide general and informal educational opportunities.

### Teleconferencing

Teleconferencing refers to "interactive electronic communication among people located at two or more different places." There are four types of teleconferencing based on the nature and extent of interactivity and the sophistication of the technology:

(a) Audio conferencing involves the live (real-time) exchange of voice messages over a telephone network.
(b) Audio-graphic conferencing: When low-bandwidth text and still images such as graphs, diagrams or pictures can also be exchanged along with voice messages, then this type of conferencing is called audio graphic. Non-moving visuals are added using a computer keyboard or by drawing/writing on a graphics tablet or whiteboard.
(c) Videoconferencing allows the exchange not just of voice and graphics but also of moving images. Videoconferencing technology does not use telephone lines but either a satellite link or television network (broadcast/cable).
(d) Web-based conferencing, as the name implies, involves the transmission of text, and graphic, audio and visual media via the Internet; it requires the use of a computer with a browser and communication can be both synchronous and asynchronous.

Teleconferencing is used in both formal and non-formal learning contexts to facilitate teacher-learner and learner-learner discussions, as well as to access experts and other resource persons remotely. In open and distance learning, teleconferencing is a useful tool for providing direct instruction and learner support, minimizing learner isolation.

## Computers and the Internet For Education

There are three general approaches to the instructional use of computers and the Internet, which are as follows:

### Learning about computers and the Internet

Learning about computers and the Internet focuses on developing technological literacy. It typically includes:

1. Fundamentals: basic terms, concepts and operations
2. Use of the keyboard and mouse
3. Use of productivity tools such as word processing, spreadsheets, and data base and graphics programs
4. Use of research and collaboration tools such as search engines and email
5. Basic skills in using programming and authoring applications such as Logo or Hyper Studio
6. Developing an awareness of the social impact of technological change.

### Learning with Computers and the Internet

Learning with the technology means focusing on how the technology can be the means to learning ends across the curriculum. It includes:

1. Presentation, demonstration, and the manipulation of data using productivity tools.
2. Use of curriculum-specific applications types such as educational games, drill and practice, simulations, tutorials, virtual laboratories, visualizations and graphical representations of abstract concepts, musical composition, and expert systems.
3. Use of information and resources on CD-ROM or online such as encyclopedia, interactive maps and atlases, electronic journals and other references. Technological literacy is required for learning with technologies to be possible, implying a two-step process in which students learn about the technologies before they can actually use them to learn. However, there have been attempts to integrate the two approaches.

## Learning through Computers and the Internet

Learning through computers and the Internet combines learning about them with learning with them. It involves learning the technological skills "just-in-time" or when the learner needs to learn them as he or she engages in a curriculum-related activity.

## Role of Teachers in Ict Environment

Learning and Teaching has undergone a tremendous change due to the emerging technologies. Because of the advances in the technologies, the teaching profession is evolving from an emphasis on teacher-centered, lecture based instruction to student-centered, interactive learning environments. The responsibility of the teacher has changed from knowledge transmitter to that of learning facilitator, knowledge guide and co-learner with the students in ICT environment. The modern teacher in the ICT age acts as a guide rather than a knowledge transmitter. In fact, with the introduction of ICTs in the classroom, we can say that the teaching and learning process has been modified from blackboard to keyboard.......from pen to pen drives......and from chalk to mouse......

Because of the rapid change and uncertainty, there is one thing of which we can be sure, that the teachers need to adapt to change if they are to survive and keep pacc with new methods and technologies. The teachers should adapt current teaching skills and practice to accommodate the introduction of ICT in all their academic efforts. These efforts are in bringing changes in teaching methodology, assessment of learning, student tracking, communication and evaluation.

## Ict in Education: the Indian Perspective

Though the potential and capability of open and distance learning was realized in early sixties across the globe however, it got national acceptance and recognition with the emergence of Indira Gandhi National Open University in 1985.

IGNOU and ISRO share a common vision of creating Educated India. And to achieve this, ISRO and IGNOU have been collaborating in the use of satellite communication to enrich learning processes and increase access to education through distance mode. Under ISRO-IGNOU collaboration, IGNOU has developed capability for four TV-channels and two interactive networks dedicated for education. In order to fulfill the requirements of education for all, the Indian Parliament took a major decision in the year

2001 whereby education was made compulsory for every Indian in the age group of 6 to 14 years. This task is to be accomplished by the year 2015 under the initiative Sarva Shiksha Abhiyan. The massive educational setup required to handle such large numbers requires development of effective satellite communication systems with extensive point-to-point reach covering the whole country. In this initiative, some successful joint interventions between ISRO and IGNOU and a few other educational institutions and organizations propelled the idea of designing and developing a dedicated satellite for education by ISRO. Within a short period of less than 2 years, ISRO successfully designed, developed and launched a dedicated geo-stationary satellite on September 20, 2004, EduSat, dedicated exclusively for Education. India is unique in the world in this respect and it is expected that this capability will immensely support the mission to provide seamless education and to accomplish the target of education for all.

Overall, India is graduating at a steady pace towards implementation of various ICTs at all levels of education which will soon be taken as a standard by other countries desirous of achieving this goal.

## Conclusion

The one fact that emerges in the relatively brief history of ICT use in education is that “It is not the technology but how we use it”. Technology should not drive education; rather, educational goals and needs, and careful economics, must drive technology use. Only in this way can educational institutions in developing countries effectively and equitably address the key needs of the population, to help the population as a whole respond to new challenges and opportunities created by an increasingly global economy. Indian Education System has a bright future in terms of Information & Communication Technology, as that it will enhance the speed of providing education even to remote areas of the country. Let’s wait for the dawn when education will become a familiar term to all the Indians.....

## Bibliography

1. Ali Amjad, “Internet and University Libraries”, University News, 39(17), April 23-29, 2001, pp06-10.
2. Angelo S J Fr Rex, “Rethinking Pedagogy for Our Digital Age”, University News, 47(06), February 09-15, 2009, pp14-16.
3. Baruah Kuin, “Information Society and its Impact”, University News, 39(13), March 26-April 1, 2001, pp 07-09.

4. Chaudhary Sohanvir S, "In Search of Online Learning in India", University News, 48(36), September 06-12, 2009, pp01-07.
5. Ganesan S, "Mobile Learners in Open and Distance Learning System: Challenge of Growing Numbers", University News, 44(27), July 03-09, 2006, pp 09-11.
6. Goel D.R., Goel Chhaya & Das Anshuman, "Realisation of Liberal and Technical Teacher Education", University News, 39(17), April 23-29, 2001, pp11-13.
7. Harishankar Bharathi V, "Virtual Education Initiatives at the University of Madras", University News, 44(36), September 04-10, 2006, pp65-66.

# 51

# Role of Ict in Education

## Introduction

In the modern era the role of ICT, especially internet in the education sector plays an important role, especially in the process of employing the technology into the educational activities. Education sector can be the most effective sector to anticipate and eliminate the negative impact of ICT .Internet technology can be the most effective way to increase the student's knowledge. In course of industrial, scientific and technological development, ICT has become an inevitable means of pedagogy in education.

## Different Types of Icts their and in Education

1. Radio and television have been used widely as educational tools since 1920s and 1950s, respectively. There are three genera approaches to the use of radio and TV broadcasting in education; direct class room teaching ,where broadcast programming substitutes for teachers on a temporary basis; school broadcasting ,where broadcasting programming provides complementary teaching and learning resources otherwise not available and general educational programming over community ,national and international; stations , which provide general and informal educational opportunities.

2. Teleconferencing enables one to “interactive elect4ronic communication among people located at two or more different places “. There are four types of teleconferencing based on the nature and extent of interactivity and the sophistication of the technology (i) audio conferencing (ii) audio-graphic conferencing (iii) video conferencing and (iv) Web-based conferencing.

3. There are general approaches to the instructional use of computers and the internet ,namely learning about computers and the internet in ,which technological literacy is the end goal; Learning with the help of computers and the internet in which the technology facilitates learning across the curriculum and learning through computers and the internet ,integrating technological development skills with curriculum applications.

4. Learining with the technology means focusing on how the technology can be the means to learning and across the curriculum.

5. Many higher educational institutions offering distance education courses have started to leverage the internet to optimize quality of their programmes.

6. ICT gives students the opportunity to collaborate with scientists in conducting earth science research. Participating students periodically take measurements of the atmosphere, water, soils and land around their schools .It also provides teachers with guidelines and materials for structured learning activities that take off from the student’s hands-on experience.

7. ICT provides e-journals, which cover all aspects of information and communication technology theories and applications.

8. People learn with ICT and digital media as an integrated aspect of everyday course of living whether in school at home or at work.

9. ICT provides Blended Learning which refers to an educational experience created cost-effectively using a mix of integrated distance learning technologies such as video conferencing, e-learning, videos and CD-ROM

## Advantages of the use of Ict in Education:

ICT encompasses all those gadgets that deal with the processing of information for better and effective communication. In education, communication process takes place between teachers, students, management and administrative personnel which requires plenty of data to be stored for retrieval as and when required, to be disseminated or transmitted in the desired format. The hardware and software like OHP, Television, Radio, Computers and related software are used in the educational process. However ICT today is mostly focused on the use of Computer technology for processing the data. In this context, advantages of ICT in education can be listed down as follows:

- **Quick access to information:**

  Information can be accessed in seconds by connecting to the internet and surfing through Web pages.

- **Easy availability of updated data:**

  Sitting at home or at any comfortable place the desired information can be accessed easily. This helps the students to learn the updated content. Teachers too can keep themselves abreast of the latest teaching learning strategies and related technologies.

- **Connecting Geographically dispersed regions:**

  With the advancement of ICT, education does not remain restricted within four walls of the educational institutions. Students from different parts of the world can learn together by using online, offline resources. This would result in the enriching learning experience. Such collaborative learning can result in developing.

- **Divergent thinking ability in students,**
  - Global perspectives
  - Respect for varied nature of human life and acculturation.

- **Facilitation of learning**

  ICT has contributed in shifting the focus on learning than teaching. ICT helps students to explore knowledge to learn the content through self study. Teacher can help the students by ensuring the right direction towards effective learning. Situational learning, Programmed learning, many Online learning courses are some of the example of self learning strategies that are being utilized with the help of ICT.

- **Catering to the Individual differences:**

  ICT can contribute in catering to individual needs of the students as per their capabilities and interest. Crowded class rooms have always been a challenge for the teacher to consider the needs of every student in the class.

- **Wider range of communication media:**

With the advent of ICT, different means of communication are being introduced in the teaching learning process. Offline learning, on line learning, blended learning is some of the resources that can be used in educational institutions. Collaborative learning, individualized learning strategies can enhance the quality of group as well as individual learning with the real society. This can ensure the applicability of knowledge.

- **Facilitation of learning**

ICT has contributed in shifting the focus on learning than teaching. ICT helps students to explore knowledge to learn the content through self study. Teacher can help the students by ensuring the right direction towards effective learning. Situational learning, Programmed learning, many Online learning courses are some of the example of self learning strategies that are being utilized with the help of ICT.

- **Catering to the Individual differences**:

ICT can contribute in catering to individual needs of the students as per their capabilities and interest. Crowded class rooms have always been a challenge for the teacher to consider the needs of every student in the class.

- **Wider learning opportunities for pupils**

Application of latest ICT in education has provided many options to the learners to opt for the course of their choices. Many Online courses are available for them to select any as per their aptitude and interest. Students can evaluate their own progress through different quizzes, ready to use Online tests. This can ensure fulfillment of the employment required in the job market thus minimizing the problem of unemployment. It can also provide more efficient and effective citizens to the society as per the changing needs. There are many important dimensions to ICT education, including:

1. ICT/Digital Literacy – Today, everyone needs a basic understanding of ICT and how to make productive use of it, just to be good students, workers and citizens. Teaching people how to be competent basic users of ICT technologies is an important role of ICT education, so

they will be successful in their academic and work careers, and so they can efficiently participate in modern technical society. As part of its study validating U.S. Department of Labor IT Competency model content in California, MPICT determined with 99% confidence California employer agreement with the following statements regarding Digital Literacy:

2. "Information and communication technologies (ICT) competencies are increasingly important for most of our employers, regardless of role. If there was an agreed-upon standard for "digital literacy", or ICT competencies expected of all workers, regardless of workplace role, my organization would value a credential based on that standard as a way of validating ICT skills for non-ICT workers." (70.5% agree or very much agree)
3. "In the 21st century, an ability to work with information and communication technologies is becoming as essential to education, life and workplace success as "reading, writing and arithmetic"." ICT Digital Literacy should be considered a basic skill by educational systems, something taught to and assessed for all students. (85.2% agree or very much agree)
4. This study details 49 competencies for ICT User level knowledge and skills, as an actionable, teachable and assessable definition of what people need to know and be able to do to be "digitally literate."

**ICT Infrastructure and Support Applied Technologists** – Beyond a basic user competency, our society also needs more knowledgeable and capable technical people to deploy, manage and maintain ICT equipment, software and systems, so they work well for users. In all industries, these people manage computer and communications hardware, software and applications; networked systems; online information sharing, communication and commerce systems; business processes making use of these systems; and user support.

## Conclusion

To summarize, when using ICTs in your adult learning work, make sure and

1. ICT and e-learning offers opportunity to raise educational standards in schools
2. Large range of ICT tools are available for teaching and learning
3. Closes the gap of "Digital Divide"
4. Involvement of teachers and parents is important

5. Schools will need funding, access and training
6. Mix, supplement with different media
7. Mix and experiment with formats and treatments
8. Greater emphasis upon substance, less on style
9. Use of graphics, animation
10. Summarizing and recap of main points
11. Build in interactivity

## References

1. Digital Media and Learning. The John D. and Catherine T. MacArthur Foundation
2. Digital Learning (India) December 2011
3. Victoria L.Tinio,'ICT in Education Sector', Inside Magazine
4. Society for ICT 2002.Basic Principles.

# 52

## Flipped Classroom: A New Paradigm

The flipped classroom is a pedagogical model in which the typical lecture and homework elements of a course are reversed. Short video lectures are viewed by students at home before the class session, while in-class time it is devoted to exercises, projects, or discussions. The video lecture is often seen as the key ingredient in the flipped approach, such lectures being either created by the instructor and posted online or selected from an online repository. While a prerecorded lecture could certainly be a podcast or other audio format, the ease with which video can be accessed and viewed today has made it so ubiquitous that the flipped model has come to be identified with it. The notion of a flipped classroom draws on such concepts as active learning, student engagement, hybrid course design, and course podcasting. The value of a flipped class is in the repurposing of class time into a workshop where students can inquire about lecture content, test their skills in applying knowledge, and interact with one another in hands-on activities. During class sessions, instructors function as coaches or advisors, encouraging students in individual inquiry and collaborative effort. There is no single model for the flipped classroom—the term is widely used to describe almost any class structure that provides prerecorded lectures followed by in-class exercises. In one common model, students might view multiple lectures of five to seven minutes each. Online quizzes or activities can be interspersed to test what students have learned.

Immediate quiz feedback and the ability to rerun lecture segments may help clarify points of confusion. Instructors might lead in-class discussions or turn the classroom into a studio where students create, collaborate, and put into practice what they learned from the lectures they view outside class. As on-site experts, instructors suggest various approaches, clarify content, and monitor progress. They might organize students into an ad hoc workgroup to solve a problem that several are struggling to understand. Because this approach represents a comprehensive change in the class dynamic, some instructors have chosen to implement only a few elements of the flipped model or to flip only a few selected class sessions during a team.

## Introduction

The flipped classroom model encompasses any use of using Internet technology to leverage the learning in the classroom, so we can spend more time in interacting with students instead of lecturing. This is most commonly being done using teacher created videos that students view outside of class time. It is called the flipped class because the whole classroom/homework paradigm is "flipped". What used to be class work (the "lecture") is done at home via teacher-created videos and what used to be homework (assigned problems) is now done in class.

Flipped teaching often involves students watching lecture videos as homework. Flipped teaching is also known as flip teaching, reverse teaching and the inverted classroom. The main goal of flipped teaching is to make time for meaningful discussions, interaction, activities and application of course content during face-to-face sessions.

In class students apply the knowledge by solving problems and doing practical work, the teacher tutors the students when they become stuck, rather than imparting the initial lesson in person. Complementary techniques include differentiated instruction and project-based learning. Flipped classrooms free class time for hands-on work. Students learn by doing and asking questions. Students can also help each other, a process that benefits both the advanced and less advanced learners. Flipping also changes the allocation of teacher time. Flipping changes teachers from "sage on the stage" to "guide on the side", allowing them to work with individuals or groups of students throughout the session. Rosenberg, Tina (October 23, 2013).

The flipped classroom describes a reversal of traditional teaching where students gain first exposure to new material outside of class, usually via reading or lecture videos, and then class time is used to do the harder work of assimilating that knowledge through strategies such as problem-solving, discussion or debates.

## PURPOSE OF FLIPPED CLASSROOM

The purpose of flipping the classroom is to shift from passive to active learning to focus on the higher order thinking skills such as analysis, synthesis and evaluation (Bloom). Flipping the Classroom: Simply Speaking (Penn State), students access key content individually (or in small groups) prior to class time and then meet face-to-face in the larger group to explore content through active learning and engagement strategies.

In the flipped classroom, the roles and expectations of students and teachers change where:

- Students Take More Responsibility For Their Own Learning And Study Core Content Either Individually Or In Groups Before Class And Then Apply Knowledge And Skills To A Range Of Activities Using Higher Order Thinking.
- Teaching 'One-to-many' Focuses More On Facilitation And Moderation Than Lecturing, Though Lecturing Is Still Important. Significant Learning Opportunities Can Be Gained Through Facilitating Active Learning, Engaging Students, Guiding Learning, Correcting Misunderstandings And Providing Timely Feedback Using A Variety Of Pedagogical Strategies,
- There is A Greater Focus On Concept Exploration, Meaning Making And Demonstration or application of knowledge in the face-to-face setting.

Educational technologies are an important feature of the flipped classroom as they can be used to:

1. Capture key content for students to access at their own convenience and to suit their pace of learning (e.g. lecture material, readings, interactive multimedia),
2. Present learning materials in a variety of formats to suit different learner styles (e.g. text, videos, audio, multimedia),
3. Provide opportunities for discourse and interaction in and out of class (e.g. polling tools, discussion tools, content creation tools),
4. Convey timely information, updates and reminders for students (e.g micro-blogging, announcement tools),
5. Provide immediate and anonymous feedback for teachers and students (e.g. quizzes, polls) to signal revision points,

6. capture data about students to analyse their progress and identify 'at risk' students (e.g. analytics).

## Flipped learning in higher education

Flipped Learning is particularly well-suited to higher education settings for a variety of reasons. The in-class discussion and enrichment activities allowed by moving content delivery outside of class time provide opportunities for students to develop vital skills needed in the 21st century, including critical thinking, creativity, communications, and collaboration.

### *KEY ELEMENTS OF THE FLIPPED CLASSROOM*

1. Provide an opportunity for students to gain first exposure prior to class.
2. Provide an incentive for students to prepare for class.
3. Provide a mechanism to assess student understanding.
4. Provide in-class activities that focus on higher level cognitive activities.

## Benefits of Flipping a Classroom

1. The flipped classroom maximizes the face-to-face time for discussion where students are able to ask questions and interact in real-time with their instructors and fellow classmates.
2. The ability to shift the lecture outside of the classroom time allows time for increased active learning and engagement through the professor's expertise, facilitation, and guidance. Because face to face time is limited, flipped classrooms can also provide the ability to cover more material during the semester.
3. Students can also take their time to complete their notes, reflect, pause, replay, and re-listen to the lectures to spend time digesting complex lecture based topics by watching the lectures online, outside of class.
4. Students are able to better prepare for classroom discussions - and engage in them - through being better informed of the main topics and concepts before coming to class.

## Conclusion

Flipped classroom allows students to get individual time in class to work with their teacher on key learning activities. Although students' thinking about their own learning is not an inherent part of the flipped classroom, the higher cognitive functions associated with class activities, accompanied by the ongoing peer/instructor interaction that typically accompanies them, can readily lead to the meta cognition associated with deep learning. By providing an opportunity for students to *use* their new factual knowledge while they have access to immediate feedback from peers and the instructor, the flipped classroom helps students learn to correct misconceptions and organize their new knowledge such that it is more accessible for future use. Furthermore, the immediate feedback that occurs in the flipped classroom also helps students to recognize and think about their own growing understanding.

## References

1. Lage, M. J., Platt, G. J., & Treglia, M. (N.d.). Inverting The Classroom. A Gateway To Creating An Inclusive Learning Environment, 31(1), 30-43.
2. Marco Ronchetti (June 2010), “Using Video Lectures To Make Teaching More Interactive”, International Journal Of Emerging Technologies In Learning
3. Rosenberg, Tina (October 23, 2013). “In ‘Flipped’ Classrooms, a Method for Mastery”. New York Times

# 53

# New Ways of Tomorrow Learning and Teaching Environment

## Introduction

Traditionally, behaviouristic models have been used for the design of many interactive learning environments. In contrast, we propose a pedagogical model based on social constructivism and Phenomenography, which we believe is more adequate when, for instance, information seeking and the use of the WWW are natural components in the learning situation. To see learners as persons who continuously alter their conceptions and ideas by working with data, information and knowledge, i.e. to see learners as knowledge workers, corresponds well with social constructivism and Phenomenography. Frequently, the design of interactive learning systems focuses exclusively on computers and the virtual environments they provide, excluding the physical environment. We believe that the design of learning environments based on a combination of physical and virtual artifacts will enhance the learning experience. In this paper we present our efforts in exploring the implication of two learning theories, Phenomenography and social constructivism, for the design of learning environments that combine physical and virtual (computer-based) media.

There is general agreement as we approach the next century and next millennium that our society is changing into a knowledge and information society. The world is constantly evolving now at a faster pace than ever before, creating the challenge for individuals and organizations to deal with changes and for schools and universities to prepare people for changes. There is trend indicating that the amount of people working with knowledge and refinement of data and information is increasing. More and more of the laborers can be categorized as knowledge workers, hence knowledge workers is a group of workers who is growing in size and importance. Scientists, stockbrokers and journalists are examples of knowledge workers of today. The fact is that many tasks traditionally performed in physical environments are now done in virtual (electronic) environments, or they have been altered to fit to the new premises of emerging physical-virtual environments.

## Knowledge Work

"The manual worker is yesterday. The basic capital resource, the fundamental investment, but also the cost centre for a developed economy is knowledge worker who puts to work what he has learned in systematic education, that is, concepts, ideas and theories, rather than the man who puts to work manual skill or muscle. History also indicates the existence of such metaphors, where the users have more control over the working situation, as in the case with craftsmanship a knowledge worker metaphor.

## Pedagogical Issues

What kind of pedagogical framework has the ability to cope with the educational requirements that arise from this increasingly important group of laborers? A point of departure for this paper is a view on learning based on the following definition: "Learning is an active, constructive, cognitive and social process where the learner strategically manages available cognitive, physical, and social resources to create new knowledge by interacting with information in the environment and integrating it with information already stored in memory".

## Furthermore, we assume that learning can be characterized by the following features:

### Learning is embedded

Learning will take place in a situation we learn out in the real world where the knowledge and skills are needed to solve problems. "We must, therefore, attempt to use the intelligence in the learning environments to reflect and support the learner's or user's active creation or co-production, in situ, of idiosyncratic, hidden models and concepts, whose textures are developed between the learner/user and the situating activity in which the technology is embedded."

## Learning is a constructive process

As indicated by the fact that learning is embedded, we should view learning as a constructive process rather than a passive absorption of facts and rules. The view that the learner should acquire the expert's knowledge does not necessarily acknowledge this constructive perspective. Knowledge and skills are gained and regained over and over in an on-going process between the learner and situations in which the knowledge and skills are required. The central notion is that understanding and learning are active, constructive, generative processes such as assimilation, augmentation, and self-reorganization.

## Knowledge is very much a question of understanding phenomena

The area of pedagogy traditionally takes a positivistic and quantitative view on knowledge. Phenomenography in contrast takes quite different view knowledge is understandings of phenomena, and learning is viewed as a process where these understandings are changed; this is a central principle. Other important characteristics are the analysis of the outcome of the learning process in qualitative terms, the move of focus from the "teacher-side" to the "learner-side" of the learning situation and the view on learning as a generative process, which is constantly going on.

## Active learning is good for the quality of the outcome

A deep-directed level of processing is characterized by an active way of processing the material active reading. Beside internal and external factors of relevance, the researchers have found the vicarious relevance important. Active reading has at least four components:

1. **Explore;** The ability to study the topic partly in the course material and partly by searching for material that is relevant in the learner's personal context.
2. **Form;** adding notes, making references to other relevant material, by changing the structure of the texts, change the text to fit the learner's understanding and previous knowledge, and more.
3. **Analyses;** The ability to analyze the topic and or the intended meaning of the text, ask oneself processing questions, working with the structure of the text, or by analyzing how one and other learners have worked or processed the material.

4. **Administrate;** The ability to keep track of the exploring, forming and analyzing activities by administrating references, recording how one have worked with the text, which questions one has asked oneself, etc.

## New Ways of Learning and Teaching

In order to better prepare for lifelong learning activities, learners must be exposed to learning activities that require them to take on and develop many of the responsibilities normally afforded to educators. To achieve this requires moving away from a view of learning that is controlled outside the individual by a teacher, trainer, instructional designer, or subject matter expert to a view of learning that is internally controlled by the individual. As mentioned above, IT plays an important role in the working situation for the knowledge worker of tomorrow. How and why should we use information technology in learning environments? These are two relevant questions to ask in this context. In this section we discuss these two questions putting our main focus on the "how question", although the "why question" is first briefly discussed. We believe it is important to give a historic perspective on the use of IT for the design learning environments in order to identify how and why to use modern IT in many educational settings.

### Why

Traditionally there are three major motives behind the use of IT for learning: economical and efficiency motives have traditionally played a big role, and also the possibility to bridge distances in time and space. It is necessary to extend the concept of distances to also include distances between the ways of study or learning and distances between documents. We believe that an elimination of distances in learning environments, for instance, by forcing learners to study at the same location and time, and use the same material and study it in the same manner mainly have negative effects for learners' situation. Consequently IT plays a very important role for the learning situation of tomorrow, and must be viewed as a natural part of the learning environment.

### How

Skinner, Pavlov, and Piaget all played important roles as founders of theories of learning. Skinner's and Pavlov's ideas about the way we learn things, based on the stimulus-response concept, were one source of inspiration for programmed learning or programmed instruction. Those theories have been used as the foundation for the design of the first generation of computer-based learning environments. Using this pedagogical model a huge industry of learning grew up during the early.

## The First generation of ILE

Computer Assisted Instruction systems (CAI) are a kind of interactive learning environment based on programmed learning, which became common in the period from the mid of the 60s to the early 70s. Still, many projects are based on behaviouristic ideas. This seems strange since these ideas and all what they stand for have been almost completely rejected in traditional classroom learning environments. At the same time, there is a very simple explanation: two of the major advantages with programmed learning are the possibility of self-administration of a course and the simplicity of implementing a computer-based learning environment with a behaviouristic control mechanism, see Figure 2. Therefore, it is not hard to see the possibilities to make it serve as a basis for computer-based learning environments.

## The Second Generation of ILE

Even if one can get positive results with regard to learning in these learning environments, there is much one can do to speed up the process of learning. One of the major drawbacks of these learning environments is the lack of individualization. The learning situation is one-to-one, but all learners are still running through the course in the same order.

## The Third Generation of ILE

The ITS approach has many good results to show, although it has also been criticized for a long period. Much of the criticism has concerned the possibilities to trace learners' state of knowledge.. Cognitive tools are artifacts that amplify, support, and unburden the user. They have the possibility to affect the task, and the user's state of knowledge. In some sense they amplify and unburden the user in the same manner that the winch amplifies our ability to lift things (heavy things), a backpack unburdens the carrier, and the hammer supports nailing. The cognitive tools approach has its pedagogic base constructivist ideas of knowledge and learning, where the learners consider as active knowledge constructors.

## Learner centered design

Not many of the approaches used for the design of ILEs are able to meet the demands and requirements of tomorrow's learning situations. In these situations the integration of physical and virtual work as well as theoretical and practical work is very natural.

1. **Growth;** At the core of education is the growth of the learner; promoting the development of expertise must be the primary goal of educational software. Rather than just support "doing" tasks, software designed for learners must support "learning while doing."
2. **Diversity;** Developmental differences, cultural differences, and gender differences play a major role in the suitability of materials for learners. To be usable by all learners, a range of software tools that address these differences must be available.
3. **Motivation;** In contrast to software developed for professionals, the student's initial interest and continuing engagement cannot be taken for granted.

## IT-augmented

In fact, we have to take future information technology into consideration because it will have a major influence on the conditions for future knowledge work and learning. Information access everywhere, through new 'physical' devices with computational power, will contribute to bridge the gap between the physical and virtual worlds. New tools will so close to our cognition and perception that they almost become part of our personalities. These new computerized environments will complement and eventually replace the desktop PC as provider of cognitive tools. All these aspects will cause a new knowledge reorganization that should not be ignored.

## The Way We Use Computers

Using IT for learning has a long tradition but we need new ways of doing it mainly because many of the traditional approaches of involving IT in learning situations do not meet the requirements of future more dynamic physical-virtual learning environments. A futuristic learning environment should include elements where learners can put the topic into a context and relate it to things, situations, and events that are relevant to them — promote active learning. One such element for instance, could be an open hypertext environment; open meaning that there are possibilities to search for information external to the course material, possibilities like those offered by the World-Wide-Web. It would also be open in a wider meaning, letting the learner view how other people (learners and teachers) have worked with the topic. Learning in such environment demands much support from the system, in order to help the learners to manage the new kind of learning situation. This support could be of the kind of: to establish goals, to manage goals, to manage the in-stream of information, searching for relevant information, etc.

## Conclusion

To be able to meet the challenges for the design of tomorrow's learning environments we propose a pedagogical framework based on knowledge work approach to learning. This framework has its base in five cornerstones: Knowledge work tasks are those that most likely many people will be doing in the future. There is continuous knowledge reorganization in the society partly caused by the use of new technologies. People in the future will become more and more IT-augmented. The use of computers for learning purposes is still in its infancy.

## Refercnces


1. Broberg, A. (1997) Cognitive Tools for Learning. Licentiate thesis. Umeå University, report UMINF 97.18.
2. Cochinaux, P & de Woot P. (1995). Moving Towards a Learning Society. A CRE-ERT Report on European Education.
3. Drucker, P. F. (1973). Management: Tasks, Responsibility and Practices. New York: Harper & Row.
4. Drucker, P. (1993). The Post Capitalist Society, Editorial Sudamericana.
5. Gentner, D., & Nielsen, J. (1997). The Anti-Mac Interface. In Communications of the ACM, August 1997/Vol. 39, No 8, pp70-82.
6. Hoyles, C., & Noss, R. (Eds.). (1992). Learning Mathematics and logo. London: The MIT Press.
7. Kidd, A. (1994). The Mark are on the Knowledge Worker," presented at The Human Factors in Computing Systems (CHI'94), Boston.